The Church in a Secular Age

Princeton Theological Monograph Series

K. C. Hanson, Charles M. Collier, D. Christopher Spinks,
and Robin A. Parry, Series Editors

Recent volumes in the series:

Riyako Cecilia Hikota
And Still We Wait:
Hans Urs von Balthasar's Theology of Holy Saturday
and Christian Discipleship

Guillaume Bignon
Excusing Sinners and Blaming God:
A Calvinist Assessment of Determinism, Moral Responsibility,
and Divine Involvement in Evil

Jeff McDonald
John Gerstner and the Renewal of Presbyterian and
Reformed Evangelicalism in Modern America

James P. Haley
The Humanity of Christ:
The Significance of the Anhypostasis and Enhypostasis in
Karl Barth's Christology

Karlo V. Bordjadze
Darkness Visible: A Study of Isaiah 14:3–23 as Christian Scripture

Graham H. Twelftree
The Nature Miracles of Jesus: Problems, Perspectives, and Prospects

William M. Marsh
Martin Luther on Reading the Bible as Christian Scripture:
The Messiah in Luther's Biblical Hermeneutic and Theology

Benjamin J. Burkholder
Bloodless Atonement?
A Theological and Exegetical Study of the Last Supper Sayings

The Church in a Secular Age
*A Pneumatological Reconstruction of
Stanley Hauerwas's Ecclesiology*

SILJE KVAMME BJØRNDAL

FOREWORD BY AMOS YONG

☙PICKWICK *Publications* · Eugene, Oregon

THE CHURCH IN A SECULAR AGE
A Pneumatological Reconstruction of Stanley Hauerwas's Ecclesiology

Princeton Theological Monograph Series 233

Copyright © 2018 Silje Kvamme Bjørndal. All rights reserved. Except for brief quotations in critical publications or reviews, no part of this book may be reproduced in any manner without prior written permission from the publisher. Write: Permissions, Wipf and Stock Publishers, 199 W. 8th Ave., Suite 3, Eugene, OR 97401.

Pickwick Publications
An Imprint of Wipf and Stock Publishers
199 W. 8th Ave., Suite 3
Eugene, OR 97401

www.wipfandstock.com

PAPERBACK ISBN: 978-1-5326-3279-2
HARDCOVER ISBN: 978-1-5326-3281-5
EBOOK ISBN: 978-1-5326-3280-8

Cataloguing-in-Publication data:

Names: Bjørndal, Silje Kvamme. | Yong, Amos, foreword.

Title: The church in a secular age : a pneumatological reconstruction of Stanley Hauerwas's ecclesiology / Silje Kvamme Bjørndal ; foreword by Amos Yong.

Description: Eugene, OR : Pickwick Publications, 2018 | Princteon Theological Monograph Series 233 | Includes bibliographical references and index.

Identifiers: ISBN 978-1-5326-3279-2 (paperback) | ISBN 978-1-5326-3281-5 (hardcover) | ISBN 978-1-5326-3280-8 (ebook)

Subjects: LCSH: Hauerwas, Stanley,—1940–. | Church. | Holy Spirit.

Classification: BT121.3 .B66 2018 (print) | BT121.3 .B66 (ebook)

Manufactured in the U.S.A.   09/19/18

*To all those who wander
but yet are not lost
because they belong*

Contents

Foreword by Amos Yong | ix

1. In the Beginning | 1

Part I: A Secular Age: Taylor's Framework | 17

2. Taylor's Secular Age | 19
3. Challenging the Church | 34

Part II: The Church as Community: Hauerwas's Ecclesiology | 49

4. The Church as a Storied Community | 51
5. The Church as a Defining Community | 67
6. The Church as a Performative Community | 84

Part III: The Church by The Spirit: A Pneumatological Reconstruction of Hauerwas | 97

7. Engaging Hauerwas's Critics: A Critical Discussion | 99
8. Introducing the Pneumatological Reconstruction | 126
9. The Church as a Storied Community by the Spirit of Rationality | 139
10. The Church as a Defining Community by the Spirit of Relationality | 149
11. The Church as a Performative Community by the Spirit of *Dunamis* | 158

Part IV: Explorative Proposal: Crucial Practices | 167

12   Practicing Church in a Secular Age | 169

13   In the End | 205

Bibliography | 209
Index of Authors | 217

Foreword

SILJE KVAMME BJØRNDAL HAS a fearless imagination, an expansive intellectual capacity, and visionary theological instincts. The majority of doctoral theses in theology if focused at all on leading thinkers, will grapple with one major interlocutor. Some of the more daring might bring two leading lights into dialogical conversation. Bjørndal here takes on not one or two but three philosophers and theologians, each with very different agendas and dispositions, and does it seamlessly but no less acutely and with a great deal of sophistication and nuance.

Charles Taylor might appreciate how Bjørndal uses his work to set the broader context and parameters for her own exploration even if he may also feel that there are more theological resources to be mined within his own *oeuvre* for responding to the questions raised than she actually engages. On the other hand, to the degree that the focus here is specifically ecclesiological rather than more widely cultural, there is justification to allow Taylor to set the stage upon which more specifically theological perspectives might then resound. Yet it is also precisely on this front that Stanley Hauerwas might counter: starting philosophically already prejudices theology's perspective, so why not foreground theological assessment of secularism (which is precisely what Hauerwas has done) rather than subordinating the Hauerwasian resolutions to the Taylorean analytic? Yet—and this is precisely the strength of our author—what emerges is a systematic analysis of late modernity and a robustly ecclesiological response, on that is attentive to both to the overarching commitments and the depth intuitions of these intellectual giants while at the same time forging her own constructive frame. In other words, the achievement before us is that Bjørndal helps us to understand both Taylor and Hauerwas on their own terms while also bringing them together in a complementary but yet creative fashion. She accomplishes this no mean task via a mastery of the full scope of their work (no mean feat!) which allows her to focus on those threads relevant to her own project while yet respecting the gifts she derives from her sources and managing to situate them appropriately for the purposes of this book.

If Hauerwasians might nevertheless read the Taylor-Hauerwas transition carefully to ensure that the latter's theological convictions retain their polemical edge rather than being blunted by alien categories, then they might also be surprised to find not just that the project initiated by America's best theologian—identified by *Time* magazine in 2001—remains unfinished (that is the nature of theological endeavors) but also that the assist Bjørndal proposes in the major part of her work derives from the Pentecostal sector of the contemporary theological academy: the work of yours truly. What hath the pneumatological dynamic of Azusa Street brought forward one century to do with the ecclesiological vision emanating from the Duke University theologian?! It will be fascinating to follow how readers assess Bjørndal's effort to direct Hauerwas and Yong's voices in her ecclesiological orchestra, but even if there are discordant notes, the performance is nothing short of brilliant. Furthermore I can say this: Bjørndal has been one of my most incisive readers and interpreters. She has both gone to the core of my theological project and grasped the breadth of its scope, both discerned its aesthetic sensibilities and identified its aspirational trajectories. This allows her to handle the potencies of pneumatology in a tempered and restrained manner, yet channel them appropriately and productively as well. Those who are familiar with my work will not be surprised then that I am recommending Bjørndal as one who is supplying the pneumatological perspectives crucial for the present and future theological task.

In all of this, Bjørndal has emerged in her own right as a leading Pentecostal and pneumatological theologian. Some might think then about these elements parochially: that she then speaks only for her own Pentecostal church (surely needed in any case, especially in the Norwegian context wherein she works) or that her work covers just a narrow swath of the theological landscape (focused on the doctrine of the Spirit). But those who make this mistake are not aware that pneumatological theology is not equivalent to pneumatology, and these same persons also have a reductive comprehension of Pentecostal. Instead, this book positions Bjørndal as one capable of contributing to the so-called Third Article theology that is today revisiting the systematic and dogmatic loci of the Creed from a perspective not only after Christological commitments (which is what the Reformation did) but also from the perspective of the person and work of the Holy Spirit. Further, if all theological reflection emerges not just after Easter but also after Pentecost, then Christian theology from whatever venue is Pentecostal in that sense, and we are now just beginning to realize how such an initiative invites reconsideration of the theological tradition from this pneumatically charged site. *The Church in a Secular Age* takes a major step forward toward this essential formulation of a pneumatological ecclesiology, a theology of the church that is shaped and driven by Pentecostal resources, one needed for the third millennium.

Amos Yong

I

In the Beginning

1.1 *The Backdrop*

THE CORE TASK OF the systematic theological discipline of ecclesiology is to identify the *ekklesia* in ecclesiology by asking questions such as: What is a theological understanding of church?[1] What, if anything, differentiates the church from any other sociological grouping of people with a common interest? How should the church relate to the particular context in which it finds itself? Spending most of my youth in a Pentecostal church, my sense of what the church is about was early grounded in spiritual practices and personal devotion. The church did not depend on formalized structures, churchly offices, or even sacraments, but on the gathering of the faithful, among whom the Spirit abides. This rather limited understanding of church was considerably challenged during my theological studies at a predominantly Lutheran, yet ecumenically inclined, institution. Realizing that the Pentecostal way is neither a homogeneous way, the only way, nor necessarily the most "authentic" way of being church, several questions emerged that turned out to be questions of ecclesiology.

In order to say something truthful, relevant, and hopefully, even interesting about the church, it is imperative that theologians engage in

---

1. I do not differentiate between "a church" and "the church" in a substantial or theological sense. Rather, it is a matter of linguistics and readability. Thus, I am not indicating a particular church denomination in the book title or chapter titles, although phrasing them with the definite article. By the term church I am referring to the many Christian congregations from various denominations, i.e., the empirical church. In the following, however, it will be further clarified who I address with the term church. When referring to various denominations, I specifically use "denominations" and not "churches" in plural, and when I refer to a particular denomination, this is clearly qualified, e.g., the Roman Catholic Church, the Pentecostal Church. Also, when addressing the category of the local church community, I use "congregation," with the Christian affiliation implied, however, not implying that all "congregations" adhere to congregationalism (see Volf, *After Our Likeness*, 12–13., for what he calls the process of "congregationalization").

contemporary discussions that enable us to contribute to the church's staying aligned with its purpose and being, as well as with its particular situation.[2] On that premise, this book intends to contribute to a more adequate contemporary ecclesiology for the church as challenged by the altered conditions for religious belief and practice in a secular age.[3] In his magnum opus *A Secular Age*,[4] Canadian philosopher Charles Taylor outlines a genealogical account of how secularity, in the term's various forms, came to be descriptive of the North Atlantic countries. Although not disputed, Taylor's account offers by far the most comprehensive, and convincing I would add, explanation of what he claims to be a complex development taking us from a theistic to an atheistic starting point for our reasoning. In so doing, I will argue that he offers a framework conducive to understanding how a secular age challenges the church.

With the objective of contributing to the church's navigation of the challenges of a secular age, I turn to one of the most significant and prolific contemporary exponents for what I will call a particularistic ecclesiology:[5] the North American theologian and ethicist, Stanley Hauerwas.[6] Hauerwas is (in)famous for his insistence that the church's primary task is not somehow to translate Christian faith for the world to understand, but simply to be

---

2. Thus, I assume that it is constructive to strive for an articulation of a common purpose and being for the church catholic, although acknowledging that such articulations must be contextually interpreted and further developed, and therefore will be provisional in a sense.

3. Other terms used to define the contemporary culture in the North Atlantic part of the world are "postmodern," "post-Christendom," or "post-secular." The point is not, however, the term, in and of itself, but the content of the term and in my opinion Taylor's framework for secularity offers a content that can constructively be engaged in the ecclesiological effort of this book. Interestingly, the challenges for the church that I articulate from Taylor's framework are similar to what Sigurdson suggests in what he calls a "post-secular political theology" (Sigurdson, "Beyond Secularism?," 193–94), thus exemplifying that different terms may well carry similar contents and descriptions.

4. Taylor, *A Secular Age*.

5. The term "particularistic ecclesiology" is employed in the minimalistic sense of emphasizing the particular and distinct nature of the church. It has been used to describe Hauerwas's position as an alternative to a protestant liberalism position, which emphasizes church in continuity with and as a contributor to liberal societies (Mortensen and Nilsen, *Walk Humbly with the Lord*. Hauerwas does not use this exact phrasing, but often speaks of the "particular community" of the church (e.g., Hauerwas, *Character and the Christian Life*; Hauerwas, *Suffering Presence*; and Hauerwas, *In Good Company*).

6. I assume Hauerwas's particularistic ecclesiology to be important due to his considerable influence even beyond the theological academia, primarily in the North American context, but also beyond. See chapter 1.3 for further introduction of Hauerwas and his work.

the distinctly Christian community that the church is supposed to be. Based on this assertion, that the church must be the church and thus preserve the Christian community's particularity, his ecclesiological insights offer what I find to be both challenging and controversial perspectives. These will be critically engaged, in dialogue with Taylor's theoretical framework for secularity, as well as with other theological perspectives.

While acknowledging that, like any other book on theological matters, this investigation is conditioned by contextual factors, like the theological, denominational, cultural, historical, geographical, and academic situatedness of the author, the scope of the book is not limited to a particular denomination, but to any church community that recognizes the challenges outlined in the first part of the book. The framework for the ecclesiological discussion will therefore be defined by a common horizon of understanding, rather than being demarcated along denominational, geographical, or theological lines. Thus, with the term church I address the church catholic, in the broadest sense of the meaning. However, the selections of both the questions and material addressed in this book will resonate better with some quarters of the church catholic than others.[7] In that regard, I assume that the addressees for this book primarily, not exclusively, identify with the manifold Protestant part of the church, and geographically are based in the North Atlantic part of the world. Before presenting the selected material any further, it will be beneficial to state the questions at hand more clearly, in order to assess how the material may contribute to address these questions in a fruitful manner.

1.2 *The Big Question*

The book addresses the following main question:

> How can a particularistic ecclesiology help the church in navigating the challenges of a secular age?

This way of constructing the question assumes that a particularistic ecclesiology actually has something to offer the contemporary church as it is faced with the challenges characteristic of a secular age. As well, it is implied that the secular age poses challenges that the church needs to navigate.[8] Whether these assumptions are correct, remain to be seen in the

---

7. For reflections on the "ecumenical claims" of Hauerwas's theology, see Rasmusson, *The Church as Polis*, 23.

8. Navigate is employed as a dynamic term, entailing at times navigation as critical *appropriation* of the premises of the challenge, and at other times, navigation by critical *countering* of the premises of the challenge. As such, navigation is understood as acknowledging, relating to, and moving beyond the presented challenge.

work ahead. The subquestions, as summarized below, are intended to explicate further the correlation between a particularistic understanding of the church, as represented by Hauerwas, and its potential contribution to the church when challenged by the altered conditions for religious belief and practice in a secular age, as portrayed by Taylor:

a. What are the altered conditions for religious belief and practice in a secular age, according to Taylor, and how do they challenge the church?
b. What are the characteristics of the church, according to Hauerwas, and how can they contribute to the navigation of secular challenges?
c. How can a critical discussion and pneumatological reconstruction of Hauerwas's ecclesiology offer a more precise ecclesiological contribution to the church in a secular age?
d. What are the practical implications of this ecclesiological contribution for the church as it navigates the challenges of a secular age?

The book is designed to address the main question in a purposive and argumentative order. Overall, the inquiry is organized into four main parts, corresponding to the four subquestions: part I presents the theoretical framework of a secular age; part II presents Hauerwas's particularistic ecclesiology; and part III consists of the critical discussion of Hauerwas's project, as well as the subsequent pneumatological reconstruction of his ecclesiology. Finally, part IV is an explorative proposal in need of further elaboration and research. Before the structure and procedure of the book are explicated, the research material will be presented.

1.3 *The Main Material*

Stanley Martin Hauerwas (born 1940) is a North American theological ethicist who is widely read, and cited, by friends and foes alike.[9] Since his work is the main material of this book, it seems fitting to present him first. Hauerwas grew up in Texas, and with his family he attended a local Methodist Church there. After finishing his theological studies at Yale, he went to teach at Notre Dame. It was there that he encountered the writings of John H. Yoder, a Mennonite theologian, who challenged Hauerwas's ecclesiological understanding in several ways.[10] Yoder has since become one of

---

9. Hauerwas, *The Hauerwas Reader*, 3.
10. On Hauerwas's own account, Yoder was initially "a pill I had no desire to

the most important influences on his theological formation.[11] While both his connections to Yale and Yoder, and respectively, the postliberal theology and Anabaptism, are important in order to contextualize Hauerwas's project, equally important are his opponents. They have influenced his work both in terms of content and style, the latter having been described as combative.[12]

Raging against what he argues has been the church's collapse into the North American project, Hauerwas is firmly positioned in said political and theological context.[13] He claims, against the position of the influential North American theologians Reinhold and H. Richard Niebuhr, that the work of theologians must be to show how Christian commitments make all the difference for theological ethics.[14] Rather than attempting to translate theologically grounded moral convictions into non-theological idioms, which leaves one wondering about the use of the theological premises in any case, Hauerwas insists on the importance of a distinct Christian community that makes theological convictions intelligible by its practices. Enter Hauerwas's particular ecclesiology. Critical of an ecclesiology that turns the church into a modern liberal project, while underwriting human reason as the starting point for theology, Hauerwas argues the church must follow Barth, who "refused the crumbs that modernity offered to sustain an attenuated Christianity. Reclaiming the scriptural and theological resources of the Christian tradition, Barth imagined the visibility of the gospel after Christendom."[15] Hauerwas thus claims that the scriptural and theological resources of the Christian tradition must be reclaimed and made visible by the church.

It is perhaps ironic, considering his emphasis on the church, that he seems to be somewhat ambiguous about his own ecclesial identity. Expressing both Catholic and Mennonite sympathies, he still considers himself a

---

swallow" (Hauerwas, *The Peaceable Kingdom*, xxiv). However, Yoder turned out to be the pill that convinced Hauerwas of the centrality of nonviolence for the Christian life.

11. Rasmusson, *The Church as Polis*, 21.

12. Wells, *Transforming Fate into Destiny*, 2.

13. For an outline of the North American social ethical quarrel that Hauerwas is a part of, see ibid., 3–9.

14. Hauerwas engages and critiques the Niebuhrs, as well as offers his view on North American social ethics, in the essay "On Keeping Theological Ethics Theological" in Hauerwas, *Against the Nations*, 23–50. Hauerwas also comments on his ambivalent relationship to the works of H. Richard Niebuhr in *The Peaceable Kingdom*, xx–xxi.

15. Hauerwas, *With the Grain of the Universe*, 240. Although concurring with Barth on this, Hauerwas critiques Barth for his alleged allowance for the church to "leave the world alone" (ibid., 202).

Methodist, but remains somewhat ecclesially eclectic.[16] Likewise, Hauerwas has been reluctant about settling into any academic or political camp, managing to provoke both conservatives and liberals alike with his anti-Americanism on the one hand and harsh critique of liberalism on the other. Obviously, to those who have read Hauerwas, these criticisms are two sides of the same coin, as he views the American project to be liberal modernism at its most contemptuous. While this would qualify him for the conservative camp, his unrelenting pacifism and antifoundationalist stance prevent his welcome there.

Unlike Taylor, Hauerwas has no magnum opus on his record; however, he has published over 30 books and 350 articles.[17] His works range widely, and include medical ethics, public theology, narrative theology, and ecclesiology. Instead of the expected specialization in a narrow ethical subfield, he insists on seeking the larger perspective and evaluating the "big picture." When the Christian community is liberated from the Enlightenment agenda, and instead preserves its particular identity as a people of peace in a world of war, only then can it recover the integrity to be a kingdom agent who expresses God's grace to the world through communal practices: "The church does not have an alternative to war. The church is our alternative to war."[18] Even though Hauerwas has not explicitly articulated his work as a negotiation effort with contemporary culture, some would argue the opposite. I think this brief presentation has demonstrated that his project is indeed shaped by his context, which also is profoundly shaped by the secular age, as outlined by Taylor. Thus, my contention is that a critical appropriation of Hauerwas's work might offer valuable contributions to the church challenged by a secular age.[19] In this regard I join the ranks of several

16. Hauerwas, *The Hauerwas Reader*, 24.

17. Ibid., 3.

18. Hauerwas, *Against the Nations*, 16.

19. Considering Hauerwas's comprehensive list of publications, and in line with the purpose of my book, I will delimit the primary material for the following inquiry to his most important works (both according to his own admission and to the readership it has garnered). These are books from the period where he established his position, and they are all published during the decennial between 1980 and 1990, with particular emphasis on *The Peaceable Kingdom: A Primer in Christian Ethics*. Of the latter book, Hauerwas has said: "I suspect it is all 'there' in *The Peaceable Kingdom*. Most of what I have said since, I said there" (*Hannah's Child*, 136). Additionally, and when necessary for a fuller argument, I refer to other works, but primarily to his books. I have considered co-publications only as supporting literature, in the interest of focusing on what might be considered as Hauerwas's position. However, this book is not a book on Hauerwas *per se*, but rather his is referred to in order to address a particular problem, and make a convincing argument for an ecclesiological position. Thus, I do not attempt to present a complete presentation of his theological profile, or a genealogical outline of his development as a theologian.

theologians who have worked with Hauerwas's theology, some of them also from the Nordic countries.[20]

Turning to Taylor, I will start with a brief consideration of why the theoretical framework for this book has been selected from a philosophical work, although it is a theological question that is being addressed. First, as previously mentioned, Taylor's *A Secular Age*[21] is by far the most comprehensive account of both the historical complexities preceding the secular age, and the conditions and content of the contemporary predicament of secularity.[22] Limitations notwithstanding, this work has garnered recognition from many quarters, as well as generated hosts of commentaries and discussions in its wake.[23] The widespread interest in Taylor's project, I think, is partly due to his ability to articulate experiences and phenomena that his extensive readership recognise, and thereby also perceived as accurate and credible.

This is another reason for paying attention to Taylor: his wide-ranging influence that reaches far beyond the philosophical field, attracting the interests of theologians, sociologists, and historians, to mention but a few. Also, Taylor's is the most suitable theory of secularization, considering the big question of this book, as it accounts for the conditions by which ideas, convictions, and paradigms remain in a state of flux, which differs from sociological accounts that investigate empirical effects, such as a decline in church attendance. Finally, Taylor's effort to establish a convincing

---

20. It is not within the scope of this book to offer a comprehensive account of the reception of Hauerwas's work, but I will refer to secondary literature where it can contribute with constructive input or perspectives to the analysis at hand. However, it is worth noting that Hauerwas has gained traction also in the Nordic context, which the following works are examples of: Swedish Arne Rasmusson (Rasmusson, *The Church as Polis*), Finnish Miika Tolonen (Tolonen, *Witness Is Presence*), and Danish Andreas Østerlund Nielsen (Østerlund Nielsen, *Missional Transformation*). Not all of these works are specifically addressing the Nordic and Lutheran context, but for a constructive proposal in favour of Hauerwas's relevance as critique of the Nordic "folk church"-ecclesiology, see Hagman, *Efter folkkyrkan*. A critical engagement with Hagman's proposal can be found in Fagermoen, "Etter Folkekirken?"

21. From now on referred to by the abbreviation *ASA*.

22. For more on why Taylor's work is particularly adept as a contributor to the church in mapping the challenges of a secular age, see Stassen, *A Thicker Jesus*.

23. Some of the limitations to Taylor's project are voiced by the contributors to Warner, VanAntwerpen, and Calhoun, *Varieties of Secularism*, wherein Taylor willingly admits that *ASA* is an attempt "to lay out a basis of conversation" that he acknowledges is incomplete and in need of amendments (ibid., 321). For more critical engagements with Taylor's *ASA*, see the symposium in *Modern Theology*, where also Hauerwas contributes: Hauerwas and Coles, "Long Live the Weeds and the Wilderness Yet"; and the book discussion of *ASA* in *Journal of Religious Ethics*, starting with Kavka, "What Is Immanent in Judaism?"

framework for how religious faith can remain a valid option in a secular age offers, in my opinion, rewarding and constructive insights for any religious community attempting to navigate the challenges of a secular age.

While *ASA* is considered the pinnacle of his career as a philosopher, Taylor has previously contributed extensively to various philosophical discussions, e.g. to the interpretation of the human self and identity.[24] He manages to incorporate several perspectives from a wide-ranging field of disciplines into his reflections, which *ASA* also demonstrates. In this book, Taylor offers a genealogical account of the secularization process in the North Atlantic world (or the Western world), as well as his take on the secular age we find ourselves in. Part of this entails a careful analysis of the term secularity, and what it actually means to be secular. Throughout his argument he consistently confronts the notion of what he calls subtraction stories.[25] *Pace* the presupposition that the secularization of the West has merely consisted in the liberation from clerical restrictions on knowledge, he argues that it has been a complex process, fueled by a combination of new inventions and new forms of human self-understanding. Although *ASA* is a theoretical work, which by nature involves abstractions and generalizations,[26] it is firmly rooted and related to the phenomenology of human life experiences. This suggests a case in point for my own intention: While the book is a systematic theological work, it aims at being pertinent to actual practicing church communities.

1.4 *The Structure*

This book is divided into four main parts. Part I starts with what I will argue is a suitable and convincing framework for understanding the altered conditions for religious faith in a secular age, offered by Taylor in *ASA*. In Taylor's account of how secularization[27] has captivated people in a picture, he refers to what he calls closed world structures (CWS). These structures arise within the so-called immanent frame, which consists of various conditions for belief that contribute to a closing off of our imagination toward the transcendent, thus blinding us to alternative ways of understanding the

---

24. Most notably in Taylor, *Sources of the Self*. See also his *The Ethics of Authenticity*, where he provides a nuanced and challenging analysis of modernity's malaises and opportunities for ethical selfhood.

25. Taylor, *ASA*, 22.

26. That this also pertains to *ASA* is admitted by Taylor, e.g., ibid., 557.

27. The terms secularization and secular will be discussed and defined in chapter 2.2.

world.[28] Chapter 2 sketches the social imaginary of a secular age, and points to correlated implications for the church regarding secular notions of truth, self, and belief. In doing so, central terms and concepts for the remaining discussion are defined. Chapter 3 is my attempt to articulate some concrete challenges that the church in a secular age must navigate: 1) the deconstruction of truth; 2) the detachment of self; and 3) the disembodiment of belief.

Part II presents three central features of Hauerwas's ecclesiology, in chapters 4–6: 1) the church as a storied community; 2) the church as a defining community; and 3) the church as a performative community. These features are presented neither by Hauerwas, nor in this book, as exhaustive or definitive marks of the church, but as central, and I will argue, particularly so in the contemporary situation that Taylor describes as secular. Relating Hauerwas to the challenges outlined above, I contend that his ecclesiology circumvents them in the following way: 1) church as a storied community navigates the challenge of deconstructed truth; 2) church as a defining community navigates the challenge of the detached self; and 3) church as a performative community navigates the challenge of disembodied beliefs. While the terms storied, defining, and performative are not specifically theological, the content of the story, definition, and performance that these descriptors refer to in Hauerwas's work is. As will be apparent in the analysis, these terms are present and clearly derived from his terminology and argument.

The third and most comprehensive part of the book, consisting of chapters 7–11, is my constructive contribution, starting with a critical discussion of Hauerwas's ecclesiology, which engages his most prominent interlocutors. Having attended to the charges of fideism, sectarianism, and pragmatism, I then suggest that a pneumatological reconstruction might sharpen the ecclesiological contribution to be gained from Hauerwas's work, while also accommodating some of the critical charges. With the intent to do so, I turn to the Pentecostal scholar Amos Yong, whose wide-ranging theological work is thoroughly embedded in his foundational pneumatology, which will be the main reference for the pneumatological reconstruction I endeavor.[29] Reading Hauerwas's ecclesiological features through Yong's pneumatological categories of Spirit as rationality, relationality, and *dunamis* offers the following pneumatologically recon-

---

28. The conditions of the "immanent frame" are outlined in chapter 2.4. For the definition of transcendence, see chapter 2.2 n. 20.

29. Considering Yong's substantial contribution to the pneumatological reconstruction, his work could arguably be presented in this introductory chapter. However, regarding the flow of the book's argument and design, I found it more conducive to introduce his work in chapter 8.3, when introducing the reconstruction.

structed ecclesiological features: 1) church as storied by the Spirit of rationality; 2) church as defining by the Spirit of relationality; and 3) church as performance by the Spirit of *dunamis*.

Finally, based on the systematic reconstructive effort, the fourth part of the book is an explorative venture seeking to operationalize the pneumatologically reconstructed ecclesiology in consideration of three concrete church practices. The selected practices are not intended to be exclusive, but representative and essential, tested against Taylor's secular signposts (ref. part I, chapter 3) and my ecclesiological findings. Thus, I propose that 1) the church practicing religious dialogue, as a storied community by the Spirit of rationality, navigates the secular challenge of deconstructed truth; 2) the church that practices meeting the marginalized, as a defining community by the Spirit of relationality, navigates the challenge of the secular detached self; and 3) the church, as a performative community by the Spirit of *dunamis*, must practice liturgical living in order to navigate the secular challenge of disembodied beliefs. Bringing extra-theological perspectives into consideration, I also attempt to further the conversation on these practices. Obviously, these incipient proposals warrant both practical corroboration and further research.

1.4.1 Outline Illustration

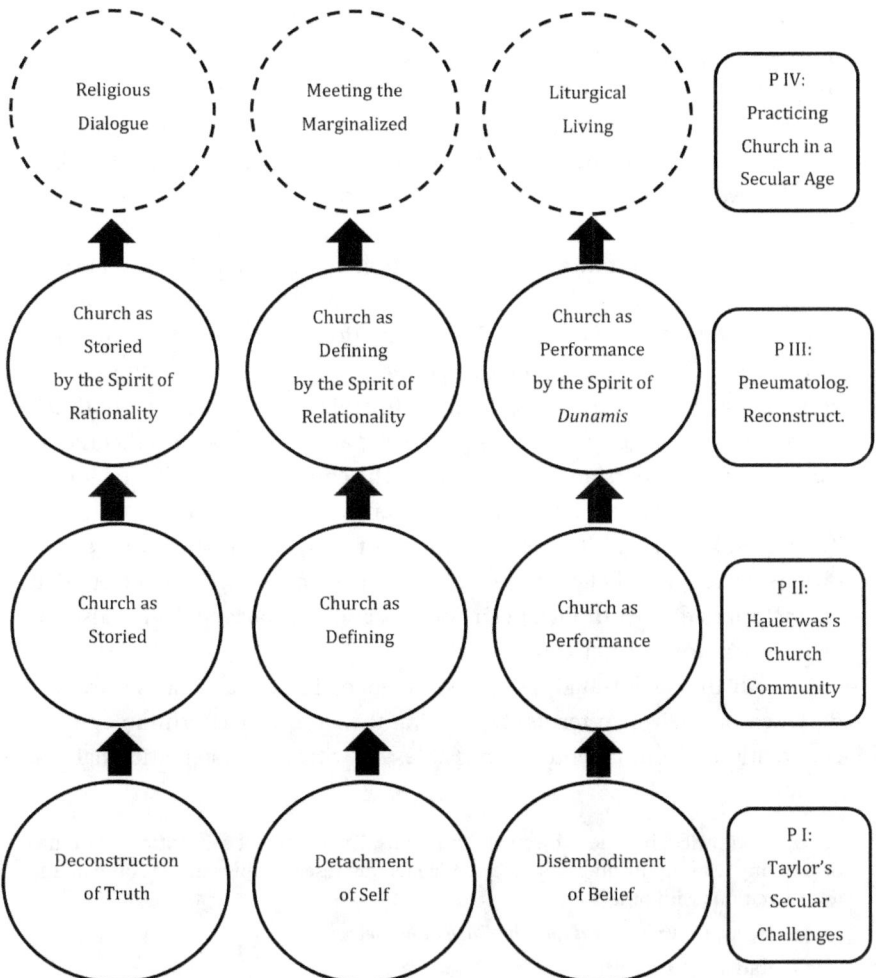

1.4.2 Reflections on Procedure

The procedure of this book reflects some fundamental convictions about ecclesiology and ecclesiological method:[30] A) Ecclesiological methods are interdependent on convictions about church.[31] How a theologian approaches ecclesiology correlates to what she thinks can and should be said about

---

30. These reflections are largely inspired by the works of Nicholas M. Healy in Healy, *Church, World and the Christian Life*, and Harald Hegstad in Hegstad, *The Real Church*.

31. Healy, *Church, World and the Christian Life*, 1.

the church.[32] B) Pre-understandings should be acknowledged and transparent, as far as possible, and revisable.[33] C) Ecclesiology should contribute to the health of the church, and as such it must contend with the thoroughly human complexities of which the concrete church is a part.[34] D) While fully aware of the tentative character of every theological and ecclesiological project, systematic efforts in ecclesiology should aim at articulating normative and universal claims about what the church should be.[35] E) Such claims must, however, be sensitive to the empirical reality and various contexts of the concrete church communities across time and geographical space.[36]

Having already offered a brief reflection on my own point of departure into the field of ecclesiology, I will in the following present the argumentative procedure of this book.[37] It is a question-driven quest, progressing in three stages wherein the first stage includes parts I-II, and the second and third stages correlate respectively to the third and fourth parts outlined above. The first stage starts with a systematic analysis of Taylor's theoretical framework for understanding secularity. The choice to start with Taylor reflects my E) conviction, about the importance of the context of the church. To my best knowledge, Taylor offers the most adequate portrayal of the conditions for religious belief and practice in the so-called secular society that characterizes the North European context, and to a varying degree also for Hauerwas's North American context.

Both the Taylor-analysis and subsequent Hauerwas-analysis are undertaken on their own terms, explicating their respective terminologies as coherently and immanently as possible. As with any systematic analysis,

---

32. Acknowledging the subjective limitations, I will attempt self-critical examinations of my readings by querying relevant Hauerwas-research, in order to compare my interpretations with others.

33. Healy, *Church, World and the Christian Life*, 2.

34. Ibid., 2.

35. Hegstad, *The Real Church*, 6–7. In Norway, Hegstad's ecclesiological proposal has been critically assessed, e.g., Johannesen, "Menighetsutvikling for Folkekirken"; Bunkholt, "'Den virkelige kirke' og embetet"; Haga, "Hegstad og den lutherske embetsteologien"; Njå, "Den virkelige kirke og kirkens virkelighet." Hegstad offers a response in Hegstad, "Den virkelige kirke og den virkelige lutherdom." This critical exchange demonstrates how the ecclesiological conversation in Norway is situated in a predominantly Lutheran context. Due to the ecumenical intention of this project, I will not enter into the Lutheran discussions, *inter alia* of how the church should understand the two kingdoms theory in our contemporary context.

36. Hegstad, *The Real Church*, 7.

37. The intent of the following reflections is not to propose some sort of objectivity for the research process, but rather to strive for transparency, which I think is closer to any researcher's attainability.

intelligibility[38] is a crucial criterion for the convincingness of the argument. For a theological systematic analysis, however, will the criterion of faithfulness, or authenticity, to the Christian tradition[39] come as an addendum. Together they monitor the first two parts of the book. Where logical or theological inconsistencies occur, I will make a brief note, but leave the further discussion for the ensuing part III.

Moving on to the second stage entails a procedural move to the constructive part of the book. By "constructive" I mean that at this stage, my analytical terminology is developed in order to gain critical distance from the material, and to offer constructive suggestions on how the main question can be better and more precisely answered. "Better and more precisely" here refers to the mentioned criteria of intelligibility and authenticity, but at this stage and for the remaining parts of the book, a third criterion of applicability is more actively engaged, in form of the question "How does the pneumatologically reconstructed ecclesiology contribute to the church's navigation of the challenges of a secular age in a better way?"[40]

---

38. Regarding criteria like intelligibility and faithfulness I partially agree with George Lindbeck that "intelligibility comes from skill, not theory, and credibility comes from good performance, not adherence to independently formulated criteria" (Lindbeck, *The Nature of Doctrine*, 117). His claim is related to his understanding of religion in a cultural-linguistic mode, as part of the so-called postliberal approach (ibid., 18ff). While I subscribe to the thrust of Lindbeck's concluding claim on methodology: "the norms of reasonableness are too rich and subtle to be adequately specified in any general theory of reason and knowledge" (ibid., 116). I am critical to aspects of his program that stands in danger of casting the cultural-linguistic view of religion as a self-enclosed system of both intelligibility and faithfulness. Since Hauerwas's project has been charged for similar problems, I will return to discuss these matters critically in part III of the book. Also, I do not find Lindbeck's juxtaposition of intelligibility as skill against intelligibility as theory convincing. Rather, I would suggest that theory is part of the skill Lindbeck appreciates. Thus, intelligibility can, and should, in my opinion, in addition to the pragmatic reference, also entail more theoretical criteria such as consistency of argument.

39. Faithfulness to the Christian tradition is of course not a mere matter of conforming to a specified set of criteria, but for the purpose of this book, which does not include thorough discussions of "tradition," suffice it to say that the criterion of faithfulness entails adherence to the lowest common multiple of the Apostle's Creed. Although it is a thin description, it says something crucial about transcendent beliefs, as well as the centrality of the Christ event. For more on the challenges of claiming the Christian tradition as criterion, see Jeanrond, *Theological Hermeneutics*, 165–69.

40. The criterion of applicability is considered by Lindbeck to judge "how relevant and practical they [theologies] are in concrete situations as well as how well they fit the cultural-linguistic systems whose religious uses they seek to describe" (Lindbeck, *The Nature of Doctrine*, 110). In this book, the challenges of a secular age make up the "concrete situation" for the church (and ecclesiology), and to what degree the ecclesiological project of Hauerwas fits "the religious uses it seeks to describe" (insofar as it is descriptive, and not merely normative) will be considered in the critical discussion

Thus, I have arrived at the pneumatological reconstruction of Hauerwas's ecclesiological features which, based on the critical inquiry, I argue, will result in a contribution that better addresses the big question of the book. At times I develop intuitions present in Hauerwas's work, and at other points I concur with his critics engaged in previous chapters about finding his project wanting. This systematic pneumatological reconstruction is the main contribution of the book, and builds as such on the preceding analyses made in the first part, as well as constituting the basis for the final part (IV) of the book.

While there are limitations to every theological project, based on my D) conviction, the intention is still to articulate ecclesiological insights of normative relevance even for the church at other times and places.[41] However, at this third and final procedural stage (which pertains to part IV of the book), as mentioned above, I venture a more explorative proposal as to what kind of practical implications the systematic ecclesiology attempted in this book might have for the church in a secular age. At this point I mostly employ my own analytical terminology accrued from the pneumatological reconstruction, in engagement with extra-theological perspectives, continually guided by the book's big question. In so doing, the concluding effort is motivated by my ecclesiological C) conviction about contributing to the health and practice of the concrete church, and aspiring to avoid both the extremes of utopian ecclesiology and mere descriptive ecclesiology.[42]

1.5 *The Aim*

At the end of the day, and at the end of this book, I hope to have contributed helpful suggestions for how the church should navigate the challenges

---

ahead. Thus, "navigating the challenges of a secular age in a better way" implies this kind of practical relevance, as well as a theological faithfulness (see n. 39 above on the meaning of "faithfulness").

41. It might appear self-defeating for a project setting out to contribute to the church's navigation of contextually specific challenges, to claim normativity. However, I will argue that it is precisely in tension with particular conditions and situations that normative theological insight is best gained. Reflecting on these issues, I have found Healy's argument quite helpful in claiming that the ecclesiological inquiry should "include *explicit* analysis of the ecclesiological context as an integral part of properly *theological* reflection upon the church" (Healy, *Church, World and the Christian Life*, 39, italics original).

42. The various movements of this book, and particularly this third stage, also echo the practical-theological program of Don S. Browning, which emphasizes the importance of researching and considering church from various angles and disciplines (Browning, *A Fundamental Practical Theology*).

of a secular age. Not presuming to come up with anything revolutionary, I do think the way I analyze and reconstruct the theory at hand offers constructive and fresh perspectives for the contemporary church's self-understanding and practice, with regards to the secular challenges, which is my primary and most important aim. Secondarily, the critical discussion and subsequent pneumatological reconstruction of Hauerwas's work aims to contribute to the ecclesiological Hauerwas-research, or even more broadly, to particularistic ecclesiology. Finally, the ecclesiological appropriation of the pneumatological work of Pentecostal scholar og pneumatology, Amos Yong, aims also to contribute to both Pentecostal theology and pneumatological ecclesiology.

PART I

A SECULAR AGE: TAYLOR'S FRAMEWORK

Taylor's Secular Age

CHARLES TAYLOR (1931–) IS Professor Emeritus of Philosophy at McGill University in Montreal, Canada.[1] He has authored several influential books, most notably *Sources of The Self*[2] and *A Secular Age*.[3] The latter will be the main object for this presentation, as it aspires to argue "what a convincing theory of secularization might look like."[4] Taylor is primarily concerned with secularity in a Western, or North Atlantic, context, though he is well aware that the phenomenon in no way is delimited to this part of the world. Therefore, a number of issues that are considered in this comprehensive work may still be of relevance on a global scale by virtue of being universal human concerns, although the immediate focal point for Taylor is the civilization rooted in Latin Christendom.[5]

A prerequisite for the project of this book is a theory of secularization, which provides a framework and conversation partner for an ecclesiology that aspires to be both intelligible in a secular age and truthful to the Christian convictions. In order for a constructive exchange and critique to proceed, such a theory should not dismiss religion and spirituality *a priori* as irrelevant to the understanding of human experience in a secular society. On the contrary, a theory is needed which argues that secularity is not merely about the decline, or even irrelevance, of religious prominence in a society, but as much about the changed conditions for religious practices and convictions in a given context. Enter Taylor, whose contention about secularity being descriptive of a social imaginary more than a social theory is an imperative incentive for preferring his secularization theory (or put differently, his social imaginary).[6]

1. For a broad overview of Taylor's work and thought, see Abbey, *Charles Taylor*.
2. Taylor, *Sources of the Self*.
3. Taylor, *ASA*.
4. Ibid., 21.
5. Ibid., 21.
6. Says Taylor, a social imaginary is "broader and deeper than the intellectual schemes people may entertain when they think about social reality in a disengaged

In the following presentation of Taylor's theory of secularization, I will outline his main arguments about what it means to live in a secular age, or put in his own words, to live in the social imaginary of a secular age. Several lines of argument are deliberately omitted, such as the extensive outlining of the historical backdrop going back to the fifteenth century, as well as his analysis of the many facets of modernity leading up to, and permeating, our contemporary secular age. This is done with reference to the question at hand, as well as for delimiting concerns. However, in order to adequately convey his theory, I will summarily refer to points made in these overarching lines of argument when required for a sufficient understanding of the particular point under consideration. Based on these limitations, my focus in this analysis will be part V of *ASA*, which is titled "Conditions of Belief."[7] This part is, according to Taylor, his attempt to present a picture of the spiritual shape of the secular age.[8]

Preceding and preparing for this presentation is Taylor's aforementioned chronological telling of the story of how we became a secular society, which he claims is critical in order to comprehend our current predicament: "Our past is sedimented in our present, and we are doomed to misidentify ourselves, as long as we can't do justice to where we come from. This is why the narrative is not an optional extra, why I believe that I have to tell a story here."[9] His emphasis on the narrative nature of social imaginaries, as well as human identity, brings me to the second incentive for preferring Taylor's project. Even though his work is comparably far more comprehensive in style (and arguably, in influence) than Hauerwas's, there are several points of convergence with Hauerwas's project, notwithstanding their diverse academic fields and frequently differing conclusions. In order to clarify why I consider Taylor to be the most convincing option for my purpose in this book, I will sketch out the relevant points of convergence, as well as note the divergences that matter in relation to the subsequent analysis. Such a brief comparison also works to anticipate some of the important foci in the Hauerwas-analysis.

---

mode. I am thinking, rather, of the ways people imagine their social existence, how they fit together with others, how things go on between them and their fellows, their expectations that are normally met, and the deeper normative notions and images that underlie these expectations" (*Modern Social Imaginaries*, 23). He goes on to compare and differentiate the social imaginary from social theory.

7. Taylor, *ASA*, 539ff.
8. Ibid., 539.
9. Ibid., 29.

2.1 Taylor and Hauerwas

While Hauerwas and Taylor might arguably share the context of Western secular society, there are imperative differences between the North American and Canadian settings, including social, political, religious, and academic variations. However, by briefly examining the central convergences and divergences between their projects, I intend to make a sufficient case for my initial hunch about their compatibility in this book.[10] Their convergences are presented in the form of common friends and foes, while the main divergence I will argue concerns how to deal with the latter lot.

Going back to the philosophical titans, they are both self-confessed Aristotelians, viewing humans as social animals who are dependent on the community of which they are a part.[11] The foundational conviction about the sociality of human beings is evidenced in their shared interest in notions such as virtue ethics and embodied (practical) wisdom. Assuming wisdom and knowledge to be thoroughly embodied, they share a common enemy in the modern concept of rationality understood as a form of detached reasoning uninformed by subjective moral, religious, or otherwise embodied experiences. Both thus critical of Kant's project, they find variable amounts of solace in Hegel.[12] Taylor, whose doctoral thesis argued for Hegel's continued relevance,[13] has obviously the most articulated relation to Hegel's thought, but it has been argued that Hauerwas also is indebted to Hegel, albeit less directly. Particularly, I think the Hegelian term *sittlichkeit* as descriptive of the ethical life as communally determined, rather than rationally willed, undergirds Hauerwas's project in a crucial way.[14]

---

10. It is important to note that this compatibility is not reviewed as if this were a comparative study of Hauerwas and Taylor, but rather the question is whether their projects are sufficiently within a shared paradigm, making it reasonable to attempt a conversation with Hauerwas within Taylor's framework. Another objection could be that such compatibility is not a requirement for a fruitful exchange to happen. However, I do think the following commonalities are advantageous for what I am attempting in this project.

11. Taylor, *Philosophy and the Human Sciences*, 190.

12. Kant, of course, had several projects, but they correlate and overlap. Thus when e.g., Hauerwas critiques Kant's categorical imperative in ethics, he implicitly disagrees also with the epistemological basis for that project.

13. Taylor, *Hegel*, 537ff.

14. For Taylor's explication of Hegel's alternative to Kant, see ibid., 377–78. Regarding Hauerwas and Hegel, Gale Heide suggests that Hegel's influence on Hauerwas follows the argumentative lineage through Kierkegaard's critique of Danish Hegelianism, via Barth's appropriation of Kierkegaard (Heide, *Timeless Truth in the Hands of History*, 186–206). While this is not the only way to trace Hegel's influence on Hauerwas, I find it convincing, ref. Hauerwas's engagement with and appreciation of Barth (e.g., Hauerwas, *With the Grain of the Universe*, chapters 6–7).

Camping with modern rationality, and thus equally an enemy of both Taylor and Hauerwas, is the concept of liberal universalism. Skeptical of the possibility and product of so-called universal reasoning, à la Rawls and (early) Habermas, they insist on the import of tradition, narrative, and language for moral reasoning. Following this, they are both, more-or-less self-admittedly so, regarded as communitarians. Taylor has long voiced his critique of the liberal universalism, and since the early 1980s been a prominent advocate for a communitarian counterpoint. Hauerwas has been about as vocal in his critique of liberal universalism, but somewhat hesitant in his unequivocal support of communitarianism.[15] His hesitancy offers a hint about where Hauerwas and Taylor part ways, which is when it comes to the way in which they respond to the things they often recognize on similar terms, such as the perils of modernity.

Hauerwas actually denies the general value of notions like narrative, community, or tradition, without the qualifiers of *theological* narrative, *church* community, and *Christian* tradition. In light of this emphasis on the particularity of church community and Christian existence, he offers a wholesale condemnation of the many ills of modernity, while Taylor consistently seeks the *via media*, attempting to retrieve what he finds valuable from both sides.[16] For example where Hauerwas adamantly warns against the terminology of "universal" human rights, Taylor argues that our only option in today's pluralistic world is to find out how a modified version of Rawl's overlapping consensus can work in order to sustain such a thing as universal human rights.[17]

Beyond these overlapping interests, and in spite of some significant differences, the benefit of putting Taylor and Hauerwas together must be proven in the work ahead. As mentioned above, I will now turn to Taylor's theory of secularization, starting with some important definitions, then moving on to his concept of the immanent frame, which presupposes the dualism of immanence and transcendence.[18] The so-called CWS spin our reading of the immanent frame toward closure on any transcendent no-

15. Hauerwas, *Dispatches from the Front*, 156–163.

16. Says Taylor: "Modernity urgently needs to be saved from its most unconditional supporters . . . Understanding modernity aright is an exercise in retrieval" (Taylor, *Sources of the Self*, xi).

17. Bhargava, *Secularism and Its Critics*, 53. I suspect their differing takes on the pragmatics of politics and consensus-making reflect their different levels of engagement with public policymaking. While Taylor has been, and continues to be, engaged in practical politics, Hauerwas has argued for the church as an alternative polis, whose ethos constitutes an alternative political engagement, not subservient to state or nation.

18. His use of this dichotomy has been critiqued, e.g., by During in Warner, VanAntwerpen, and Calhoun, *Varieties of Secularism*, 111–12.

tions of fullness, or meaning. Taylor, however, claims that the CWS are not self-evident, and when put under scrutiny they rightly appear as potential interpretations of reality, rather than the only possibility. In conclusion of this part, I will articulate three critical challenges facing the church in a secular society, based on the preceding analysis of Taylor's deconstruction of the CWS.

2.2 Defining Secularity

In order to present Taylor's framework for understanding a secular society as such, it is required first to outline the distinctions he makes between three different designations of the term secularity.[19] In the first sense, secularity is descriptive of public spaces being "emptied of God" and of references to a transcendent reality.[20] Thus, in each sphere of activity there is an "internal rationality" that becomes the guiding principle for people when deliberating their actions within that sphere. In the business sphere this guiding principle may be maximum profit, while in politics it may be the greatest benefit for the greatest number, and so forth. Common for these, however, is that they generally do not refer to God or any religious beliefs, which stands in stark contrast to previous periods when religious references were present and authoritative also in what are considered to be neutral domains of contemporary society.[21]

The second way of understanding secularity relates to the decline in church attendance, and other religious practices. Those concerned with this development worry, or alternatively appreciate, the "falling off of religious belief and practice" on the private scene of piety and faith. However, a society may very well be secular in the first sense, but still have the majority of people believing and practicing religious faith. The most striking example of this would be the United States, which is the Western society with the

---

19. I deliberately leave out discussions of the terms secularism and secularist, since I am not interested in theorizing about the doctrine or ideology of secularism. For more on the development of the terms secularism and secularist, see Asad, *Formations of the Secular*, 23–25, and also, see my reference to Stout's comment on "the ideology of secularism" versus secularization in the critical discussion below, chapter 7.2.1. In the following, I concur with Taylor's use of "secular" and "secularization" as grammatical inflections of "secularity."

20. "Transcendence" for Taylor must be understood in three dimensions: 1) the sense of a higher (transcendent) good, beyond human flourishing; 2) belief in a higher power, i.e., God; and 3) expectation of extended life beyond "this life" (Taylor, *ASA*, 20).

21. Ibid., 2.

highest numbers for religious practice and belief, even though church and state are separated.[22]

Taylor then adds a third kind of secularity, the existence of which he sets out to argue, at the same time examining the significance of this secularity for the Western world. Secularity in this third sense is, according to Taylor, about the changed conditions for belief and religious faith. From being unchallenged and unproblematic, belief in God has become not only one option among others; it is the least eligible option to many people. Taylor's self-imposed task is thus to trace and define how the context of understanding has changed and caused belief in God to go from being axiomatic to becoming merely a human possibility. By "context of understanding" he refers to both explicit factors, such as the plurality of options, and more implicit matters, such as the unfocussed background for how people search spiritually and construct their religious experiences. According to this definition of secularity, a society would be so inclined by virtue of the conditions for searching after, and experiencing, what is conceived as spiritual or transcendent.[23]

2.3 *Defining Religion*

All these three definitions of secularity relate to religion in one way or another, but since this term refers to a varied spectrum of phenomena, Taylor also seeks to clarify his use of the term religion.[24] In line with his geographically and culturally delimitation of his project, Taylor opts for a reading of religion in terms of the differentiation between immanence and transcendence.[25] Religion is therefore understood as belief in the transcendent. Taylor readily admits, however, that this is an elusive and vague definition, partly because the distinction between immanent and transcendent has been construed primarily in the context of modernity, and thus it is far from the case that religion in general can be understood in this manner.

In addition to this account of religion, Taylor also considers people's perception of their practical context. This entails what they perceive to be a fulfilled, meaningful, and admirable life—in short, how they answer the question of what human flourishing is about. Taylor then distinguishes between those who would answer that a fulfilled life is merely about human

---

22. Ibid., 3.
23. Ibid., 3.
24. For more on the interdependence of religion and the secular, see Asad, *Formations of the Secular*, 22.
25. Taylor, *ASA*, 15.

flourishing, and those who would point to ultimate goals beyond this, mostly pertaining to religious beliefs. In the Judeo-Christian tradition worshipping God is the ultimate goal; however, this God is portrayed as willing human flourishing, but worshipping him is not considered contingent on this.[26] Another example that Taylor mentions is Buddhism, where followers are called upon to detach themselves from their own flourishing in order to attain true bliss and to enter a state of Nirvana.

Taylor claims that the development of modern secularity (in the third sense) has been coterminous with an emergence of the societal conditions for self-sufficient humanism to be accepted as a valid option, which is, according to Taylor, a historical first.[27] While previously the general understanding of the human predicament did not place humans at the top of the order, humanism, in the purely self-sufficient sense, accepts no final goals or allegiances beyond human flourishing. It could then be added to the understanding of a secular age as "one in which the eclipse of all goals beyond human flourishing becomes conceivable; or better, it falls within the range of an imaginable life for the masses of people."[28]

To summarize, Taylor defines "religion" as relating to the following three dimensions of transcendence: 1) the notion of a higher good, beyond (immanent) human flourishing, which in the Christian tradition offers a possibility of transformation through the love of God. Closely associated with this is 2) the belief in a higher power, i.e., the transcendent God of faith, who appears in most religions. 3) Finally, there is the dimension of extended life beyond "this life." In order to adequately understand the debate between religion and unbelief in the secular society, Taylor claims that religion has to be considered as a combination of these three dimensions of transcendence.[29]

2.4 The Immanent Frame

Central to a secular society, and contrasting the religious relation to transcendence, is what Taylor calls the immanent frame. This frame consists of various conditions for belief that I will outline in the following.

---

26. Ibid., 17.
27. Ibid., 18.
28. Ibid., 19–20.
29. Ibid., 20.

2.4.1 From the Porous Self to the Buffered Self

Following his definition of secularity (3), an important condition for belief that has changed is the replacement of the porous self by the buffered self.[30] While the pre-modern porous self was vulnerable to extra-human agencies that could alter and change her spiritual and emotional condition, the modern buffered self has been given the opportunity to disengage from everything outside her own mind.[31] The latter condition is linked to the supposition that all thought, feeling and purpose must be in her mind, and thus distinct from the "outer" world. Because such a buffered self can view itself as the master of the meanings things have for it, as well as being able to define an inner base area with clear boundaries from outside emotions, this understanding lends itself to individuality and atomism.[32] Contrasting this, the porous self inherently existed and survived in a social mode, as exemplified by the collective rites and allegiances that were supposed to ensure the weal of the community.[33]

Along with the buffered identity came the focus on discipline, self-control, and programs of self-fashioning.[34] Taylor traces the first individualism through the developing significance of self-examination, self-development, and ultimately, authenticity. He sees this in light of the process of Church Reformation, which above all invoked the individual responsibility to adhere to God, Christ, and the church in the form of a personal commitment. Instrumental individualism emerged from the corresponding conception of society (and social groups such as the church) as comprised by individuals, thus replacing the notion of a cosmic order. Taylor also links instrumental individualism to the secularization of time.[35]

2.4.2 The Secularization of Time and Instrumental Individualism

Before looking closer at how Taylor connects the instrumental individualism with secular time, I will outline in brief what the meaning of "secular time" is in Taylor's project. In order to explicate this term, he opposes secular, or ordinary, time with what he calls "higher times." In philosophical and

---

30. Ibid., 539.
31. Ibid., 38.
32. Ibid., 41.
33. Ibid., 42.
34. Ibid., 112.
35. Ibid., 541.

theological language, this is referred to as eternity; however, since eternity is neither a univocal term, nor exhaustive for higher times, he prefers the latter. The function of higher times in the pre-modern era was to be the organizing field for ordinary time, and as such higher times gathered and punctuated secular time. Describing time as secular in this context is thus to express how some people are embedded in the ordinary time, as opposed to those who seek to live closer to eternity, or higher times. The former is concerned with things related to ordinary time, while the latter is concerned with matters of eternal value.[36] According to Taylor, while in the pre-modern era, secular time was grounded in higher times, the immanent frame of the modern age has caused a marginalization of higher times, which contributes to the modern experience of the world as entirely immanent.[37]

The subject of higher times versus secular time resurfaces throughout Taylor's project, and he relates it to various aspects, such as the change from viewing the world as part of an ordered and meaningful cosmos to seeing it as an insignificant fraction of an unlimited and chaotic universe.[38] However, for a fuller understanding of Taylor's argument, I will, in the following, outline his brief account of the Christian notion of time. According to Taylor, early Christianity developed a particular idea of eternity. Because of the Incarnation and God's entrance into ordinary time, the previous concept, following Plato, of reaching God in rising above time obviously had to be replaced. This new formation evolved gradually, and Taylor suggests Augustine as the main author of the reconception of eternity as what he called gathered time.

By this, Augustine departed from the Greek tradition of viewing time objectively, and understanding eternity as a model of perfect immobility and impassivity. Instead, Augustine outlined a model of God's eternity that does not abolish time, but gathers it into an instant. In examining lived time, his notion of an instant draws together the events of the past with present actions in order to project a future. Thus, there exists simultaneity between the agent's current situation, as it emerges from her past, and her actions that are consistent with the planned future. Following Augustine, all times are gathered into God, who holds them in his extended simultaneity, and the only way for humans to access this instant is by participating in God's life. Ordinary time, on the other hand, is for Augustine to lose the unity by

---

36. Ibid., 54–55.
37. Ibid., 376.
38. Ibid., 60.

being cut off from the past and out of touch with the future, and thus people get lost in their own limited parcel of time.[39]

Now, returning to the question of how Taylor connects ordinary, or secular, time with the instrumental stance: Reinforced by a society that considers time a measured resource, which we have to make the most of, the dominance of rational instrumentality is woven together with the pervasiveness of secular time.[40] In my understanding, Taylor points out how this instrumental approach toward secular time, which is emblematic for modern people, results in their getting lost in their own little parcel of time, referring to Augustine, and thus they also lose the ability to even imagine the existence or relevance of higher times.[41]

2.4.3 Immanence versus Transcendence

These conditions for (un)belief—the transition from a porous to a buffered self-understanding, the secularization of time, related to instrumental individualism—are central features of the immanent frame, often conceived as the natural order, which Taylor contrasts with the transcendent world. He traces the clear distinction between natural and supernatural as championed by Latin Christendom in the Middle Ages, via the rise of post-Galilean natural science, to the modern concept of the physical universe as governed by invariable laws that can be seen to reflect the wisdom of a creator, but not necessarily so. In bringing together the life of the buffered self, the secularization of time, and the instrumental stance, Taylor demonstrates how the immanent frame came to be enabled as a self-sufficient paradigm of experience.[42]

The newfound authority of science gave the theoretical framework to this idea of a self-sufficient immanent order, while the life of the buffered self, living without reference to or dependence on extra-human agencies, constituted the practical experience of this realm as immanent. Following this is a new understanding of our lives as taking place within a constellation of impersonal and immanent orders. Among these is the social order, which can be seen as offering a blueprint of the providential plan, but such a blueprint can also be attributed to Nature, which again can be identified

---

39. Ibid., 56–57.
40. Ibid., 542.
41. For more on the modern inability to imagine alternative realities, see Taylor's discussion of why the immanent frame remains closed for many modern people (ibid., 549).
42. Ibid., 542.

as identical with God, and then Taylor observes that we end up with a plan without a Planner. Furthermore, when humans see themselves as adhering to the Plan through the process of civilization and Enlightenment, then the notion of a blueprint can be considered fully immanentized, no longer to Nature but to human development.[43]

However, the thrust of Taylor's argument is that even though the immanent frame may be lived as closed to the transcendent, as exemplified above, one may as well prefer to live it as open to something transcendent. He goes on and asks the question: How does the immanent frame remain open? Basically, this is answered by outlining various forms of consubstantiality between "the highest good" and transcendence (e.g., God). When people link their strong evaluations, which Taylor describes as how we distinguish good from evil, noble from base, virtuous from vicious, with God, then an openness to the transcendent seems necessary and right. Obviously, more so is this the case when the notion of the highest good has been formed in religious settings, perhaps even before any conscious deliberation has been undertaken about God's being consubstantial with this good. Another version of the individually made strong evaluations is the collective experience of the good, which may be national, ethnic, or religious.[44]

2.5 Closed World Structures (CWS)

Subsequently, after arguing that a proper understanding of the immanent frame allows for either an open or a closed reading of it, Taylor goes on to explore why the latter has come to be seen as the natural and obvious reading of immanence.[45] This is done by articulating some of the worlds, in Heidegger's sense—i.e., in its meaning for us, where the open reading seems invalid and unjustifiable.[46] Although such articulation inevitably entails generalizations and an intellectualization of the issues at hand, Taylor still contends that it may be conducive to enable us to discover alternatives to the picture that may hold us captive, following Wittgenstein.[47] Thus, it is also possible to gain increased understanding of the varieties of experience and thought when the differently structured pictures are revealed.[48]

43. Ibid., 543.
44. Ibid., 544–45.
45. Ibid., 550–51.
46. Ibid., 556.
47. Wittgenstein, *Philosophische Untersuchungen*, 53, paragraph 115.
48. Taylor, *ASA*, 557.

The four worlds he outlines are termed closed world structures (CWS) by Taylor, and refer to axiomatic and unchallengeable understandings in the modern world, presupposing a closed reading of the immanent order. His aim is to demonstrate that even though these CWS may be considered as obvious and unshakeable, they are rather grounded on simplified and illegitimate naturalizations of what in fact are, according to Taylor, complex cultural developments. While sketching out four different CWS, he maintains they are all linked together by the common narrative of maturation.[49] This narrative portrays religion as emanating from a childish need for comfort and a soothing environment, which the belief in a benign God supervising a providential world supposedly provides.

2.5.1 CWS 1: The Death of God

The first CWS, which Taylor simply refers to as "the death of God," relies heavily on the assumption of religion's intellectually inhibiting disposition.[50] A central feature of the phrase "God is dead," both as it was made famous by Nietzsche and as it is currently interpreted, is that it is impossible in our modern world to be a rational and honest person—and still believe in God. This conviction is argued mainly on two fronts, according to Taylor—one being the idea that modern science has delivered us from superstitious belief and mythical explanations that resist the truth, and the other that to be a delivered unbeliever is to face reality, which is that human beings are on their own, yet still affirm the worth of humanity and fight for human good, however, now without any false pretenses.[51]

Taylor questions this modern humanist tendency to view all-around materialism as an inevitable corollary to modern science. Materialists seem too eager to accept what Taylor calls inconclusive arguments, and he claims that the reason for this hesitation about looking too closely at the details is that this CWS defines the human ethical predicament as being able to form our own beliefs.[52] Further, conversion stories about people of faith who had to bow to the facts, often reluctantly, serve as accreditation for the impression of this understanding as being epistemically driven.[53]

---

49. Ibid., 589–90.
50. Ibid., 560.
51. Ibid., 562.

52. Taylor here either presumes that these apparent "inconclusive arguments" are obvious in their nature to the reader—or he simply neglects to expound on this matter, which I believe weakens his argument. He does refer to Alister McGrath on the matter in a footnote, see ibid., 562 n. 27.

53. Ibid., 563.

2.5.2 CWS 2: The Subtraction Story

The second CWS is the subtraction narrative. Taylor announces early on his opposition to subtraction stories that describe secularity, or modernity, as the happy result of humanity finally liberating itself from the limited knowledge and illusions pertaining to religious beliefs.[54] According to this subtractionist view, modern humanism emerged when old horizons were wiped away, and thus it is unthinkable to retain any old beliefs if one is to be fully with the modern age. As concern with the transcendent reality is sloughed off, people are left with the human good, which seems to be the only legitimate concern for modern societies.[55]

Taylor questions two of the central premises that ground the subtraction narrative. First, the subtraction narrative rests on a particular conceptualization of religious belief as being the result of deprivation and lack of human hope, resulting in misery and strict self-renunciation, which represent the exact opposite of the idea of human flourishing.[56] Second, the subtraction story tends to present the coming of modernity as changes in belief, against the fuller account of complex cultural changes, such as new understandings of self, society, and time. Related to this latter critique lies one of the strongest currents in Taylor's work as I view it. By delineating the broader strokes of the ways in which the Western experience of the human condition has changed, e.g., as autonomous agents and masters of their destiny, he challenges the shortcut version of the subtraction narrative.[57]

2.5.3 CWS 3: Modern Social Spaces

The third kind of CWS Taylor refers to is related to social and political formation. He describes the historical transitions moving from a narrower world of close-knit networks, entailing hierarchical and claustrophobic systems of relations, to the modern liberation into a broader terrain, where people overcame old distinctions and got together as fellow citizens.[58] In order for this to happen, a new kind of space with new forms of justice, liberty, and solidarity had to be established, in opposition to the structures and rules of the ancien régime. While Taylor readily admits the religious leaders' adherence to several of the counter-values, such as structures based on cos-

---

54. Ibid., 22.
55. Ibid., 572.
56. Ibid., 572.
57. Ibid., 573.
58. Ibid., 575.

mic orders or the condemning of certain human goods, he still maintains that the rise of modern social spaces did not rest on the battle against religious views. In support of this claim, he argues that Christian thinkers have certainly contributed to modern ideas, such as Christian democracy and modern moral order (e.g., Locke). Most importantly, though, Taylor wants to point out how the anti-religious versions of the social and political transition stories too easily become self-evident and uncontested.[59]

2.5.4 CWS 4: The Self-Authorization Story

Finally, the fourth CWS is a ubiquitous facet of secularity, which Taylor considers particularly important in explaining why the closed reading of the immanent frame has become so obvious: the notion of human self-authorization. It can be seen as a radicalization of the pusillanimity argument undergirding the maturation narrative, but it is not only about outgrowing immature illusions; humans have now come to establish the true facts and values by which they live, without any reference to (or alleged inference from) extra-human authority. Humanity's search for meaning in a supposedly indifferent universe is certainly convoluted but, according to Taylor, also unavoidable.

In illustrating how self-authorization may materialize when facing the force of meaninglessness, he refers to Albert Camus' form of humanism. Camus articulated a shift in the human condition, from being confident in religious-metaphysical illusions to being left with "the unreasonable silence of the world."[60] He maintains, like Taylor, that a crucial part of the human experience is the call to make sense of the world and our existence in it, but as this call can no longer find answers in a transcendent providential order (and on this Taylor obviously is at variance with Camus), Camus argues that humanity ought to stand tall, asserting its nobility and honor, and unite in a revolt against absurdity itself.[61] Such a revolt means fighting whatever battles we can for the provisional happiness that might be achieved, even though it is a fight that will be lost in the end.[62]

Notwithstanding their differences, Taylor sees in Camus' position an inspiring ideal of courage, as it pursues the good in the face of ultimate failure, accepting no hope beyond history but still be fully committed to

---

59. Ibid., 579.

60. Ibid., 583.

61. On the apparent contradiction of speaking about absurdity in a universe without any expectation of meaning, see ibid., 583.

62. Ibid., 585.

the right, which for Camus entailed acting for the benefit of all. Contrasting this, Taylor refers to Nietzsche's sense of self-authorization as an exhilarating emancipation in discovering that all meaning is our own to shape.[63] Taylor's claim, however, is that independently of how the story of self-authorization is told, it is too easily taken for granted as an axiomatic trait of modernity, and thereby also making the closed take on immanence seem unavoidable. But according to Taylor, the logic of the self-authorization narrative is far from self-evident: Can humans really invent their own binding values? And why would these standards command any authority and allegiance? These are some of the issues the transcendent references attempted to make sense of, and Taylor questions the presumption that secular accounts are more convincing than the traditional ones.[64] In the following, I will attend to Taylor's critique of the CWS in a systematic approach, attempting to articulate some challenges that the church in a secular age must navigate.

---

63. Ibid., 586.
64. Ibid., 588–89.

3

Challenging the Church

THROUGHOUT TAYLOR'S ACCOUNT OF the immanent frame and its CWS, he returns to a cluster of related critiques intended to contest the CWS reviewed above. He repeatedly affronts the assumption that the immanent frame prescribes closure toward a transcendent faith and, in examining the CWS, Taylor argues that these structures are disguised in a bogus neutrality that naturalizes the closed perspective. The CWS naturalize certain views by conveying that this is simply how things appear when prejudices are removed. Thus, other contributing preconditions are occluded and sometimes also discredited as being in opposition to what appears to be natural, such as the social reconstruction of human identity, which Taylor claims is decisive to the attractiveness and convincingness of the CWS.[1]

This chapter is structured around three challenges I have articulated based on my analysis of Taylor's critique of some of the presuppositions of the CWS. The analysis proceeds according to three movements: first, Taylor's point of critique is presented as clearly and accurately as possible. Second, Taylor's argument is examined in order to determine which of the CWS are most effectively contested by the various points of critique. At this stage I will distinguish and point out when Taylor himself addresses an explicit CWS in his argument, versus when I consider his critique to implicitly pertain to any of the CWS presented in the previous chapter. Thus, displaying how the CWS can be contested in order to open up the immanent frame toward transcendence, I provide in this second movement the necessary groundwork for the third movement, which is to articulate challenges that the church in a secular age needs to navigate. Substantiating this third move is the premise that the only way for the church's belief and practice to be both intelligible in a secular age and faithful to Christianity,[2]

1. Ibid., 560.

2. "Christianity" refers to the many-faceted tradition that in its multiplicity adheres to the lowest common multiple of the Apostle's Creed. While such a qualification can be contested on various grounds, e.g., that it is too theoretical or general, I still think it works as a theological demarcation (see a related consideration made above, chapter 1.4.2, n. 39).

is if the immanent frame can be opened toward transcendence by convincingly contesting the CWS.

All three movements will be carried out through the optic of the book's big question, necessitating that my emphasis is put on the aspects that most clearly offer relevant and challenging findings in order to address that question. A related premise for the articulation of the challenges (to the church) is that, as a theologian whose interest is to explore the contributions of a particularistic ecclesiology for the church in a secular age, I will intentionally articulate the challenges in order to bring out what I consider to be the most constructive insights of my main material, which is Hauerwas's ecclesiology. However, it is with deep respect for the integrity of Taylor's text and argument, I do so, and therefore I have verified my readings with other sources, while choosing not to beleaguer the analysis with such secondary references. With these introductory comments in place, I turn to the first facet of Taylor's critique, which assesses the central principles of modern epistemology.

3.1 The Challenge of the Deconstructed Truth

3.1.1 Taylor's Critique of Modern Epistemology

Epistemological questions are relevant to ecclesiology, since asking about the church's identity and practice also raises the valid question of how we know what we claim to know about the church and its identity (i.e., practices and beliefs). Taylor argues that modern epistemology offers a picture of knowledge and understanding as gains pursued by individuals, who rationally gather information which they subsequently structure and combine according to inner representations. These inner representations may be either mental pictures, or propositional truth-sentences. An example of a mental picture functioning as an inner representation, which, Taylor claims, directs and structures how people think and reason, is modern epistemology itself.[3]

Taylor explains pictures as what make up the background for our understanding, and refers to Ludwig Wittgenstein's notion of picture, which is described by Taylor as a largely unarticulated and therefore unrivalled outlook that delimits and determines our thinking.[4] In the preceding

---

3. Taylor, *ASA*, 557. For a more detailed critique of modern epistemology, see *Philosophical Arguments*, 1–19.

4. Taylor, *ASA*, 549.

paragraphs in Wittgenstein's *Philosophische Untersuchungen*,[5] which Taylor explicitly refers to, Wittgenstein points out that propositions seem obvious to us because we naturalize their content by repeatedly assuming their correlation to reality. But the propositions merely describe the frame through which we look at reality, or what Wittgenstein terms nature. And similar to Taylor's emphasis on our inability to question the background, partly because it often remains unacknowledged, Wittgenstein argues that the picture that captivates us is embedded in our language, and therefore impossible to escape.[6]

The picture of modern epistemology is characterized by a series of priority relations, which says something both about the sequential order of what is known before what, and about what kind of knowledge can be derived from other kinds of knowledge. First, there is the knowledge of self and its conditions; then, on basis of this primary knowledge of self, knowledge of outer reality and others may be attained. The outer reality, or things of this world, is viewed as neutral and representing the natural order. To this neutral reality is then attributed diverse values and meanings. Finally, if any inference about transcendence is attempted, it is drawn from our knowledge of the natural order. Thus, Taylor concludes, according to modern epistemology, any intimation of transcendence belongs to the most tenuous end of the series of priority relations.[7]

From within the modern epistemological picture this series of priority relations seems unproblematic, like most CWS, often because they come across as obvious results from scientific discoveries. In Taylor's examination of the CWS, he wants to display their attractiveness and convincingness, as well as present contestations that demonstrate some of the ambiguities of the CWS. However, when questioning the epistemological series of priority relations, Taylor refers not merely to ambiguities but also to Heidegger's comprehensive refutation of modern epistemology, reiterated in brief by Taylor in the following four points.[8]

1. Our inner representations of the external reality, best understood as sentences held true, make sense only as part of the ongoing activity of coping with the world (and our existence in it), as bodily, social, and cultural beings.

---

5. Wittgenstein, *Philosophische Untersuchungen*.
6. Ibid., 53, paragraphs 114–15.
7. Taylor, *ASA*, 558.
8. Ibid., 558–59.

2. The coping activity is primarily a social activity into which individuals are more or less consciously initiated. The sociality of the coping practices does not exclude the claims that may be laid on individuals through such practices.

3. Our coping deals with *pragmata*, things that have relevance and meaning for us from their first occurrence in our world. Later, we attain the ability to distance ourselves from the *pragmata* and consider them without relations to coping activity.

4. The *pragmata* may include focal points of higher valor that serve to structure our whole way of life. This fourth stage is the most controversial, and it is possible to concur with the three stages above without conceding to the idea of a higher (and structuring) focal point.

With Heidegger's assistance, Taylor argues that as knowing agents we do not follow a series of priority relations, since the allegedly inferred values and meanings are prerequisites for our knowing and grasping the external world. Thus, there is no neutral knowledge of reality, but what we know we get to know as part of being inducted into the collective coping practices in which we engage as cultural, social, and bodily beings. This also means that there is no temporal priority of self-knowledge over knowledge of reality and others, since our sense of identity is primarily shaped by the social action of which we are part.[9]

3.1.2 Contesting CWS 1 and 4

A central premise of the priority relations of modern epistemology is that our knowledge of outer reality is conceived as objective and neutral knowledge, upon which we may infer values and potentially, but tenuously, relations to the transcendent. In his attempt to overturn modern epistemology, Taylor challenges this understanding of neutral knowledge as a prior qualification to other forms of knowing, related to beliefs and values. Following his claim that what we come to know is preconditioned and construed in an ongoing coping activity, which also relates to Taylor's argument of holding together altered beliefs and altered experiences below, the modernist review of the death of God CWS as grounded in objective knowledge must be re-evaluated. If the question of God's existence, or alternatively death, is raised within the picture of modern epistemology, it is compellingly refuted by referring to the priority relations that determine religious knowing to

---

9. Ibid., 559.

be at the tenuous end of the epistemological chain of knowledge, and thus lacking credible status as knowledge.

However, Taylor's critique explicitly challenges the established logic of modern epistemology and argues that what we consider to be knowledge, or sentences held true, has to be explicated as part of the broader framework of coping practices, including social constructions and experiences. Based on this argument, the convincing power of the first CWS comes not from actually representing objective or isolated knowledge in prepositional form, but can best be understood within the enabling framework of secular constructions and practices. With this critical approach, Taylor diminishes the apparently unassailable science-driven status of the first CWS.

A similar charge can be raised against the CWS of human self-authorization, I will argue, since it is a corollary to the first CWS. If science has proven religious belief about God to be illusory, then humans are finally free to ascertain the true facts and values of this world. We are not only free to do this but also bear the responsibility of so doing. However, Taylor claims that we clearly do not decide facts and values for ourselves, but rather exchange one authority for another. The secular predicament is that we have exchanged a transcendent and religious authority for the authority of scientific facts and investigations.[10] This exchange overlaps with the entry of modern epistemology and its priority relations, being based on the same arguments of humanity's maturation and capability. Modern epistemology starts out with knowledge of self and its conditions, confident of the human ability to attain neutral knowledge, and the self-authorization story line is based on the concurring logic that with God's demise we are the only capable authorizing agency remaining.[11]

Since the self-authorization story depends on scientific knowledge being considered as neutral and prior to inferences about values and transcendent beliefs, Taylor's critique of the priority relations of modern epistemology contests a crucial premise when insisting that there is no such thing as neutral knowledge. Rather, we get to know what is true by being habituated to collective coping practices as cultural, social and bodily beings. If the tenets of the self-authorization story are based on knowledge that turns out to be a corollary to certain collective coping practices, then it cannot remain enveloped in a science-driven invulnerability, but must be considered as one social construction among others.

---

10. Ibid., 580.
11. Ibid., 588.

3.1.3 The Challenge of the Deconstructed Truth Summarized

Within the picture of modern epistemology, and its priority relations of knowledge, religious claims are accused of being comforting illusions maintained by an immoral and cowardly escape from reality, while scientific claims are accepted as obvious and self-evident truths.[12] Taylor's contestation, which he calls a deconstruction of epistemology,[13] questions the priority relations of modern epistemology, including the self-evidency of science. This deconstruction of epistemology pertains to the church in two ways that I consider relevant in order to articulate the challenge: First, Taylor's critique of modern epistemology applies to the church, in its more-or-less successful attempts to adapt Christian beliefs to the modern understanding of natural science as "the royal road to truth in all domains."[14] It follows that any experience related to religious belief can only be considered as relevant in an argument about transcendent realities if it has already been scientifically validated, which significantly weakens the epistemological import of experiences.

Secondly, and subsequently, if the church has embraced the premises of modern epistemology too uncritically, Taylor's attempt to overturn those premises opens up an opportunity for the church to retrieve a fuller and more experience-near epistemology. Based on these two observations, and following Taylor's deconstructive critique, the challenge of a deconstructed epistemology must be navigated by the church in a secular age. Since human understanding of truth and how we acknowledge something to be true, is decisive for what we hold to be true, I will in the continuing discussion refer to the deconstructed epistemology of truth by the shorthand *deconstructed truth*. In the later chapter on Taylor's critique of the excarnation of religion, a related challenge is articulated but with a specifically theological angle rather than primarily epistemological.

3.2 *The Challenge of the Detached Self*

3.2.1 Taylor's Critique of Secular Constructions of Human Agency and Fullness

According to Taylor, a crucial condition of modern epistemology, together with several of the CWS, is that certain pretenses are accepted as the

12. Ibid., 561–62.
13. Ibid., 559.
14. Ibid., 568.

inevitable corollary to scientific discoveries. One such pretense is what Taylor calls the story of adulthood, which claims that the courageous embrace of science and reason is part of humanity's maturation and liberation from religious superstition. Part of the attack on religion since the Enlightenment follows this line of argument, claiming that religion expresses an immature and childish resistance to the truth. Much like children who seek comforting illusions in a dangerous and threatening world, but then when they grow up they have to adjust to most of reality as indifferent to them, so also religious people should realize that religion and the idea of a benign God emanate from the lack of courage to mature into adulthood.[15]

Thus, Taylor argues that the story of adulthood appears as part of the unquestioned background for our understanding, or like a Wittgensteinian picture, which most often goes unnoticed, yet influences how we think, experience, and reason. Taylor remains convinced of the value of articulating how various pictures may hold us captive, for the sake of both understanding our predicament as well as gaining insight into why different people or groups of people may find it difficult to communicate. Various pictures structure our way of thinking, experiencing, and arguing differently, and Taylor's point is that when such a picture is assumed to be merely the sum of scientific discoveries, it closes off the option or ability to see how every picture consists of several constructs that enable that particular picture to appear obvious and unassailable.[16]

Returning to the story of maturing into adulthood, Taylor argues that its credibility lies not in its scientific discoveries, but rather in a carefully constructed moral agency that idealizes the courageous affirmer of human good without the need for any false consolation or transcendent authority.[17] With this change in the construct of moral agency, the human proclivity toward transcendent belief, which previously was assumed to express the drive toward truth, is now interpreted as a dangerous and cowardly temptation.[18] However, to make the claim that something passed off as simply registering discoveries is, in fact, about replacing constructions, does not disallow the role of science and reason related to the issues at stake. The emphasis on constructions that are replaced, including our sense of human agency, complicates the notion of rational human beings who simply register scientific discoveries and their consequences.[19]

15. Ibid., 561.
16. Ibid., 557.
17. Ibid., 562.
18. Ibid., 563.
19. Ibid., 565.

3.2.2 Contesting CWS 1, 2, and 3

Within the picture portraying scientific discoveries as the principal and unquestioned authority and driving-force in history, several CWS are assumed to be indisputable consequences of registering such discoveries. Taylor refers explicitly, as an example, to the first CWS presented in the previous chapter (i.e., the death of God) as a property of the universe the way science has discovered it to be.[20] This argument is, according to Taylor, a severe short-circuiting, which leaves the CWS in no need of defense. If the conclusion about a godless universe appears to be driven by science, there is a certain and indisputable objectivity related to it. The scientific objectivity is, however, compromised if the link from scientific discoveries to the death of God-claim turns out to be less convincing than proposed by notorious atheists such as Richard Dawkins.[21]

Taylor questions the logic of this link by pointing out that a scientific understanding of the human capacity to investigate and control nature, through the use of disengaged reason, may well be coupled with the transcendent belief in a benevolent creator. And if Taylor is right about his claim that scientific discoveries do not make up a conclusive case for atheism, which I think he is, then his corollary question seems important to attend to. If the arguments based on scientific discoveries are inconclusive with regard to a transcendent reality, why are they assumed to be so convincingly in favor of atheism?[22] Taylor suggests that the convincing power comes from a new construction of human identity, including moral agency, and our predicament in the world.[23] When these constructions sink to the level of a picture that makes up the unquestioned background for our understanding, we cease to acknowledge the atheist interpretation of scientific discoveries as merely one possibility among others. An important point for Taylor is that the atheist interpretation relies on compatible constructions that need to be recognized in order to be critically evaluated.[24]

Similarly, the convictions of the subtraction story (CWS 2) rest on a compatible construct of human good as an exclusively immanent concern, which stands in diametric opposition to religious belief and practice. The argument of the subtraction story maintains that when we subtract references

20. Ibid.
21. Ibid., 567.
22. Ibid., 569.
23. This claim relates to Taylor's critique of the CWS of self-authorization, but since I already pointed out the interrelatedness of CWS 1 and 4 in chapter 3.1.2, I will not repeat the argument here.
24. Taylor, *ASA*, 571.

to God and a transcendent reality, by simply registering what scientific discoveries reveal, we are left with human good as the sole concern of modern society. Taylor's critique disputes the adequacy of this story by pointing out that such demands as universal justice and benevolence are not sufficiently warranted by referring to the mere subtraction of what was previously considered to be good or valuable. To be rid of transcendent concerns does not automatically make human welfare, equality, and freedom the new goals for humanity. The inference of the subtraction story—that when religious beliefs are cast off humanity can realize a better existence—is thus grounded in a picture of, among others, human motivation and flourishing. For Taylor, this picture is made up of replaced constructions that enable the logic of the subtraction story.[25]

The third CWS, consisting of the understanding of our social and political condition, I will argue also is affected by Taylor's deconstructive argument about the importance of replaced constructs.[26] A common conception of the modern society in a secular age is that it is made up of equal individuals who have been liberated from claustrophobic and hierarchical relations in order to gain unmediated affiliation with larger wholes such as nation, economy, or public sphere.[27] The modern concept of social and political spaces is based on the constructs of certain ideals of human agency and individualism, and is not merely the result of a society liberated by scientific discoveries from religious notions of transcendent goods and hegemonic church structures. According to Taylor, rather than seeing the benchmark values of modern social spaces, commonly known as liberty, power, mutual benefit, and reason, as threatened by and in opposition to religious notions of transcendent good, the latter may offer important insight into the limitations of these "Enlightenment" values.[28]

3.2.3 The Challenge of the Detached Self Summarized

When Taylor, in this contestation of the CWS, argues that several of the atheist claims assumed to be grounded in scientific discoveries are in fact a chosen interpretation based on replaced constructions, he contributes to an

---

25. Ibid., 572.

26. In Cavanaugh, *Theopolitical Imagination*, William Cavanaugh argues that the concepts of state and civil society primarily presuppose our collective disciplined imagination. He also argues that these notions entail abandoning theological anthropology in favor of seeing self and other as individuals with certain rights that "serve only to separate what is mine from what is thine" (ibid., 44).

27. Taylor, *ASA*, 575.

28. Ibid., 578–79.

open reading of the immanent frame that conditions how people's convictions about self and society are shaped in a secular age. How, then, can this part of Taylor's contribution represent a challenge for the church in a secular age?

In order to articulate how the church is challenged by the replaced constructions, it is necessary to clearly define what constructions Taylor is referring to, and what constructions I will refer to in the following. Taylor's review of the constructions of human agency and human good/fullness I consider to be of crucial importance for my purpose in this book, due to their historic relation to the church and their general correlation to religious beliefs and practices. According to Taylor's genealogical account, both the constructions of human agency and human good/fullness were previously related to a transcendent reality, but have been replaced by constructions that are closed off toward transcendence. He argues that it is possible to live within these new constructions and simultaneously to maintain rival notions of good/fullness, which may be related to religious beliefs, and thus may function as a limit and modifier for the immanentist/materialist constructions. However, if the latter constructions are made exclusive, they have a self-affirming effect, which then entrenches us in a picture that becomes unchallengeable.[29]

With this analysis, Taylor's conception of human agency seems to follow the modernist view of the individual as a rational and decisive agent, who freely can choose whether to maintain rival notions of good besides the immanentist notion of human good, or make the latter exclusive. However, he also claims that what he wants to describe is the näive construals that most people are not aware of, but live in without even articulating them.[30] In my reading, it is exactly these two presumptions that give impetus to Taylor's project, because if the constructions of human agency and human good/fullness are construals that the majority of people in a secular age naively live in, but potentially may consider inadequate if made aware of alternative constructions, then it seems imperative that they be made aware of the alternatives. It is further along this line of argument that I will articulate the relevant challenge for the church.

Taylor speaks of various forms of human agency: rational agency,[31] creative agency,[32] and collective agency,[33] among others. While these are all fac-

29. Ibid., 566.
30. Ibid., 30.
31. Ibid., 8.
32. Ibid., 597.
33. Ibid., 484.

ets of how human agency, i.e., the ability to act intentionally,[34] is practiced, I will pursue what Taylor refers to as moral agency, both due to its correlation with human good and its theological relevance.[35] He disputes whether the sociobiological or naturalist account of our moral agency sufficiently justifies the phenomenology of universalism.[36] The sociobiological argument is that the human tendency, caused by evolution, is to show solidarity with our own group, and when this group is extended in our perception, our moral commitments become universal. The "naturalist" account, following Hume, also refers to an innate human tendency to sympathy, which is extended through the progress of globalization, leading to a universal ethic. The issue at stake for Taylor is that we need an enriched ontology that resolves the lack of ability by the forementioned accounts to capture our moral life.[37]

Concurring with Taylor's request for an enriched ontology that accommodates more adequate constructions of moral agency and human fullness than those dominating in a secular age, I will argue that this constitutes an important challenge for the church. Considering that the sociobiological or naturalist constructions of moral agency eliminate any transcendent references, as do the fullness-constructions of unbelief, these constructions detach the human self both horizontally and vertically: The heroic individual may well act beneficially for others, but she is a lone hero in these modern constructions.[38] So the secular notion of a detached self presents an obvious challenge for the church, whose theological anthropology defines humans in relation to God and others. In some sense the reductive materialism affecting the secular constructions of human self and fullness presents the opposite of the religious move toward excarnation, to which I now turn my attention.

---

34. More precisely, agency is "the human capacity to employ intention, deliberation, and choice to make decision and to impose them on the surrounding world" (Smith, *What Is a Person?*, 69f).

35. Taylor has previously offered a comprehensive account of the moral sources that are constitutive for human moral agency, in Taylor, *Sources of the Self*.

36. Recent work from the biologist (and founder of socio-biology) Edward O. Wilson on social evolution and group-selection addresses aspect of this insufficiency (Wilson, *The Social Conquest of Earth*).

37. Taylor, *ASA*, 608–9.

38. Ibid., 601.

3.3 The Challenge of Disembodied Beliefs

3.3.1 Taylor's Critique of the Secular Excarnation of Religion[39]

A third facet of Taylor's contestation of the CWS is a critique of the lopsided emphasis on altered beliefs, which he claims characterizes several of the CWS, and the affiliated neglect in articulating the new ways we experience our existence in the world.[40] Following Taylor's approach to examining the secular society, which focuses on the secular conditions for our moral, spiritual, and religious experience and search, this critique echoes his concern that the predominant interest related to belief tends to be expressed in the *what*-question: What do people believe and practice? Although this is an important question, Taylor claims the answers it begets tend to be both inadequate and implausible.[41]

Therefore, he pursues a more comprehensive account of the various kinds of lived experience, e.g., as a believer, an unbeliever, or somewhere in-between. Taylor relates the various forms of lived experience to certain understandings of fullness in life, as seen above. When such places of fullness have been situated and articulated, they may offer a moral or spiritual direction to our lives. Taylor explains the expression "places of fullness" as an activity, or condition, that brings an experience of richness, wholeness, and inspiration. Thus, we identify fullness primarily through experiences that may be uplifting or sublime in one way or the other, and their ability to orient us comes from sensing what they are of, be it the presence of God, the voice of nature, or the force flowing through all that exists.[42]

A fuller conception of the secular predicament requires that we go from the CWS' emphasis on changes in beliefs to a fuller account of changed experiences. This shift is related to the previous facet of Taylor's contestation of the CWS, which calls for an argumentative move from explanations based on scientific discoveries to explanations based on replaced constructions. Both shifts are related to the overturning of epistemology, as well, with its insistence that our truth claims are only intelligible in the context of our experiences as bodily, social, and cultural beings. In the chapter summary, I will attempt to give a more detailed sketch of how the facets of Taylor's deconstruction of the CWS overlap, and hence how the challenges for the church are also variably overlapping.

39. Ibid., 613.
40. Ibid., 573.
41. Ibid., 3–4.
42. Ibid., 5–6.

3.3.2 Contesting CWS 2 and 4

As previously noted, Taylor points out that the subtraction story is contingent on replaced constructs of how human fullness and moral agency are conceived, rather than its logic being merely the result of registering scientific discoveries. Another and related facet of Taylor's contestation of the subtraction story (CWS 2) is that it gives too much credence to changes in beliefs, which are corollaries to registering discoveries at the expense of a fuller account including the altered experiences that Western modernity has brought on. These altered experiences are corollaries to replaced constructs: for instance, the *construction* of human agency as cut off from transcendent powers or ideals enables our *experience* of being autonomous agents, reveling in choices and perhaps even in control of history.[43]

If we ignore how the replaced constructs influence and alter our experiences, we are left with an account solely of altered beliefs, which Taylor considers an unconvincing master narrative. Acknowledging the postmodern dispute over the concept of master narratives, he argues that they are still essential to the way we think, and therefore it is imperative to be aware of what master narratives we depend on, as well as being willing to debate them openly.[44] All the four CWS outlined in the previous chapter are components of such a master narrative which, according to Taylor, precludes an open reading of the immanent frame. Through the somewhat haphazard contestation of the CWS Taylor offers an alternative master narrative that allows for an open reading of that immanent frame.

Taylor is critical of the lopsided emphasis on changed beliefs, and repeatedly challenges the argument of the subtraction story that assumes certain beliefs of the secular society have merely been subtracted and adapted to accommodate scientific discoveries. While this may be an accurate assumption to a certain extent, according to Taylor, the subtraction story offers an insufficient portrayal of the modern changes in convictions because it does not account for how altered experiences and sensibilities function as vital corroborators to such changes. Together with the reminder of the import of replaced constructions, his critique of the subtraction story exposes argumentative deficiencies that positions it as merely one potential social construct among others.

Previously, I argued that Taylor's critique of modern epistemology contests the fourth CWS (self-authorization story), by challenging the delimited view of knowledge processes expressed in the priority relations. Following Heidegger, Taylor rebuffs the subjectivist view of the human capacity for knowledge as based on a cognitive method, which ignores the

---

43. Ibid., 573.
44. Ibid.

social, bodily, and cultural aspect of human knowing. Taylor's critique of the secular over-emphasis on changes in beliefs is thus related to the epistemological argument, since both points of critique rest on an insufficient account of the modern construction, and following experience, of human self-authorization. Similar to the way in which modern epistemology gives the self-authorization story a science-driven invulnerability by undermining important aspects of human knowing and knowledge, the emphasis on the altered beliefs of modernity undermines the significance of altered experiences in giving the self-authorization story (CWS 4) credibility.

Taylor points to the modernist experience of being delivered from any transcendent authority, or the experience of being courageous in facing existence's absurdity, as examples of experiences that enable and "naturalize" the conception of humanity as self-authorizing.[45] These experiences are dependent on the replaced constructs discussed in the previous facet of Taylor's deconstruction, and thus the overlapping and correlation of his critical arguments are in evidence. Similar overlaps and correlations can be found in the challenges I have articulated based on my analysis of Taylor.

3.3.3 The Challenge of Disembodied Beliefs Summarized

According to Taylor, there has also been a push toward what he calls excarnation in the Reform of Latin Christendom, and I will argue that this is closely related to the amplified focus on how our beliefs change. The excarnation of religion, which Taylor discusses, is characterized by a religious life residing "in the head," and is concerned with proper beliefs, unlike a religious life which is embedded in bodily forms of ritual, worship, and practice, and thus induces altered life experiences.[46]

The push toward the excarnation of Christianity is accompanied by the Cartesian ideal of the disengaged and rational self, which distances itself from the embodied understanding and experience of things, in order to gain clear knowledge.[47] According to Taylor, the Cartesian ideal is also reflected in the aspect of human linguistic–communicative activity that has been emphasized by modern Western religion, which is one of prose and descriptive language, as opposed to the aspects of bodily habitus and symbolic expressions. In his critique of the modern Western religious tendency to focus on propositional truth at the expense of right worship, Taylor also

---

45. Ibid., 583.
46. Ibid., 613.
47. Ibid., 614.

offers a critique of the church and its inability to maintain the imperative correlation between beliefs (reason) and experiences (action).[48]

Following both Taylor's critical argument highlighting the unacknowledged significance of altered experiences in a secular age and his claim about the excarnation of religion, I will suggest that the church needs to navigate *the challenge of disembodied beliefs*.[49] Correlated with the challenge of deconstructed truth, they both problematize the reductionism of understanding truth and belief as primarily, and even entirely, residing "in the head."[50] However, Taylor acknowledges that there have been movements trying to counter this excarnation, ranging from yogic practice to religious forms of embodied rituals such as fasting, healing, or kneeling prayer.[51] Thus, he emphasizes the complexities that are not reflected in ideal types that are intended to portray an overall direction of development. I would add that this disclaimer is relevant as well for my presentation of Taylor's framework, as my goal has been to articulate challenges that are representative for a direction, but not to offer a comprehensive critical assessment of either Taylor or the secularity he attempts to explain.

3.4 *Summarizing Taylor's Secularity*

The task of this chapter has been to articulate some challenges that the church in a secular age must navigate by way of attending to Taylor's contestation of the CWS that prevent the immanent frame from being lived as open toward transcendence. Briefly recapping, the CWS were described under the following headlines: 1) the death of God; 2) the subtraction story; 3) modern social spaces; and 4) the self-authorization story. Tracing Taylor's contestation, which rests on a basic opposition to the crude reductionism he argues that the CWS presuppose, I articulated three challenges for the church in a secular age, related to: 1) the deconstruction of truth; 2) the detachment of self; and 3) the disembodiment of beliefs. It is the task of this book to explore how a particularistic ecclesiology, represented by Hauerwas, might contribute to the church in navigating these challenges, so to his brand of ecclesiology I now must turn.

48. Ibid., 615.

49. For a convincing argument of the necessity for the church (particularly in Europe) to return to the social and political embodiment of its faith, see Sigurdson, "Beyond Secularism?" However, he argues not for any nostalgia on the church's part, but for a redefining of the church as a pilgrim in a post-Christian society (ibid., 188).

50. Taylor, *ASA*, 613.

51. Part of this counter movement can be found in Pentecostalism, with its focus on embodied symbols and practices such as glossolalia and healing. For more on the embodied and experiential nature of Pentecostal rites, see Albrecht, *Rites in the Spirit*.

PART II
THE CHURCH AS COMMUNITY: HAUERWAS'S ECCLESIOLOGY

Each chapter of the following analysis of Hauerwas's ecclesiology will proceed in three steps: First, the ecclesiological feature is presented; second, it is summarized and briefly problematized as an anticipation of the critical discussion in part III; and finally, the third step consists of arguing how Hauerwas's ecclesiological feature relates to the challenges of a secular age. While I attempt to remain close to Hauerwas's terminology in this part, there will be some anticipatory comments, particularly in the second step of summarizing and problematizing, functioning as promissory notes for the critical discussion ahead.

4

The Church as a Storied Community

> We are "storied people" because the God that sustains us is a "storied God" . . .[1]

AS AN ETHICIST, HAUERWAS started out by critiquing the kind of ethical reasoning that assumes the world to be "made up of hard facts that are easily recognizable by reason."[2] By focusing on ethics as rational decisions, the import of moral notions gathered from everyday experiences and embodied in language was, at best, underdetermined and at worst, ignored completely.[3] These incipient convictions about the import of considering ethics in relation to whole ways of living mark Hauerwas's ecclesial program, as well. In a similar manner he claims that moral life and Christian existence both depend on how we see. And how we see is determined by the story that forms our experiences, and eventually our character.

In this chapter, Hauerwas's understanding of church as storied will be presented through approaching the topic from various, but interrelated, angles, starting with the concept of narrative itself. Second, his emphasis on the correlation between story and ways of living is outlined under the heading "Embodying the story." Finally, epistemological issues regarding the potential truthfulness of the Christian story are considered in the form of an excursus, intended to shed light on Hauerwas's implicit epistemology. This excursus also points ahead to the subsequent chapter on church as defining, since questions of truth and truthfulness continue to be relevant, particularly when considering the meaning of a truthful tradition.[4]

---

1. Hauerwas, *Vision and Virtue*, 91.
2. Ibid., 13.
3. Ibid., 20.
4. Hauerwas's notion of tradition is defined and discussed in chapter 5.2.3.

4.1 The Concept of Narrative in Hauerwas's Project

In order to appreciate why Hauerwas argues for the church as a storied community, it is beneficial to start with his understanding of narrative and its importance for theology.[5] While apprehensive about the concept of narrative theology, due to what he considers to be a potential slant towards scholarly narcissism, he acknowledges the importance of (re)discovering the narrative character of biblical texts. Scholarly narcissism (in theology) is, according to Hauerwas, a corollary of abstracting narratives from the concrete people, i.e., the church, who acknowledges the authority of the Bible.

Hauerwas avers that theologians' emphasis on narrative only makes sense in an ecclesial context, and thus he critiques attempts to develop general hermeneutical theories that are not anchored in church practice.[6] Concurring with Hans Frei, he warns about making narrative a general category prior to theological claims. This is poignantly expressed in the claim "Jesus is prior to story, though Jesus' life and resurrection can only be displayed narratively."[7] In the following, I will outline the main points relevant to Hauerwas's understanding of narrative, and how this relates to the church as a storied community.

4.1.1 Narrative as Moral Experience

Principles are not sufficient to a moral language, according to Hauerwas.[8] Rules are dependent on stories to have meaning. Since the moral task is not merely to describe the world as it is (descriptive), but also to envision what it ought to be (prescriptive), it inevitably entails the employment of stories and metaphors. It is exactly through the practice of envisioning what our moral lives should be, in a way that gives narrative coherence and meaning to our existence, that the particularity of Christian ethics is made recognizable. From this, Hauerwas proposes the church as the community wherein the particular Christian story is learned and heard. It is as part of this community that one learns how ideals such as freedom or equality translate into practices. Hauerwas insists that the Christian must first experience the

---

5. Hauerwas seems to use the terms narrative and story interchangeably in his texts, and while he discusses and defines the category of narrative, I have not seen a similar consideration of story (for the former, see Hauerwas and Jones, *Why Narrative?*). I will follow Hauerwas's apparent equating of the two, although being aware that in other contexts they may be differentiated between.

6. Hauerwas, *Christian Existence Today*, 55.

7. Ibid., 57.

8. Hauerwas, *The Hauerwas Reader*, 166.

kingdom as present in Jesus Christ, in order to know what kind of freedom and equality she is to desire.[9]

By stressing the importance of both narratives *and* principles for moral life, Hauerwas opposes the Kantian notion that underlying the variety of human actions there is a universal moral reason that everybody can and should adhere to. When Christians adopt the generalizing language of moral development as a substitute for the particular story about spiritual growth, holiness and perfection, they lose the religious content in their moral language. This is problematic for several reasons, according to Hauerwas.[10] First, Christians regard life as a gift from God, and therefore their moral life is lived in recognition of this, unlike the morality that makes autonomy its ultimate goal or necessary precondition. Hence, Christians seek to live faithfully into the conviction that they belong to the One who offered them the gift of life, which also implies that life cannot be described as an achievement, or be intended to be lived autonomously.[11]

Secondly, a general language of moral development is problematic for Christians because the moral life is learned through imitating another, and not merely by adopting and acting on principles. Proposing the opposite of Kant's assertion that first the autonomous individual chooses to live according to moral principles and then looks to other lives as confirming and instructing examples, Hauerwas argues that the Christian moral life starts with being accepted as a disciple and then starting to learn by imitating a master. Third and finally, the Christian language of holiness and perfection is far more radical than the idea of moral development. It is part of the Christian narrative, which requires conversion, confession, and Christ-imitation.[12] This new way of life that Christians are called to puts them on a path of growth that is never-ending. When stressing narrative as decisive for Christian moral formation, Hauerwas also touches upon the importance of narrative in forming the Christian sense of self, to which we will now turn.

4.1.2 Narrative as Moral Self-Formation

On the premise that our moral behaviour contributes to the formation of self, Hauerwas argues that this is dependent on the development of a character by a narrative that provides a truthful account of our existence.[13]

9. Hauerwas, *The Peaceable Kingdom*, 113.
10. Hauerwas, *A Community of Character*, 130–32.
11. Ibid., 130.
12. Ibid., 131.
13. Ibid., 136.

In analyzing problematic propositions found in Aristotle's and Aquinas's ethics, he makes the case that in order for Christians to form selves sufficiently coherent to deal with the diversity of their moral life, they are reliant on a narrative that helps them understand that they are not their own creations, but their life has been given unto them.[14]

In Hauerwas's analysis of Aristotle and Aquinas, I find three relevant points of interest that help to shed light on his understanding of moral formation. First, he acknowledges the importance of calling attention to the moral self in relation to ethical reflection. In order for a person to be able to act and take responsibility for her actions, she is dependent on a moral self that gives intelligibility to what she does and what happens to her. With this Hauerwas agrees, quoting Aquinas: "The form of an act always follows from a form of the agent."[15] However, his critique can be recapped in the following two points.

Both Aristotle and Aquinas presuppose that the agent has to act as a virtuous person, or person of prudence, which includes acting virtuously for the virtues' own sake. According to Aristotle, in order for a person to act virtuously she has to be a virtuous person. Hauerwas points to the circularity of this position, and claims there is no satisfactory solution to this from within Aristotle's position.[16] Likewise, Aquinas asserts that *how* a person acts is determinative of whether he or she is in fact virtuous, and this *how* is always marked by prudence. In other words, the practice of any virtue is dependent on prudence, yet prudence itself is dependent on moral virtue.

The second and related point of Hauerwas's complaint targets Aristotle and Aquinas's assertion that moral virtue necessarily provides a unity to the self. Though the latter differentiates between various virtues and their prominence, he still maintains there is no possibility of the virtues conflicting, thus presupposing that all men have a single last end, and the unity of virtues is but a correlative of this. Hauerwas assumes that this unity of virtues is proposed by Aristotle and Aquinas because they did not conceive that we live in a world where we are forced to choose among ways of life and virtues that are essentially incompatible. Opposing their notion of depending on the practice of rightly balanced virtues to provide us with a moral self, Hauerwas claims that the exercised virtues rather depend on a person's character for direction, and not the other way around. The virtues

---

14. Hauerwas wrote his PhD thesis on Aristotle and Aquinas, which was subsequently published as *Character and the Christian Life*.

15. Hauerwas, *A Community of Character*, 142.

16. Ibid., 140.

in themselves cannot provide us with the ability to claim our actions as our own in a self-consistent way.[17]

Based on this critical analysis, Hauerwas concludes that there is no principle or final end that can provide the self with the desired unity, but rather he suggests that the self ought to be understood as a narrative, and thus the unity of the self is like the unity of a good novel, with both subplots and characters that do not necessarily always relate to the primary plot of the novel. Normatively, a narrative is required in order to provide the skills to navigate the conflicting loyalties and roles that are part of our existence. Hauerwas further concretizes this point by telling an autobiographical story, through which he wants to illustrate how a true story provides the moral integrity to not deny the diversity of our lives, and the ability to claim as mine both what I wish I had not done as well as what I have done right.[18] Polemicizing against the notion that moral growth is about grasping principles or applying universal moral maxims, he points out that moral growth is about taking responsibility for one's own character. And in order to do that, we need a true story that generates practices of self-examination.[19]

However, it is not a matter of the individual merely choosing a story that may give meaning to her life, but rather, the Christian finds herself as being part of a community whose interest lies in the formation of a moral self and character appropriate to God's activity in the life and death of Jesus Christ.[20] The moral formation of the church is a concrete call to take up the way of life made possible by God's redemption for us. To be redeemed is to place oneself in God's history, be part of his people, and learn to trust in one's existence as a gift. Which brings us to the initial premise that life (and the self) is given to us. Hauerwas contends the need for a story to rightly understand and achieve this gift, and the church is where people are initiated into it, by learning the story and also the habits that the Christian life requires.[21]

4.1.3 Narrative as Theological Ethics

While proposing narrative as an imperative part of theological disciplines such as Christology, ecclesiology, and theological ethics, Hauerwas is explicit in underlining that theology should not be limited to narrative as a

---

17. Ibid., 143.
18. Ibid., 145–46.
19. Ibid., 149.
20. Hauerwas, *The Peaceable Kingdom*, 33–34.
21. Hauerwas, *The Hauerwas Reader*, 250–51.

genre. Therefore, he is adamant about differentiating between his own interest in narrative and concepts like story theology.[22] What is crucial is the proper object of theology, who is God. The theologian who wishes to show how God saves cannot do this without involving a story; however, it is not the story, but God who is "doing the saving."[23]

Still, Hauerwas opposes the idea that narratives are merely illustrative of propositional truths that should be doctrinally articulated in order for us to know the literal truth of theological convictions.[24] The most fundamental way to convey knowledge about God and his works is through stories. Thus, the starting point for theological ethics is a set of stories about God's dealing with creation, which constitutes the Christian tradition, and in turn forms the church community. This contention is related to his insistence on the particularity of Christian ethics. Because the Christian story is a defining story with a determinative content, intended to help the church rightly envision the world, it is meaningless to claim some sort of philosophical universality for theological ethics. Rather, it is precisely within this particular story that a person discovers herself, God, and world. The only way to see this truthfully, though, is through initiation into the community that attempts to be faithful to the Christian story.[25]

In an essay on theological ethics entitled "Reconciling the Practice of Reason: Casuistry in a Christian Context,"[26] Hauerwas traces the argument that leads theologians to assume that theological ethics must begin with metaphysical beliefs that in turn are explicated into their moral implications. By asserting that Christian beliefs are only made intelligible in the context and tradition of the church, Hauerwas refuses the presumption that theology is simply another ethical theory.[27] The issue at stake is thus for Hauerwas, whether God makes a difference for moral decisions and how they are justified.[28] He admits that this is a difficult task to prove, since even

---

22. Hauerwas argues against "story theology" as a substitute for critical analysis, which is an important skill for the theologian to acquire. He also questions the development of a "theology of story," in the sense that story simply becomes a new word for myth, which is seen as an unavoidable part of every human's life, and therefore is supposed to compel belief in Christianity by making all stories count equally (Hauerwas, *Christian Existence Today*, 25).

23. Ibid., 26.

24. Hauerwas, *The Peaceable Kingdom*, 25. I will return to Hauerwas's concept of truth in chapter 4.3.1.

25. Ibid., 29.

26. Hauerwas, *Christian Existence Today*, 67–87.

27. Ibid., 67.

28. Ibid., 68.

theologians think it a mistake to "speak on behalf of God in matters that have to do with ethics."[29]

Hauerwas, however, rarely shying away from a challenging task, proposes by way of referring to the Mennonite tradition that God indeed does make a difference.[30] His proposal of a community-specific rationality offers a critique of the tendency toward reducing practical rationality to a pattern, yet he points out that his proposal still maintains the import of giving reasons for our actions.[31] But while philosophers tend to prefer universal reasons, Hauerwas argues that the intended aim for such attempted generalizing, which is a peaceful community, actually depends on particular communities. They in turn depend on particular stories and might give particular reasons for their actions, although seeking shared understanding on concrete issues.[32] This brings Hauerwas back to the question of whether God matters for moral reasoning; unsurprisingly he tells a story to make his point that without belief in God some of the Christian community's moral choices would not be intelligible, such as seeking reconciliation with perpetrators rather than judgement and revenge.[33]

4.2 *Embodying the Story*

As I have tried to show, narrative is an imperative concept in Hauerwas's theological project. Still, for Hauerwas the *how* is what really matters, and therefore he is adamant about how the Christian story is to be interpreted and embodied.[34] As already indicated, the answer for Hauerwas as to how the Christian story can be made intelligible is within and through the Christian community—in fact, the answer *is* the Christian community. In the following, I will explicate what this claim entails by outlining how Christians come to understand the story, witness to it, and be sustained by, as well as sustaining, the story.

4.2.1 Understanding the Story

In the same manner that Christian beliefs are only made intelligible in the context of the Christian tradition, Hauerwas claims that the theological

29. Ibid.
30. Ibid., 69.
31. Ibid., 84.
32. Ibid.
33. Ibid., 85.
34. Hauerwas, *Hannah's Child*, x-xi.

emphasis on story is made intelligible only in an ecclesial context, as noted previously.[35] Relating to Hans Frei,[36] Hauerwas concurs with his appeal to the church as both the subject and agent of the Christian narrative, which indicates that it is people who refer, and not narratives.[37] The church is the community assigned to test and probe the story, which is told in faithfulness to the Scripture by the whole congregation through the office of the preacher. Therefore, the sermon is a vital communal action, since it is through hearing and understanding the word that the church is formed by it, and thus made part of God's continuing story.[38]

Another important part of understanding the story is attending to the lives of the saints.[39] It is in seeing how the story of Jesus impacted their stories that the church can begin to understand what it means and requires to be a disciple and partake in God's story. Also, knowing how our Christian ancestors were willing to sacrifice everything, including their lives, for the story about a God who is forgiveness, Hauerwas argues that Christians cannot claim this simply as one story among many.[40] Following this line of argument leads to the crucial questions of what makes a story true, and how the Christian story relates to other stories with regard to their truthfulness, which I will return to shortly.

4.2.2 Witnessing to the Story

Related to his claim about the Christian story being intelligible only in the ecclesial context, Hauerwas contends that questions of truth can only be validated through performed practice. Says Hauerwas: "Learning how Christian convictions are a morality is crucial for understanding what it means to claim those convictions are true. Too often religious belief is presented as a primitive mythical worldview, or metaphysics, that cannot be considered true in any verifiable sense."[41] Witnessing to the Christian story of God as creator and redeemer is at the heart of the church's life. However, the work of witnessing is tedious and often seemingly unrewarding.[42]

---

35. Hauerwas, *Christian Existence Today*, 55.
36. Frei, *The Identity of Jesus Christ*, 157.
37. Hauerwas, *Christian Existence Today*, 59.
38. Ibid., 60.
39. Ibid., 40.
40. Ibid., 41.
41. Hauerwas, *The Peaceable Kingdom*, 16.
42. Hauerwas, *Christian Existence Today*, 15.

Hauerwas's emphasis on witness is not argued on the basis that Christians possess some sort of universal truth.[43] Rather, his understanding of the importance of witness is based on the assumption that the only way to know truth is through the process of being confronted by it in the lives of faithful Christians.[44] The task of a storied community is therefore not to conform to any prior universal norm, but to remain faithful to the reality of God's lordship in this world.[45] Central practices for such faithful witness are taking responsibility for one's character, and the commitment to peace-making, to which I will return in the chapter on church as a performative community (esp. 6.3.2). In other words, church as storied must be enacted by the church as performance, and to witness is to perform according to Christian beliefs and commitments.[46]

4.2.3 Sustained by and Sustaining the Story

Through the practices of making the Christian story intelligible and witnessing to its truthfulness, the church is both sustaining and sustained by this story. Herein lies also the double implication of the church's being a storied community; on the one hand, it is the place where the stories of Israel and Jesus are told and enacted, primarily through the office of preaching, hearing, and interpreting the stories, and as such it is the community that has been entrusted with God's story.[47]

On the other hand, the church is the embodiment of the story it upholds, as it is created by God, intended to be a foretaste of his kingdom.[48] The stories of Israel and the gospel stories of Jesus are made intelligible within, and in relation to, the church. Church and story are thus mutually dependent, in the sense that without these stories there would be no church, but the stories of God cannot be abstracted from the teller, i.e., the church, and therefore, the teller and the tale are mutually dependent. Elsewhere, he makes this point even more starkly, by claiming that teller and tale are

---

43. Hauerwas, *A Community of Character*, 105.

44. Tolonen relates Hauerwas's emphasis on witness to the embodied character of his theology (Tolonen, *Witness Is Presence*, 21). I concur with this reading of Hauerwas, and outline my understanding of the embodiedness of Hauerwas's ecclesiology in chapter 6, on church as a performative community.

45. Hauerwas, *A Community of Character*, 149.

46. Hauerwas offers a comprehensive argument on the church's witness in *With the Grain of the Universe*, chapter 8. I will return to this text in the pneumatological reconstruction (chapter 11.3.1), with particular focus on his pneumatological references.

47. Hauerwas, *The Peaceable Kingdom*, 96–99.

48. Ibid., 98.

one.⁴⁹ This is argued on the grounds that the story the church has to tell is not just like any worldview, but in telling the story of an alternative way of life, the church *is* the story and the alternative it tells of.⁵⁰

4.3 A Truthful Story

The importance of truthfulness is a recurring subject throughout Hauerwas's project, and imperative to his conception of the Christian story.⁵¹ Says Hauerwas: "What we require is not no story, but a true story . . . Christians believe Scripture offers such a story."⁵² His focus is always on truth as transforming the self⁵³ as opposed to truth as theoretical propositions, whether he talks about how the church's story works pre-emptively against the danger of self-deception, or the value of truthful virtues such as forgiveness. In this section I will attempt a more thoroughgoing analysis of his conceptualization of truth and truthfulness, and how it relates to his understanding of church as storied, starting with how he differentiates the two terms.

It is difficult to talk about ecclesiology, and even more so ethics, without addressing epistemological questions. The church exists on the premise of the validity of particular truth claims maintained by the Christian tradition. Hauerwas recognizes this, and even emphasizes that it is crucial that the Christian convictions not only are functional, but true.⁵⁴ However, he is hesitant about adhering to a certain epistemological theory, due to his supposition that there is no way to deal with "truth as such."⁵⁵ Instead, he argues that in order to perceive the truth of Christian convictions, the self

---

49. Hauerwas, *Christian Existence Today*, 54.

50. Ibid., 54. Niels Henrik Gregersen has countered Hauerwas's claim that teller and tale are one, in a critical response to Hauerwas, arguing that the discontinuity must be recognized, which Hauerwas does better when he elsewhere claims that the church is part of the tale rather than in unity with it (Gregersen, "The Fluid Mission of the Church," esp. 79). Gregersen's qualification also bears upon Hauerwas's notion of church *as* mission, or church *as* a social ethic; both claims addressed in Gregersen's argument (ibid., 75).

51. I have reflected critically on Hauerwas's notion of the church as a truthful community in the article "Kirken som et sannferdig fellesskap." In conclusion I intimated the critical potential of developing Hauerwas's ecclesiological feature of truthfulness with a more fluid understanding of the communal boundaries and in dialogue, at times tensional, with the plurality of voices in our contemporary society. It is along these lines that I argue the pneumatological reconstruction in part III of the book.

52. Hauerwas, *Christian Existence Today*, 149.

53. Hauerwas, *The Peaceable Kingdom*, 16.

54. Ibid., 15.

55. Hauerwas, *Christian Existence Today*, 8.

must be transformed toward the ideal of *truthfulness*.[56] Hauerwas thereby seems to assume that it is possible to become truthful without (yet) being able to assess the truthfulness of the Christian propositions.[57] Also, he avers that the truthfulness of a claim can only be assessed in relation to the truthfulness of the person making the claim, which is why "the Christian doctrine of sanctification is central for assessing the epistemological status of Christian convictions."[58]

While Hauerwas has not himself worked systematically with epistemological questions, he refers to Sabina Lovibond[59] and Alasdair MacIntyre[60] as authors whose works are representative of his own epistemological position.[61] Since I consider these issues to be of importance in order to better understand Hauerwas's project, I will in the following present briefly the main points of Lovibond's epistemological arguments, and return to MacIntyre's notions of truth and tradition in the next chapter on church as defining.[62]

4.3.1 A QUALIFIED EPISTEMOLOGICAL REALISM: HAUERWAS AND LOVIBOND

Lovibond's project is both a critique of the non-cognitivist position in ethics, and a constructive contribution to a moral realism argued through a particular application of Ludwig Wittgenstein's (later) language philosophy. The non-cognitivist thesis is, according to Lovibond, that there is no

---

56. Ibid., 10.

57. E.g., Hauerwas refers to the necessity for a person to be transformed in order to realize her position as a creature; however, he does not problematize whether it is possible for a person to be thus transformed prior to being able to assess the truthfulness of mentioned propositions. This circularity strikes me as similar to what Hauerwas criticizes in his reading of Aristotle and Aquinas, which is referred to in chapter 4.1.2 above. He critiques them for determining a virtuous person by the ability to act with prudence, while simultaneously claiming prudence to be possible only for the virtuous. Likewise, Hauerwas seems to argue that a person must be transformed in order to realize her status as created, while simultaneously claiming that to be transformed is to realize that same assumption among others.

58. Hauerwas, *Christian Existence Today*, 10.

59. Lovibond, *Realism and Imagination in Ethics*.

60. Hauerwas refers explicitly to MacIntyre's essay "Objectivity in Morality and Objectivity in Science" in Engelhardt and Callahan, *Morals, Science, and Sociality*, 21–47.

61. Hauerwas, *Christian Existence Today*, 20 n. 11.

62. See chapter 5.2.3.

available moral knowledge or truths because there is nothing in this world that actually *makes* them true.[63]

Following this, no value can be both objective and intrinsic, but the notion of intrinsic value becomes instead a matter of subjective judgements. However, non-cognitivism admits the validity of factual propositions about instrumental value—i.e., it can be stated as a fact that certain means lead to certain ends, and insofar the ends are desirable, the means are good.[64] This line of reasoning is also applied to morality, which means that moral requirements cannot be considered universally binding on rational grounds (as in Kantian ethics), but must instead be commended by our reasoning about what kind of behaviour is most likely to lead to the satisfaction of our desires. In this way, non-cognitivists understand the rational individual as one who seeks to maximize her utilities, and thus get as much satisfaction as possible out of the opportunities and resources available.[65]

Lovibond then goes on to outline two common objections to non-cognitivism before proposing a 'realist' alternative, which Hauerwas also adheres to. First, there is the charge of irrationality. When non-cognitivists locate ethics and morality beyond the realm of critical thinking and argument, governed by the norms of truth and validity, their opponents claim that the unavoidable result is an irrationalism which leads to a "subjectivistic suicide of thought."[66] Correlatively, the phenomenological objection attends to the subjective consequences of such a supposedly irrationalist ethical theory: when non-cognitivists insist on the ultimate authority of the individual to place value on her own actions, their critics question whether this actually is either ideal or possible without the individual having any objectively valid references or reasons at her disposal. Thus, the concern of the phenomenological argument is that when the agent is logically disconnected from the regulation of external reality, she ends up with apathy about making choices at all.[67]

Following Wittgenstein, Lovibond constructs a realist position in opposition to the non-cognitivism briefly presented above. She describes it as a naturalistic realism in the way that it conceives moral discourse as embedded in the physical world.[68] The essence of this position is a materialist understanding of language as rooted in a shared way of life, which for Witt-

---

63. Lovibond, *Realism and Imagination in Ethics*, 1.
64. Ibid., 2.
65. Ibid., 4.
66. Ibid., 6.
67. Ibid., 8–9.
68. Ibid., 25.

genstein means that language-acquisition for a child consists in a process of training that leads to initiation into a language-game. This is argued in contrast to the empiricist view of language-acquisition as a theoretical instruction, in which the child is taught the names of objects and then facts about these objects.[69] Lovibond sums up the realist rejection of empiricism by referring to the realist subscription to an expressivist theory of language, a non-foundationalist theory of knowledge, and a non-transcendent theory of rationality.[70]

Thus, the realist position admits the notion of recognition-transcendent truth, in the sense that it does not consider the moral judgement of all individuals on equal footing.[71] Furthermore, moral excellence is more about the ability to assess situations truthfully and without self-deception than it is about exercising an unconditioned will.[72] The moral evaluations that are thus required presuppose, according to Lovibond, that the individual succeeds in finding a meaning in life, because in doing so she will also be able to identify authorities with respect to morality. A crucial prerequisite enabling this process is that the individual is participating in a system of shared activities and moral institutions that provides terms by which she can conceptualize and give meaning to her life-choices and actions.[73]

This brings us back to Hauerwas, who argues his central ecclesiological theses upon a similar line of reasoning: the shared practices of the community of the church enable the individual to make truthful moral assessments. While adhering to the notion of recognition-transcendent truth, his emphasis is consistently on the kind of truth that is embodied by truthful living.

4.4 Summarizing and Problematizing the Church as a Storied Community

Hauerwas's emphasis on the narrative aspect of the church's identity and practice, and his related claim that the church is both the teller and part of the tale, exposes Hauerwas to criticism from various angles. In the critical discussion, I will address one of the crucial sets of problems related to his understanding of church as storied, pointed out by critics and gathered

69. Ibid., 30–31.
70. Ibid., 45–46.
71. Ibid., 72.
72. Ibid., 190.
73. Ibid., 223.

under the heading of fideism.[74] By so doing, there are several arguments regarding narrative theology and the storiedness of the church that are left unmentioned.[75] The former Hauerwas-teacher and ethicist James Gustafson is one of those who has voiced concern regarding the narrative emphasis in Hauerwas's work. Gustafson claims that the status given to narrative by Hauerwas implies a self-justifying property, which immunizes the narrative and its interpretation from correction outside the community sustaining the narrative. I will return to Gustafson's critique, but mention it here both as a foreshadower of the critical discussion and as a reminder of some of Hauerwas's main points.

First, he insists that the church's task is to embody the story. Hauerwas argues that the church is storied in the sense that it is the teller of a story in which it plays an arguably central role. He is careful to underscore that to be a teller is to practice the story, and not merely rehearse a tale. In this, he admits to taking clues from Wittgenstein, *inter alia* regarding the import of social and practical initiation into a particular language and grammar.[76] As for Gustafson's concern, Hauerwas acknowledges that the Christian convictions are self-referential in the sense that they refer to what he argues is the Christian way of living. However, he rejects the notion of Christian convictions as self-referential propositions.[77]

Hauerwas further argues why and how the church has no better alternative than to be the witness testifying to the truthfulness of its story. No scientific investigation can prove that Jesus is Lord, and no philosophical theory can teach someone how to love her neighbour, but this is part of the grammar that the church practices. To know what it means to confess Jesus as Lord requires that someone lives a life under Jesus's lordship. However, Hauerwas distances himself from the sort of pragmatism that William James advocated,[78] among others, because he maintains that Christian convictions do involve truth claims that in principle are open to challenge.[79] Also, the

---

74. See chapter 7.1 below.

75. For an anthology that attempts to provide "a glimpse into the debates about narrative's significance," see Hauerwas and Jones, *Why Narrative?*, 5.

76. Hauerwas, *The Peaceable Kingdom*, xxi. For more on Wittgenstein's influence on Hauerwas, see Hauerwas et al., *Unsettling Arguments*, chapter 1. Also, see Kallenberg, *Ethics as Grammar*, 1–9.

77. Hauerwas, *Christian Existence Today*, 10.

78. See *With the Grain of the Universe*, 43ff, for Hauerwas's exposition of William James' faith.

79. Hauerwas, *Christian Existence Today*, 9.

content of a community's convictions as they are practiced must stand challenge scientifically, metaphysically, and morally.[80]

Second, the eschatological argument running through Hauerwas's ecclesiology places the church in a plot that makes claims on reality that cannot possibly be self-referentially argued for. A central point for Hauerwas is that the church, in witnessing to the Christian story, points beyond itself to an eschatological reality and the promise of a kingdom made present in Christ's life, death, and resurrection. This is a crucial premise for both his ethics and his ecclesiology; however, it seems to me it is underdeveloped and therefore I will later argue how Hauerwas's eschatological underpinnings have potential for pneumatologically reconstructing his ecclesiology if further developed.[81] When he claims that narrative is essential in order to display how Christian existence has a teleological nature, Hauerwas assumes the reality and significance of God's eschatological kingdom for the church's identity and practice, and as such the church is mutually sustained by and sustains the Christian story. Obviously, the credence of such an argument rests on a willingness to accept the tentative nature of teleological and eschatological claims.

4.5 Church as Storied Navigates the Challenge of the Deconstructed Truth

Hauerwas's understanding of church as storied navigates the challenge of deconstructed truth by assuming what Taylor calls the deconstruction of modern epistemology. Taylor questions the priority relations of modern epistemology, with its correlated reductive expositions of humanity's progress and existence.[82] I will argue that in his insistence on truth as storied in the context of community, Hauerwas navigates the secular challenge by critically appropriating the premise of the deconstructed epistemology of truth.

The challenge of deconstructed truth was in the preceding analysis derived from Taylor's critique of the CWS entitled death of God and self-authorization story. The question remains, however, whether Hauerwas's ecclesiological deliberations related to the challenge of deconstructed truth do not end up suggesting a mere reversal of the CWS, which critics claim inevitably entails a fideist stance. Anticipating the critical discussion, it is my opinion that Hauerwas, as a contemporary theologian struggling with

---

80. Ibid., 10.

81. See chapter 11.3 for my proposal on the pneumatological-ecclesiological potential in Hauerwas's eschatological underpinnings.

82. Taylor, *ASA*, 559.

the challenges of modernity and a secular age, attempts to do exactly that, through engaging such varied disciplines as ethics, political science, philosophy, and literature, he argues that theological truth can only be intelligible in the context of the church's story and practice. With his emphasis on church as a storied community, Hauerwas thus proves that he is not subscribing to an understanding of Christianity as mere truth claims, which arguably has been motivated by the modern priority relations of epistemology. Cognizant of the sort of philosophical underpinnings that uphold the CWS of the death of God and the maturation story, Hauerwas makes the case that it is as a storied community that the church can best maintain the truth of the Christian faith.

For the church to be a teller of the Christian story entails practicing a grammar that is taught by the church and intended to be performed as peaceable living in a world of war.[83] Facing the objection that the church does not consistently succeed in living such lives, Hauerwas, following Aquinas, insists that if God is the church's *telos*, virtues such as charity, generosity, and peaceableness will follow.[84] Not automatically, but by being initiated and habituated into the community of the church, the Christian self and character will be defined. To the ecclesiological feature of being defining I now will proceed.

---

83. Hauerwas seems to use "peaceable" and "peaceful" interchangeably. E.g., Hauerwas, *The Peaceable Kingdom*, 12, where he claims ". . . we lose the means to be a peaceable people," and then in the next passage: ". . . a saviour who teaches us how to be peaceful in a world in rebellion against its true Lord."

84. The objection concerning Christians' inability to lead truthful lives will be further discussed in chapter 7.3 below.

5

The Church as a Defining Community

> Therefore the first social task of the church—the people capable of remembering and telling the story of God we find in Jesus—is to be the church and thus help the world understand itself as the world.[1]

CENTRAL TO HAUERWAS'S PROJECT is the differentiation between the church and the world. He underscores the particularity of theological ethics, the Christian story, and thus also the Christian community called church. To state this according to the logic of Hauerwas, Scripture tells a defining story that sustains a defining community, which defines the world by being the church. However, the ecclesiological feature of defining also entails that the church defines Christian character. In this chapter, I will investigate what it entails for Hauerwas to claim that the church is a defining community by exploring two aspects: how the church defines the world, and how the church defines Christian character. However, the defining language of the church is crucial to both, and this is therefore where I must start.

5.1 *The Defining Language of the Church*

Understanding the role of language in Hauerwas's work demands some form of contextualization, which is why I make a "postliberal excursus" after briefly mapping Hauerwas's theological conception of the church's language. The engagement with George Lindbeck is intended to place Hauerwas's thinking in relation to the influential current of postliberal theology, which has also been termed the Yale school.[2]

---

1. Hauerwas, *The Peaceable Kingdom*, 100.
2. For observations about "postliberal theology," the "Yale school," and its main protagonists, see Lindbeck et al., *Postliberal Theology and the Church Catholic*, 3–8.

5.1.1 Pentecost and the Birth of the Church

In "The Church as God's New Language"[3] Hauerwas begins the essay with a Pentecost sermon that speaks about the birth of the church. According to Hauerwas, this was God's undoing of the Babel event in which He confused the peoples' languages in order to scatter them and prevent their concerted effort to "make a name for themselves."[4] The problem at Babel was not that they used their skills in a collaborative venture but that they failed to acknowledge God as the Creator and their dependence on his grace and gifts.[5] Only by appreciating the Old Testament story of Babel can the significance of Pentecost be fully understood. Hauerwas calls it the climax of the Christian year, through which all is summed up in God's creation of the church, by the Spirit.[6] This was the creation of not only a people, but also a language. As Babel was the climax of primeval history, resulting in the dispersal of the peoples through linguistic confusion, so Pentecost was a climax that prefigures the unity of humanity through the Spirit and event of common understanding. The Jews of the diaspora, who had been spread out and learned different languages, suddenly heard the disciples of Jesus praising God in their own language.[7]

This new defining language of the church was not intended to be some "artificial Esperanto that denies the reality of other languages,"[8] but this language was, according to Hauerwas, intended to be more than words. Instead of attempting to achieve unity by concealing differences, God created a church whose language extends beyond individual histories and whose memory of the risen Christ enables these very differences to contribute to the unity of the people. Much as how Hauerwas insists on the church as both telling about *and* partaking in the Christian story, he argues that the church is not only a community with a defining language, but that the church in fact also *is* this language, bearing witness to the God who heals our separateness.[9]

---

3. Originally published in a Festschrift for Hans Frei (Green and Frei, *Scriptural Authority and Narrative Interpretation*, chapter 10), and reprinted in Hauerwas, *Christian Existence Today*, 47–65. The following references are to the latter version. It was also published in Hauerwas, *The Hauerwas Reader*, 142–62.

4. Hauerwas, *Christian Existence Today*, 49.

5. Ibid., 48.

6. Ibid., 47.

7. Ibid., 50.

8. Ibid., 53.

9. Ibid., 53–54.

However, for the church to be this language, Christians must be formed in order to use the language rightly.[10] According to Hauerwas, one crucial formative action is the sermon. In this regard, he makes the interesting claim, with regard to my reconstructive purpose, that it is the Holy Spirit who enables the church to hear the word of God rightly. But in the next sentence, he inserts "the word" as the active agent, and he claims that "Put differently, the preached word's power is its capacity to create a people receptive to being formed by that word."[11] Thus, when Hauerwas seeks to explain what is meant by the Spirit making the church capable of hearing the word rightly, and consequently enabling the right use of the language, he comes back to the power of the word.

Hauerwas's emphasis on language and the sermon is closely related to his understanding of church as a storied community, a correlation that is further warranted by his concluding reflections in this essay.[12] In these reflections, he states that the stress on narrative is intended to make clear the import of where the story is told, which is in the church;[13] how the story is told, which is in faithfulness to Scripture; and who tells it, which refers to the preacher but also assumes that the whole church engages in the telling through the office of the preacher.[14] Hauerwas shares this emphasis on language and story with several theologians, often referred to as "postliberal." It is therefore useful to take a closer look at the central thought of Lindbeck, as he coined the term postliberal and his work sheds light on that of Hauerwas.[15]

5.1.2 A Postliberal Excursus: Hauerwas and Lindbeck

Hauerwas's understanding of the church as both having and being a defining language is linked to his notion of truth, which I addressed in the previous chapter on the church as a storied community.[16] His claim that it is only in the context of a particular story and language that a statement can be considered true or untrue corroborates an overlap with the program of

---

10. Ibid., 60. I will return to the gist of this argument when outlining what Hauerwas means by saying that the church is defining for Christian character, in chapter 5.3.

11. Ibid., 60.

12. "The Church as God's New Language," see n. 3 above.

13. From the context, it seems that Hauerwas refers to what he calls "the churchly event" of the sermon (Hauerwas, *Christian Existence Today*, 60), when he uses the preposition "in" the church (ibid., 61).

14. Ibid., 61.

15. Lindbeck et al., *Postliberal Theology and the Church Catholic*, 6.

16. See chapter 4.3.

Lindbeck, who was a proponent of the postliberals, as outlined in *The Nature of Doctrine*.[17] As the title implies, this work explores various approaches to doctrines, more specifically doctrinal agreements and disagreements among Christian confessions. Renowned for and motivated by his engagement with ecumenical dialogue, this is a notable current that runs through Lindbeck's seminal yet relatively small book. In order to better frame Hauerwas's understanding of the church as storied, defining, and performing, I will provide a short summary of Lindbeck's main points regarding the two key concepts of doctrine and truth.[18]

First, Lindbeck presents three approaches to doctrine that correspond to three periods: 1) the cognitive-propositional approach, which corresponds to the pre-Enlightenment period; 2) the experiential-expressive approach, which corresponds to the Enlightenment period; and 3) the cultural-linguistic approach, which corresponds to the post-Enlightenment period. The cognitive-propositional approach can also be seen as a preliberal method, as it focuses on the correlation between the language of the Bible and the world it describes. Thus, it sees religion as a series of truth claims about objective realities.[19] Rivalling this approach is the experiential-expressive (and liberal) method, which interprets doctrine as non-discursive symbols of inner feelings and existential orientations. The public facets of religion are merely objectifications of what is considered personal experience, which in turn leads to the conclusion that a Buddhist and a Christian may fundamentally have the same faith.[20]

Lindbeck goes on to propose a postliberal alternative, the cultural-linguistic approach, which is his contribution to facing the dilemmas of ecumenical disagreements and interreligious disputes regarding truth claims. If doctrines are seen as language rules, the primary center of Christianity will be found neither in propositional truth claims nor deep within the self of the believer but rather in the actual discourse, practice, and worship of the Christian community.[21] While the experiential-expressive approach assumes religious patterns are derived from a common inner experience, the

---

17. Lindbeck, *The Nature of Doctrine*.

18. Topically, this excursus overlaps with the analysis of Lovibond's critical realism above (chapter 4.3.1), but as I consider Lindbeck's work to be quite informative for understanding some important premises of Hauerwas's ecclesiology, it is still given considerable space.

19. Lindbeck, *The Nature of Doctrine*, 2–4.

20. Ibid., 3.

21. Ibid., 19.

postliberal approach assumes the exact opposite; namely, it assumes that the internal experience is derived from external religious practice.[22]

To appraise the truth of a religion, Lindbeck suggests three approaches, which are correlated to the three approaches to religious doctrine. First, the cognitive-propositional approach is related to an understanding of truth as propositional (i.e., religious statements are appraised according to ontological correspondence).[23] Each statement either does or does not correspond with the structure of reality, which leaves no room for variations or degrees in propositional truth. Second, the experiential-expressive approach is related to an understanding of truth as a function of symbolic efficacy.[24] The truth of a religion is appraised according to how effective its symbols are at articulating the inner experience of the divine, which is fundamentally common to all religions. Third, the cultural-linguistic approach is related to an understanding of truth as categorial adequacy, which means that in order to appraise the truth of a religion one must focus on its "grammar."[25] Categorial adequacy is measured by the ability of a systematic set of categories to interpret reality, thus enabling propositional, practical, and symbolic truth. For example, in order for it to be meaningful to speak of one thing as larger than another, we are dependent on the category of size. Likewise, Lindbeck argues that religious truth should be appraised according to its categorial adequacy: Does the grammar enable meaningful references to what is most important in the universe?[26] He emphasizes that while a religion might be categorially true, this does not ensure propositional or symbolic truth.[27]

However, while Lindbeck argues for the usefulness of approaching religious truth according to their categorial adequacy, particularly in the context of religious dialogue, he allows that propositional truth should be considered possible.[28] Thus, he ventures to clarify how the cultural-linguistic approach, which is related to the categorical-adequacy notion of truth, also admits the possibility of propositional truth claims. In order to do so,

---

22. Ibid., 20.

23. Ibid., 33.

24. Ibid.

25. Ibid., 34. Says Hauerwas: "The significance of narrative for illuminating the *grammar* of religious convictions is not and should not be primarily an apologetic strategy" (Hauerwas, *A Community of Character*, 94, italics mine).

26. Lindbeck relates this to Wittgenstein's "language games," and the latter's insistence that words only have meaning in the specific context of a game. For more on Ludwig Wittgenstein's understanding of language, see Wittgenstein, *Philosophische Untersuchungen*.

27. Lindbeck, *The Nature of Doctrine*, 36.

28. Ibid., 49.

he first distinguishes between what he calls ontological and intrasystematic truths.[29] While the former refers to truth that corresponds to reality through first-order propositions, the latter points to truth that coheres with whole forms of practice.

In the intrasystematic sense, a truth proposition such as "Jesus is Lord" would be rendered falsely if used to "authorize cleaving the skull of the infidel," as it would then contradict "the Christian understanding of Lordship as embodying, for example, suffering servanthood."[30] Lindbeck avers that the cognitive-propositional approach, which is related to the notion of truth as propositional, does not allow for the decisive importance of intrasystematic truth. Lindbeck then makes a claim that I believe is crucial to Hauerwas's thinking, and thus it is worth quoting at some length: "For epistemological realists, intrasystematic truth or falsity is fundamental in the sense that it is a necessary though not sufficient condition for the second kind of truth: that of ontological correspondence. A statement . . . cannot be ontologically true unless it is intrasystematically true, but intrasystematic truth is quite possible without ontological truth."[31]

However, while Lindbeck claims that the cultural-linguistic approach to religion allows for both intrasystematic and ontological truth claims, he differentiates between cultural-linguistic conditions and the conditions of a cognitivist position regarding the utterance of such claims.[32] He collocates the cognitivist position with "technical theology and doctrine" that is concerned with "second-order discourse about first-intentional uses of religious language."[33] The cultural-linguist, on the other hand, assumes that showing whether an utterance corresponds to reality (i.e., is ontologically true) can only be done in the context of the first-intentional use of ordinary religious language, such as in prayer, worship, and preaching. Thus, the way I understand both Lindbeck and Hauerwas, neither attempt to eradicate the notion or import of ontological truth. Rather, they argue for a shift from the cognitivist approach that assumes propositions can be considered to be true without acknowledging the intrasystematic truth that presupposes an alignment between performance and propositional truth claims. For Hauerwas, such an alignment is made possible for Christians by the defining church community. In light of the postliberal approach to religion as grammar and to truth as categorical adequacy, as presented by Lindbeck and outlined

29. Ibid., 50.
30. Ibid.
31. Ibid.
32. Ibid., 55.
33. Ibid.

in this section, I think Hauerwas's position becomes clearer. Considering his understanding of the church as defining the world, the postliberal underpinnings of Hauerwas's project are further evidenced.

5.2 Defining the World

As noted above, Hauerwas argues that the church not only has a defining language, but *is* a defining language. Related to this claim is his famous dictum that the church *is* a social ethic, and its primary service to the world is simply to define it as the world. In the following, I will outline what Hauerwas seems to mean by the term world, how he argues the church should understand and relate to the world, and what the defining character of the church consists of.

5.2.1 What Is the World?

To Hauerwas, the world is not an ontological designation, which means that the distinction between the church and the world is not between realms of reality, but it is mainly about the difference between agents. On this matter he quotes John H. Yoder who said that the world is "all of that in creation that has taken the freedom not yet to believe."[34] However, according to Hauerwas, this includes the world within Christians, too, which consists of those aspects of their individual and social lives that refuse to confirm that they live in God's world. Christians ought to rely on God's care instead of their own need to control the situation, which ultimately may lead to the point where they resort to violence.

Thus, the world and the church are relational concepts, and Hauerwas even suggests they are companions that are dependent on each other for survival. The world is, like the church, also God's creation, and it is therefore all the more distorted by its sinfulness.[35] The church is not anti-world but rather an endeavor to show the world what it is intended to be as God's good creation. As noted above, and in line with postliberal theology, Hauerwas insists that the only way to verify the truthfulness of Christian convictions is to recognize the necessity of a defining people seeking to live faithfully according to the story of God, and thus clearly differentiating itself from the world.[36] The apparent self-contradiction inherent in claiming that the church must define the world by being different from it, while also suggest-

---

34. Hauerwas, *The Peaceable Kingdom*, 101.
35. Ibid., 100.
36. Hauerwas, *A Community of Character*, 91.

ing that the world is equally within Christians, is further addressed in the critical discussion below.[37]

Hauerwas readily admits that the world entails various stories that cannot always be reconciled or even related, but it is not the church's task to impose an artificial homogeneity on this plurality, but instead—by being a defining community—the church will inevitably determine the world and its dividedness as what it truly is: disobedient and sinful but still created by God.[38] In an attempt to forestall a sectarian critique, he emphasizes that to understand the church as being defined by a particular story (or stories) does not lead to tribalism, which could lead the church to withdraw from the world, but rather requires the church community to provide the world with an alternative to its own tribal existence, splintered as it is by various loyalties and divisive differences.[39] However, the divided character of the world should not come as a surprise for the church, since it is defined by a story that makes it clear that this dividedness is characteristic of not knowing God.[40]

Notwithstanding the ambiguity of Hauerwas's terminology when discussing the church-world dynamic, I argue that the majority of references are to two differentiated groups of agents despite his claim that the world is also found within Christians. Also, his overarching project depends on the sociological differentiation of the church and the world. How else can it be intelligible to demand that the church help the world understand itself?[41] To the content of this repeated mantra of his I now will move on, and thus also address the question of how the church should understand and relate to the world.

5.2.2 How Can the Church Define the World?

To claim that the first social task of the church is to help the world understand itself as the world, presupposes that the world cannot discern its own predicament without the church, and thus that the church should somehow be equipped to enlighten the world on this matter. Working from the previously mentioned assumption that the difference between the church and

---

37. See chapter 7.2.

38. Hauerwas, *A Community of Character*, 92. In this argument, Hauerwas seemingly at random refers to "the story of God" in the singular and "the stories of God" in the plural. I will return to the question of whose story the church's story (or stories) actually is in the critical discussion in chapter 7.1.

39. Ibid., 92.

40. Ibid., 93.

41. Hauerwas, *The Peaceable Kingdom*, 100.

the world consists of a difference between agents, while the world at the same time also exists within Christian agents, it seems like the church community not only defines the world as the other but also defines the other within itself. A similar principle is demonstrated by Hauerwas's notion of the stranger: "Without the constant challenge of the stranger—*who often, interestingly enough, is but one side of ourselves*—we are tempted to lose the power of Jesus' story because we have so conventionalized it."[42]

It begins with the church asking the question "what is going on?" According to Hauerwas, the answer to this question determines the question of what to do.[43] Instead of starting with an action plan on how to make the world more just, the church needs to begin by listening to and retelling the story of God, while also seeking to form their Christian lives in accordance with this story. The stories of Israel and Jesus reveal a truthful God, and these stories provide answers about what is really going on with the world.[44] However, the character of these stories demands a community whose interpretation of them is open to the continuous challenges arising from the discoveries made by those who seek to live faithfully within the Christian tradition.[45]

According to Hauerwas, a crucial premise for the church's ability to be a defining community is the sustenance of a defining tradition. As previously noted, Hauerwas's emphasis on the importance of tradition in constituting the church's character and its understanding of truth relies heavily on MacIntyre. However, it is not my intention to engage in a comprehensive and manifold theological discussion about the term and content of "tradition," as I wish to focus on Hauerwas's application of MacIntyre, and the role of tradition in Hauerwas's argument.

5.2.3 A Defining Tradition: Hauerwas and MacIntyre

Because the above analysis concludes with a precondition of the Christian tradition in order for the church to define the world as the world, it is necessary to take a closer look at what Hauerwas means by tradition. An important influence in this regard is MacIntyre's *After Virtue*.[46] Hauerwas frequently quotes him when explaining the importance of acknowledging

---

42. Ibid., 109, italics mine.

43. Ibid., 102.

44. Again, the interchangeable use of "story" in the singular and "stories" in the plural reflects Hauerwas's own use of these terms (e.g., *A Community of Character*, 91f).

45. Ibid., 92

46. MacIntyre, *After Virtue*.

the church's historicity. In *The Peaceable Kingdom* he refers to MacIntyre in order to point out that everybody is a bearer of tradition, simply by being part of a history.[47] Tradition is "the memory sustained over time by ritual and habit," and as such it "sets the context and boundaries for the discussion required by the Christian stories."[48] To be a people of tradition is thus to live through memory and to be historic in a way that maintains faithful continuity with the experiences and faithful courage of our forebears.[49]

However, Hauerwas's emphasis on the import of tradition in a community is perhaps best illustrated in his essay "A Story- Formed Community."[50] By employing the novel *Watership Down*[51] by Richard Adams, Hauerwas intends to show what some of his theses about Christian social ethics might mean in the context of a defining community. In Adams's story this community is a group of rabbits on a journey. They begin as a gathering of individuals, sharing in common only the stories about the prince of the rabbits. During their journey they become a people as they experience adventures that are interpreted through their traditional stories. It is not necessary to go into detail about how Hauerwas retells this story in order to illuminate his points; at this stage it suffices to refer to the role of tradition in Hauerwas's analysis.

Opposing the social notion that tradition mainly has a conservative effect, and therefore if anyone wants to change society the only option is to argue for a rational liberation from tradition, Hauerwas instead proposes tradition as an actual bearer of rationality and innovation.[52] He refers to a scene in Adams' story where the rabbits' tradition opens up the opportunity for the rabbits to welcome a stranger as a friend. Likewise, Hauerwas demonstrates his concerns regarding the absence of tradition by pointing to one of the warrens that the rabbits visit. In this warren, there is no chief rabbit and their story is that they need no tradition, and every rabbit is free to do whatever it wants. In the end this turns this warren into a place of deception, isolation, and lack of trusting friendship.[53] Thus, Hauerwas does not call for simply any tradition but rather for a truthful and living tradition.[54] The latter presupposes the willingness of a tradition to be part of an ongoing

---

47. Hauerwas, *The Peaceable Kingdom*, 45.
48. Hauerwas, *A Community of Character*, 92.
49. Ibid., 226.
50. Ibid., 9–35.
51. Adams, *Watership Down*.
52. Hauerwas, *A Community of Character*, 26.
53. Ibid., 22, see also 125.
54. Ibid., 14.

argument with other traditions. I will now explore further what Hauerwas means by a truthful tradition.

One condition of a truthful tradition is the recognition of its own finality and the need for change. Again, Hauerwas refers to MacIntyre in describing tradition as a pursuit of goods that extends through generations.[55] For a tradition to survive, it depends on trust between people, much as the defining people called the church depend on each other when negotiating its existence in a way that is accountable to Christian tradition. This also includes challenging and analyzing this tradition, not least through the variety of other stories and traditions.[56]

Most importantly, a truthful and defining tradition is known by its ability to enable people to understand and face the truth of their existence. In practice, this enabling is spelled out as sets of defining habits by which the church learns to live according to the stories about God's care for them, in Israel and Jesus.[57] These practices together with the defining story are what constitute the Christian tradition, and thus the defining character of church. As such, the Christian tradition is also crucial in Hauerwas's understanding of the church as defining for Christian character.

5.3 *Defining Christian Character*

As argued in the previous chapter, Hauerwas contends that the self and moral agency are narratively shaped in a storied community.[58] Engaging with the work of Aristotle and Aquinas, he argues that moral virtue does not necessarily provide unity for the self. Hauerwas assumes that Aristotle and Aquinas proposed such unity because they could not conceive of our contemporary situation, in which we live in a world where we are forced to choose among ways of life and virtues that are essentially incompatible. He concludes that the exercised virtues are directed by a person's character rather than the other way around. What follows is Hauerwas's suggestion regarding *how* Christian character is defined.[59]

---

55. Hauerwas, *The Peaceable Kingdom*, 46.
56. Hauerwas, *A Community of Character*, 95–96.
57. Ibid., 150.
58. See chapter 4.1.2.
59. Hauerwas distinguishes between various implications of the term character by referring to expressions such as "character traits" and "having character," and he argues that the latter is not concerned about particular traits but closely linked to the terms integrity and consistency (Hauerwas, *Vision and Virtue*, 53). Character, in this sense of integrity, also denotes "a more basic moral determination of the self" (ibid., 55).

5.3.1 Self-Agency and Character

In his early works, Hauerwas explores the meaning of character and the relationship between character, self, and moral agency.[60] While these are subjects that maintain importance throughout his corpus of writing, they receive most thorough attention in these early publications. By developing the concepts of virtue and character, Hauerwas offers a constructive alternative to the often problematic relationship between belief and behavior.[61] Instead of discussing whether good behavior is simply to be expected as an automatic result of belief (the Protestant tendency) or if moral theology is needed to explicate what moral behavior means for believers (the Catholic version), Hauerwas situates the locus for Christian moral growth in the moral subject, which is the self. Thus he hopes to avoid the abstraction of ethical questions of right and wrong from the agent's character development.[62]

In order to better understand his emphasis on the church as the community that defines Christian character, it is useful to revisit his incipient convictions regarding character being the qualification for agency.[63] Hauerwas subscribes to an action-oriented notion of self, arguing that self and agency are inextricably linked, as both are dependent on the concept of intentional action.[64] He argues that human actions are made intelligible by being intentional, and character is formed by the intentions embodied in our actions.[65] In this he emphasizes a strong sense of human agency and the capacity for self-determination, even in the face of events beyond our control, through the active formation of character brought about by enduring such circumstances in a particular way.[66] However, Hauerwas admits that while affirming character as a qualification for agency, he does not claim that anyone could be anything. Rather, he attempts to balance the notion of strong agency by acknowledging the passive aspects of human existence.[67]

However, while acknowledging that several dimensions to human existence are given to us, such as where and when we are born, Hauerwas

---

60. This is the main focus of his first two books: ibid. and *Character and the Christian Life*.

61. Hauerwas, *A Community of Character*, 132.

62. Samuel Wells traces how Hauerwas's project developed from arguing the importance of character and vision as ethical categories, to grounding these categories in the notions of story and community (Wells, *Transforming Fate into Destiny*).

63. Hauerwas, *Vision and Virtue*, 61.

64. Ibid., 56.

65. Ibid., 59.

66. Ibid., 56.

67. Ibid., 61.

maintains that even what appears to be passive compliance to such givens still presupposes agency, and subsequently will form the character.[68] Character is thus determined by our past history and by our agency, and it will determine our present moral behavior based on how we see the world. In other words, Hauerwas understands character as a developing moral self-orientation.[69] Character is not in itself an end, but because it is determinative for human moral agency, Hauerwas thinks it is important to query the type of character that is formed based on our way of seeing the world.[70] For a Christian, the community of the church offers determinative descriptions to view the world as redeemed in Christ, thus forming Christian character through the process referred to as sanctification.[71] I will now turn to this communal formation of Christian character, or sanctification, in Hauerwas's argument.

5.3.2 THE SELF AND THE SAINTS: A COMMUNITY OF CHARACTER

When it comes to the "how" of developing Christian character, in both the self and the community, Hauerwas returns to the importance of narrative. The self and the community are storied; furthermore, it is the storied community that permits the self to be discovered as a storied self, in relation to others. Says Hauerwas: "After all, the 'self' names not a thing, but a relation . . . who I am is a relation with others."[72] The self is thus not merely shaped by its relations, for Hauerwas, but constituted by them in a decisive manner.[73] That the self is so constituted remains closely linked to his claim that Christian ethics is a social ethics, and that character is communally shaped.[74]

As previously noted, the determinative significance of story presupposes a community that sustains, embodies, and tells the story.[75] Some of the importance of the church's story is related to the determinative descriptions it offers on how Christians should view the world, but equally important

68. Ibid., 62.
69. Ibid., 63.
70. Ibid., 66.
71. Ibid., 67.
72. Hauerwas, *The Peaceable Kingdom*, 97.
73. True to form, Hauerwas corroborates this claim by referring to two sociologists, and no theologians (ibid., 165 n. 1).
74. Elaborating on this notion, Hauerwas refers to the traditional professions of medicine and law as two of the few communities that continue to remain sufficiently coherent that they are able to develop self-esteem through the training of particular virtues and skills (*A Community of Character*, 126).
75. See chapters 4.1 and 4.2.

to these descriptions are the examples of faithful living which Hauerwas claims are found in the community of character.[76] Hauerwas's notion of saints was mentioned above in the presentation of how the church's story is embodied,[77] and I return to it now because the saints are also important in his argument that Christian character is communally formed. One crucial underlying premise is the Aristotelian notion that the moral challenge is not *what* we should do, but *how* we should do it.[78]

I will not repeat the arguments above, but rather point out one challenge that Hauerwas suggests the saints can help the church with; namely showing *how* Christians can negotiate the many stories that constitute the self.[79] In his essay "A Tale of Two Stories,"[80] Hauerwas makes this point by referring to how, for a Christian, the story of being a Texan needs to be placed in perspective by the story of Jesus.[81] Thus, he claims that "the most decisive difference and challenge the story 'being a Christian' entails for 'being a Texan' is its prohibition on the use of coercion to sustain its truth."[82] This is why, he avers, the import of witnessing is so determinative for the church, as it is the only way that Christians can attract others to the story of Jesus.

Saints are witnesses who have gone before the Christians who are currently attempting to discover what the story of Jesus might mean for the story of being a Texan.[83] By attending to how the saints' stories were defined by the story of Jesus, Hauerwas argues that the truth of the gospel is made known, since in the end it depends on the kind of lives it produces. It is by being trained to trust in God as the protector and provider that the church can learn to live peacefully in a world of competing and limited stories.[84] However, Hauerwas elsewhere makes the point that the saints depend on the church, which is in line with his overall argument that saints must be taught the story of God in and by a community, and that saints also are recognized as such by the church community.[85] In this context, Hauerwas avers

---

76. I attended briefly to Hauerwas's understanding of moral formation as dependent on discipleship, such as observing and following the example of a master, in chapter 4.1.1.

77. See chapter 4.2.1.

78. Hauerwas, *A Community of Character*, 131.

79. Ibid., 132.

80. Hauerwas, *Christian Existence Today*, 25–45.

81. Ibid., 41.

82. Ibid.

83. Ibid., 40.

84. Ibid., 42.

85. Hauerwas and Swinton, *Critical Reflections on Stanley Hauerwas' Theology of Disability*, 74.

that saints may be living contemporaries, as well as deceased witnesses, who "remind us how unfaithful we have been to the story that has formed us."[86]

5.4 Summarizing and Problematizing the Church as a Defining Community

In this chapter I analyzed what Hauerwas's claim about the church being a defining community entails, starting with his emphasis on the particular language of the church, which is crucial for how the church might be defining for the world on the one hand, and the Christian character on the other. The excursus on postliberal theology's proponent George Lindbeck aimed to clarify some of the premises underlying Hauerwas's stress on the church's defining language by tracing Lindbeck's cultural-linguistic approach to religion and his related understanding of truth claims.

Although Hauerwas, as well as Lindbeck, deny that the emphasis on the particular and performative character of a religious community, such as the church, immunizes its truth claims against external critique and prevents intelligible communication with "outsiders," a prominent charge against both is that they promote sectarianism. They argue against this, indicating that their demand that testing of the church's truth claims must be done under conditions that recognize the holistic nature of religious truth claims does not equal self-referential implications. I will return to the charge of sectarianism, as presented by Jeffrey Stout, in the critical discussion in chapter 7.2.

Hauerwas also draws considerably on the work of MacIntyre, particularly with regard to his understanding of tradition. As seen in this chapter, the church's ability to define the world depends on the church's particular tradition, which it both sustains and is sustained by. In Hauerwas's argument, a tradition consists of language, story, and practices, and it therefore works as a shorthand for all things particular about the community of the church. Thus, any critique of his emphasis on the importance of the church's particular story to some degree also implicates his stress on tradition.

Finally, Hauerwas's understanding of Christian character, as defined by the church, was explicated in terms of self-agency and the role of saints. While his emphasis on a strong sense of self and the capacity for

---

86. Ibid., 74. Hauerwas makes this argument in a critical discussion on his disability theology, which I will return to when considering the church practice of meeting the marginalized in relation to the church as a defining community (chapter 12.2.1). While I do not consider his point about the importance of the saints in that chapter, it is implicit in the notion of interdependence that is reviewed.

self-determination might seem contrary to his general communal thrust, it is by attending to the importance of intentional action in Hauerwas's notion of the self that the defining role of the community surfaces. In arguing that human actions form character through the types of intentions they embody, his insistence that the church is the community that defines the intentions of Christians becomes the link between his emphasis on self-agency and the crucial role of the saints. The lives of the saints embody *how* to live with the intentions that the story of Jesus demands of the church.

5.5 *Church as Defining Navigates the Challenge of the Detached Self*

Hauerwas's notion of the saints and their defining role in shaping Christian character is instructive for how I think his ecclesiology navigates the secular challenge of the detached self. Primarily, Hauerwas offers a critical countering of the notion of self as detached and self-authorized by arguing that we are inevitably constituted by our relations. I consider all the four CWS discussed in chapter 2.5 as being indicative of the secular detachment of the self; the first detaches the self from God, the second detaches the self from religious worldviews, the third detaches the self from the local community, and the fourth detaches the self from any transcendent moral authority. These forms of detachment are interrelated, and therefore I will argue that Hauerwas's project thus navigates the challenges they represent in an overlapping manner.

As outlined in this chapter, Hauerwas grounds his understanding of the church as being defining in its defining language and story, which are assumed under the encompassing label of tradition. It is the church's tradition that counters the secular detachment of the self, as it insists that one aspect of the relationally constituted human self consists of standing in relation to God as creator. Second, it is by standing in relation to others in the local church community that the Christian self and character is formed, which counters both the CWS of modern social spaces and self-authorization. Finally, Hauerwas argues that by attending to the lives of the saints, Christians are enabled to negotiate the many stories that make up their lives. In seeing how the story of Jesus has shaped, or shapes, the lives of saints, both the church and the world are given examples of *how* the church's constructions of human fullness can offer a more convincing story than the secular subtraction story of human existence.[87]

---

87. Following Taylor, the immanent constructions of human agency and human fullness that the majority of people in a secular age naively live within are in need of

I think Hauerwas's emphasis on the human predicament of navigating many stories to be particularly relevant in a secular age (cf. Taylor's open landscape of cross-pressures),[88] although Hauerwas insists that the church's story is defining and perspectival for all other stories that are part of the Christian self. I will return to the tensions in this claim about *the* defining story and community of the church in the critical discussion.[89] But now I will turn to the third and final feature of Hauerwas's church community, namely the church as performance.

---

being challenged by alternative constructions (see chapter 3.2.1).

88. Taylor, *ASA*, 592–93.

89. Chapters 7.1–7.2.

6

The Church as a Performative Community

> The peace Christians embody and seek is not some impossible ideal . . . It is not order that is free from conflict because it has repressed all rightful demands for justice. Rather the peaceable kingdom is a present reality, for the God who makes such a peace possible is not some past sovereign but the present Lord of the universe.[1]

HAUERWAS'S FOCUS ON THE church's practices is a decisive feature of his ecclesiology. The reason why I have chosen the term performative is that he is adamant about that practices function as a testimony to the world of Christianity's trustworthiness. Thus, they are not merely religious rituals practiced in order to sustain a tradition, God's benevolence, or other similar aims, as they have a specific performative potential and intent. If the church community is to perform according to its story, there are some foundational practices that must be enacted, drawing their intelligibility from the gospel stories and the story of Israel. Previously, I outlined Hauerwas's ecclesiological features of church as a storied and defining community, and in this chapter I will examine how the church's story is embodied in the performance of defining practices. For Hauerwas, it is the church's worship that is primary to all other practices, and so there I must begin.

6.1 *Worship as Performance*

Hauerwas insists that worship is the origin and center of the church, and therefore liturgy is a fundamental practice to the Christian community.[2] In fact Hauerwas views worship as formative and decisive in receiving knowledge of God in the first place, which in turn changes a Christian's moral and rational perspectives. The interconnectedness of worship and ethics for Hauerwas is demonstrated in his essay "The Liturgical Shape of

---

1. Hauerwas, *The Peaceable Kingdom*, 142.
2. Hauerwas, *In Good Company*, 156.

the Christian Life: Teaching Christian Ethics as Worship."[3] He outlines how ethics is about the interdependence between knowledge of God and the self, and worship is what constantly reminds the church of this. Moreover, when Christians worship the true God they are enabled to see the world as the world, and thus they can also realize how they continue to be occupied by it. Thus, for Hauerwas it is obvious that "without the virtue of worship there can be no other virtue."[4]

6.1.1 Liturgical Sacraments as Marks

Working from the assumption that the church is an empirical reality rather than an invisible ideal church, Hauerwas delineates what he calls the "marks" of the church: the celebration of the sacraments, the preaching of the word, and the encouragement and performance of upright living.[5] He does not explain why he uses quotes on "marks," but maintains that the church is known by these God-given means; however, their occurrence does not guarantee the existence of the church.[6] When it comes to the sacraments, Hauerwas is most concerned about their intent: "The sacraments enact the story of Jesus and, thus, form a community in his image. We could not be the church without them. For the story of Jesus is not simply one that is told; it must be enacted."[7] Through the rite of baptism, a Christian is initiated into the story of Jesus, thus becoming part of his death and resurrection. In the Eucharist, the church becomes part of God's kingdom, and through his Eucharistic presence He makes possible a peaceable people. These rites are essential for teaching Christians who they are as a community. For Hauer-

---

3. Ibid., 153–68.

4. Hauerwas, *Sanctify Them in the Truth*, 59.

5. Hauerwas, *The Peaceable Kingdom*, 107. Note that Hauerwas explicitly refers to preaching as a mark on its own, and thus he does not subsume it under "sacraments." Perhaps a fruitful way to systematize Hauerwas's understanding would be through the categories of prayer and preaching, since he argues several of the sacraments are actually prayers. Also, he has published books consisting entirely of sermons (*Without Apology*), prayers (*Prayers Plainly Spoken*), and both (*Disrupting Time: Sermons, Prayers, and Sundries*).

6. Elsewhere he argues that it is a common mistake to understand "the church" too restrictively, in terms of particular denominations, when in fact the "church is none of these, but rather the church is where people faithfully carry out the task of being a witness to the reality of God's Kingdom" (*A Community of Character*, 109). Similarly, he insists that even though various denominations emphasize different "marks" (his use of quotation marks), this does not make them deficient. Rather, the point is that the sum of the church exhibits these marks, of which "upright lives" is central (*The Peaceable Kingdom*, 107).

7. Hauerwas, *The Peaceable Kingdom*, 107.

was, baptism and the Eucharist are in themselves effective social works of the church, as these actions witness to God's kingdom in the world.[8]

The habits of prayer, the confession of sin, forgiveness, and reconciliation are also important parts of the church's liturgy that Hauerwas attends to.[9] However, it is the church's habit of preaching that, not surprisingly considering his narrative focus, receives the most attention from Hauerwas. Witnessing is crucial for the survival of a story, and in the act of preaching and hearing the gospel the church becomes a people of performative witnessing.[10] It is through this witnessing, generation after generation, that God creates a people who brings the story of God's kingdom to the world and to the stranger.

6.1.2 Being a Liturgical People

Hauerwas considers the stranger to be important with regard to the church's hearing the story of Jesus, because in the stranger's reception of the Christian story, "which often may take the form of rejection," the church also learns to hear it more fully.[11] Receiving and appreciating the stranger is also an act of hospitality, which Hauerwas thinks of as a crucial mark in the life that the church is called to live. To be hospitable is part of what it means to be holy. Holy people are described by Hauerwas as "a people who are capable of maintaining the life of charity, hospitality, and justice."[12] Or according to his oft quoted mantra, "the church does not *have* a social ethic, it *is* a social ethic."[13] To be a social ethic is first of all to define and understand the world rightly, as well as to understand Christian existence in relation to God's kingdom and the world.[14]

Similar to his claim that the church is a social ethic, he also claims that liturgy is, in and of itself, a social action.[15] Liturgical practices, such as baptism and the Eucharist, are not motivational means, but enactments of God's story that shape participants and help them become part of the story. Liturgical living cannot be separated from being a social witness; rather, when the church is disciplined by the liturgy it can be the witness it is called

8. Ibid., 108.
9. Hauerwas, *In Good Company*, 159.
10. Hauerwas, *The Peaceable Kingdom*, 108.
11. Ibid., 109.
12. Ibid.
13. Ibid., 99.
14. Ibid., 102.
15. Hauerwas, *Christian Existence Today*, 107.

to be through its commitment to social ethical practices.[16] What may seem like insignificant practices towards justice in the eyes of the world, such as caring for the poor and the widowed, are pertinent for the church's ability to understand what justice means.[17] Hauerwas argues that these seemingly insignificant gestures in everyday life are of utmost social-ethical significance for Christians. It is through the performance of these gestures that the church defines both the world and its limits.[18] However, such performance is made possible only by the one at the center of the church's liturgical worship: Jesus.

6.2 Jesus Makes the Church's Performance Possible

At the core of Hauerwas's understanding of Christian ethics and Christian community is his emphasis on the significance of Jesus. Even though he acknowledges the importance of Christological claims about Jesus' incarnation, death, and resurrection, Hauerwas also argues that when the first Christians told the story of Jesus, it was equally vital to show how he exemplified the standards of the kingdom he proclaimed through the life he lived, as well as through his death and resurrection.[19] The fact that the Gospels provide a narrative of a life lived is not merely for descriptive intentions, as Hauerwas believes that it provides an opportunity for Christians to position their lives in relation to Jesus' life. According to Hauerwas, this is the only way a person can know who Jesus is and what he is about: by learning to be a disciple of Christ.

6.2.1 JESUS IN THE GOSPELS

The Gospels show how the first disciples had to learn to follow Jesus, and thus be purged of their erroneous expectations about the kingdom of which Jesus preached. In like manner Hauerwas claims that Christians today have to learn what the kingdom of God is about, while observing Jesus' willingness to become subject to the powers of this world, through his capture and crucifixion. Jesus did not focus on himself, but on the kingdom as a present and future reality. Through his performance of healing, serving, teaching, and crucifixion, he made present and initiated this kingdom. However, the emphasis on Jesus as bringing the kingdom is for Hauerwas not in

---

16. Ibid., 125.
17. Hauerwas, *The Peaceable Kingdom*, 100.
18. Hauerwas, *Christian Existence Today*, 106.
19. Hauerwas, *The Peaceable Kingdom*, 74.

opposition to Jesus as Christ and salvific redeemer. He also objects to the notion that his focus on Jesus' whole life is some form of "low Christology."[20] Rather, Hauerwas argues that paying attention to the narrative form of the Gospels will serve to highlight Jesus as God's anointed.

Referring to Matthew 5:38–48, Hauerwas notes that Christians learn to be like God by following the teachings of Jesus. In this passage, Jesus calls his disciples to be perfect, as God is perfect. Hauerwas thus deduces that Christian ethics is not primarily about principles but about imitating the life and performance of He who taught that perfection was to forgive one's enemies.[21] To be like Jesus involves the rejection of the dominion that comes through coercion, and the power that comes through violence. The kind of power Jesus displayed was genuine and truthful because it never forced or tried to control anyone. This power can only be made available to those who are willing to give up whatever possesses them in this world, and thus become dispossessed.[22]

However, it is Jesus who provides Christians with this way of selfless power by being a messiah who did not use force to impose his message, or even to defend himself against his persecutors, as He instead patiently endured the violence knowing that the kingdom of God is a kingdom of peace. Hauerwas therefore considers Jesus' proclamation of the present kingdom of God to be a proclamation of the possibility for a transformed people to live peaceably in a world at war.[23] In order to understand the extent of this message, Hauerwas maintains that it is critical to understand how Israel had learned to view the world, namely eschatologically. To see their existence as such meant that the world had a beginning, a continuing drama, and an end.[24] Through Jesus proclamation, life, death, and resurrection, the world was given not only an announcement about God's kingdom, but also a claim about *how* God rules—not through the violence of the world but through the performative power of love.[25] According to Hauerwas, God's resurrection of Jesus was an affirmation of his life as a perfect proclamation of God's kingdom.

---

20. Ibid., 75.

21. Ibid., 76. Hauerwas explicitly differentiates between the Christian call to be *like* Jesus, and the misunderstanding of trying to *be Jesus*. It is impossible to simply mimic Jesus; one has to learn what it means to be like Jesus from others, and these others are found in the church community.

22. Ibid., 81.

23. Ibid., 83.

24. Ibid., 82.

25. Ibid., 79, 83.

6.2.2 The Resurrection of Jesus Makes Peaceable Performance Possible

The crucified and resurrected Jesus creates the possibility of peace through the power of forgiveness.[26] The peace Jesus proclaimed is, according to Hauerwas, a peace that comes from knowing that one's life is in the hands of God. It is the peace of those who want to make their lives a worship of God, and thus they are not driven by the notion of controlling history in order to achieve what might be perceived in this world to be optimal outcomes.[27] This peace is an eschatological peace, which is a peace not only between people, but also between people and creation.

Because of the resurrection of Jesus, Christians see the kingdom of God as a present reality, and thus also the eschatological peace. Since the church is part of this kingdom, it is committed to embodying the peace of God, by protecting life and creation.[28] Following Jesus, this means not resorting to violence or coercion, even in the face of evil or oppression. Hauerwas here quotes Yoder: "...the Gospel itself, the message that Christ died for His enemies, is *our* reason for being ultimately responsible for the neighbor's—and especially the enemy's—life."[29] To Hauerwas, this means that even though the church presently does not live in a peaceful world, its concern should be to protect life—including the life of one's enemies. Not because life in itself is sacred, but because life belongs to God, even the lives of those who do us harm. Such a commitment to nonviolence is, according to Hauerwas, a Christian act of witness to the peace that makes it possible to view the other as God's creation.

6.2.3 *The Power of Forgiveness*

One of the central premises for Hauerwas's line of reasoning on this matter is the importance of forgiveness. Only through the practice of forgiveness can peace be possible. The first task of a Christian is not to forgive but to receive forgiveness, which compels her to give up control. Hauerwas argues that because people fear the gift of forgiveness may be used against them, accepting it renders them powerless. Thus, learning to receive God's

---

26. Ibid., 89. The brunt of the following arguments rests on the presupposition of the concept of sin. See *A Better Hope*, 189–99.
27. Hauerwas, *The Peaceable Kingdom*, 87.
28. Ibid., 88.
29. Ibid.

forgiveness is necessary for Christians in order to forgive others, not from a position of power but as a fellow forgiven.[30]

To be a forgiven community entails giving up control, because one has to trust in God's providence. For Hauerwas, this also means that Christians must learn to trust each other as they have learned to trust God. Then they can be at peace with their histories and themselves, and they can thus let God's life and forgiveness determine their character. Hauerwas ties being a forgiven people at peace with their history to individuals being able to claim their life as their own, without denying the sins of the past. By seeing their lives and histories in light of Jesus' story, and not the other way around, Christians are enabled to be agents of God's peace and forgiveness. However, Hauerwas stresses that such a community of forgiveness is fully dependent on the resurrection of Jesus.[31]

It is the resurrection that gives Christians the confidence to own their sinful history, because it assures them of the eternal presence of a Lord who has inhabited our world, and in learning the story of how he after his resurrection went to his faithless followers and empowered them to forgive, the church is made an agent in the history of God's kingdom. Hauerwas thus quotes Rowan Williams on the importance of the resurrection story: "the Christian proclamation of the resurrection of the crucified just man, his return to his unfaithful friends and his empowering of them to forgive in his name offers a narrative structure in which we can locate our recovery of identity and human possibility, a paradigm of the saving process; yet not only a paradigm. It is a story which is itself an indispensable agent in the completion of this process, because it witnesses to the one personal agent in whose presence we may have full courage to 'own' ourselves as sinners and full hope for a humanity whose identity is grounded in a recognition and affirmation by nothing less than God."[32] An essential consequence of the church recovering its identity as a forgiven community is that the church will perform the practice of peacemaking, which, as will be evident in the following, is closely linked to the power of forgiveness.

6.3 *The Eschatological Presence of Peace*

For Hauerwas, it is crucial for the church that the motivation for practices like forgiveness, reconciliation, and peacemaking is primarily eschatological rather than ethical. They are so motivated, avers Hauerwas, both in the

30. Ibid., 89.
31. Ibid., 90.
32. Ibid.

sense that they depend on the eschatological community of the church to be made intelligible, and in the sense that they are intended to be declarations of the eschatological kingdom that is promised by God. First, I will explore what Hauerwas thinks it entails for the church community to make a virtue such as peacemaking intelligible. Second, his claim about the church's performance as a declaration of the eschatological kingdom will be further investigated.

6.3.1 The Church's Peaceable Performance

In his essay "Peacemaking: The Virtue of the Church"[33] Hauerwas explicates what he also has called the redemptive process of peace.[34] In the following I will structure his argument according to six points. First, he states that the virtue of peacemaking is only intelligible in the context of a community. Again referring to Aristotle, Hauerwas concurs with his insistence on the presupposition of certain relations to virtues such as friendship and justice. Building on this, he goes further in maintaining peacemaking to be not merely a Christian virtue, but "an essential characteristic of its nature."[35] Also, as this is the community of Christ, who is peace, peacemaking is the very form of the church.[36]

Second, Hauerwas outlines why and how confrontation is a critical component of peacemaking, based on Matthew 18:15-22. Rather than thinking of peacemaking as primarily the resolution of conflict, Hauerwas points out that this text from Matthew actually encourages the conflict that confrontation is bound to bring about.[37] It clearly states that if a Christian has a grievance, she is obliged to confront the one who supposedly wronged her, in order to reconcile. According to Hauerwas, the peace the church is practicing is not about the absence of conflicts, as it is about a way of life for those who are forgiven. This is also inherent in the third point: peacemaking is engendered by the community of the forgiven.

According to Hauerwas, because the church has learned that ignoring sin threatens the truthfulness and peace of the community, according to Hauerwas, it cannot afford to neglect the process of peacemaking. However, it is a practice based on the shared notion that Christians' lives are no longer

---

33. Hauerwas, *Christian Existence Today*, 89–97.
34. Hauerwas, *A Better Hope*, 209.
35. Hauerwas, *Christian Existence Today*, 90.
36. Ibid., 95.
37. Ibid., 90.

their own.[38] This entails that one cannot harbor resentment or refuse to confront a wrongdoer, since a crucial premise for the possibility of reconciliation and peace, is that forgiveness will be offered. Hauerwas thus claims that "Our ability to be truthful peacemakers depends on our learning that we owe our lives to God's unrelenting forgiveness."[39]

Fourth, the peace of Jesus is a peace of truth. Hauerwas argues that any truth worth knowing is necessarily as disturbing as it is fulfilling. Still, when failing to challenge the sinner, the Christian in fact abandons the other to her sin.[40] On the other hand, to actually be willing to do the demanding work of establishing truthful peace with someone is the attitude of someone who knows they come from the position of the forgiven rather than from a superior position of power. In particular, Hauerwas stresses the importance of truthfulness in relation to the church's task of confronting the false peace of the world. Thus fifth, the peacemaking of the church extends to those who are not within the church.

Hauerwas insists that while challenging the peace of the world, which is often built on coercion rather than truthfulness, may be hazardous, the church cannot be less truthful in relation to the world than it is with itself.[41] It is imperative that the church gives the world an example of a peacemaking community; without it, the world will resort to violence as the means to deal with conflicts. Hauerwas admits that historically the church has often failed in this task, but that does not allow it to be despairing about the possibility of peacemaking in the world. He argues that being created by God people are not naturally violent, but they need help to establish habits of peace, and this is the demanding task of the church. Sixth, being a peacemaking community of the forgiven serves the higher good of witnessing God's kingdom of peace.[42] As Hauerwas's exposition demonstrates, peacemaking is a demanding process, which is neither possible nor intended to be maintained by individuals alone, as it is a virtue of the community that is called to witness the God of peace.

6.3.2 Pacifism and the Overlapping of Ages

According to Hauerwas, the Christian commitment to nonviolence is not first and foremost an ethical principle but rather an announcement of the

---

38. Ibid., 91.
39. Ibid., 93.
40. Ibid., 92.
41. Ibid., 95.
42. Ibid., 93.

new age as a present reality.[43] He opposes the notion of a "just war" and arguments that build on our existence as being between the times of the world and the promised kingdom, and therefore presume Christians must compromise their ideals of peace in recognition of humanity's sinful condition.[44] This kind of reasoning mistakenly assumes that it is the nation-state that carries on the history that determines the destiny of the world. In fact Hauerwas asserts that the human desire to protect oneself against enemies by eliminating them expresses a claim for the power to determine destiny, and as such it is a manifestation of a hatred of God.[45]

The church, on the other hand, is living under the assumption that God is in charge of history, and his way of ruling is never through war, violence, or coercion. Rather, Hauerwas insists that Christians are offered a chance to participate as a community in the history of God's peaceable kingdom.[46] This kingdom has, according to Hauerwas's reading of the New Testament, fully come, but it currently overlaps with this world of war. He quotes Yoder approvingly: "These aeons are not distinct periods of time, for they exist simultaneously. They differ rather in nature or in direction; one points backwards to human history outside of (before) Christ; the other points forward to the fullness of the kingdom of God, of which it is a foretaste. Each aeon has a social manifestation: the former in the 'world', the latter in the body of Christ."[47]

The peace brought by Jesus' life, death, and resurrection is an eschatological peace, but for the church to view the world eschatologically is to see peace as a possibility in the present world at war.[48] He claims that the eschatology of the New Testament is not about anticipating peace, but about recognizing that the age of peace is present. In recognizing this, the church has to stand against the world's assumption that war can be an instrument of justice. Hauerwas again refers to the eschatological understanding found in the New Testament, arguing that in the same manner the early Christians

43. Hauerwas, *Against the Nations*, 194.
44. Ibid., 192.
45. Ibid., 196.
46. Ibid.
47. Ibid., 194. It is of course no coincidence that Hauerwas quotes Yoder on this, considering the latter's crucial influence on his pacifism, as previously noted (cf. chapter 1.3 nn. 10–11). However, since Hauerwas outlines the pacifism argument extensively in his works, I do not find it necessary to include an analysis of Yoder in order to understand Hauerwas's position. For Hauerwas's first essay dealing with Yoder's pacifism, see "The Nonresistant Church" in *Vision and Virtue*, 197–221. For a recent work on Yoder's post-Christendom theology, in comparison with Lesslie Newbigin, see Nikolajsen, *The Distinctive Identity of the Church*.
48. Hauerwas, *Against the Nations*, 193.

chose nonviolence on the basis of their dedication to live under God's reign, so the church is still called to live in recognition of God's reign.[49]

How then is the church supposed to perform according to God's peaceful reign in a world at war? Hauerwas both poses and answers the question, and he suggests that it comes down to the capacity to imagine peace.[50] Such imagination, however, does not come from lofty ideas or abstract principles, but from the liturgical performance of the church community. This brings the analysis of Hauerwas's understanding of the church as performance back to where it started; namely, back to the church' worship and liturgy. When Christians perform the Eucharist they offer the world an alternative to division and war. In this sacramental practice, Hauerwas proposes that the church witnesses the fact that war is not a part of God's providential care for the world.[51]

The supposition that war is unavoidable in sustaining a particular history, when encountering the threat of the other, is proven wrong by the Lord's meal, which instead reveals to the Christian how her story is enhanced by welcoming the stranger. Thus, the church can offer the world an invitation to an imaginative community, which through its story has been given resources to reject the incentives for war, however morally compelling they may be. Finally, Hauerwas counters the alleged claim that Christian commitment to pacifism necessitates withdrawal from the world and politics. Rather, it is the opposite, as the church is so convinced of the importance of nonviolence that it must engage itself in making the world less determined to go to war. However, Hauerwas maintains that even more than offering moral advice, the church is a witness to God's history which frees us from the assumption that war is unavoidable.[52]

6.4 *Summarizing and Problematizing the Church as a Performative Community*

Hauerwas's understanding of the church as a performative community can be summarized in the practices of prayer, preaching, and peacemaking. As he considers sacraments such as baptism and the Eucharist to be prayers, I think it would be accurate to describe his view of liturgical worship as prayers offered by the church to God. Preaching is for Hauerwas more than the sermon, as it is the church witnessing the story of Jesus, which can also

49. Ibid., 194.
50. Ibid., 196.
51. Ibid., 197.
52. Ibid., 198.

occur through practices such as hospitality and forgiveness. The story of Jesus is the crucial premise and motif for the church's performance. Moreover, the church's performance is "the real alternative able to free our imagination from the capacity of war."[53]

This insistence from Hauerwas on the present and real alternative offered by the church's performance has garnered critical attention in various forms. One prominent charge is that the empirical church is not a particularly extraordinary example of peaceableness or otherwise sanctified performance, and thus Hauerwas's claim about the church's performance as being decisive in the assessment of the truthfulness of the gospel becomes problematic. Another peril of Hauerwas's approach, according to critics, is that he comes close to replacing a propositional truth-emphasis with a pragmatic truth-emphasis, which results in reducing a person to physiology and belief to embodied practice. I will return to both of these charges in the critical discussion.[54]

Finally, I think it is important to emphasize how Hauerwas's eschatological argument relates to the church's performance, in particular its nonviolence and peacemaking efforts, which he adamantly promotes as crucial. Peace is not merely a promise, according to Hauerwas, but also a part of the overlapping history present in the church. Where this argument stops short is in extrapolating how the overlapping ages are made present in and through the church's performance, and so this is the inquiry I will make in the pneumatological reconstruction.[55]

6.5 Church as Performance Navigates the Challenge of Disembodied Belief

Hauerwas's understanding of the church as performance acknowledges and counters the secular tendency toward disembodying belief. It counters it by insisting that belief cannot be disembodied and remain intelligible, as it must inevitably manifest in embodied performance in order to be meaningful. Thus, by stressing the importance of the performative character of the church, Hauerwas acknowledges the necessity of reversing what Taylor considers to be the "excarnation" of religion in our secular age. What we need in a secular age, according to Taylor's analysis, is a move away from emphasizing so-called inevitable changes in beliefs and toward fuller phenomenological accounts of how experiences of human existence have changed.

53. Ibid., 197.
54. Chapter 7.3.
55. Chapter 11.

In arguing that the church's performance enables the particularities of Christian existence (e.g., the practice of peacemaking), Hauerwas attempts to explicate how the church offers this type of fuller account, enabling the transformation of imagination and experiences.

The emphasis on the church's performance continues to underline the thoroughly embodied character of Hauerwas's ecclesiology, which has been a consistent feature of the church as a storied and defining community. In his book *The State of the University*,[56] Hauerwas refers to Taylor's argument about the individual's disembodiment in a social sense.[57] Taylor avers that this disembodiment is the result of modernity's individualism and so-called freedom.[58] Hauerwas compares Taylor's disembodiment, in this social sense, to his own claim that modernity produces people who think that they do not need a story.[59] Thus, both the social and religious disembodiment that Taylor polemicizes against fit with Hauerwas's argument that the church should be a storied, defining, and performing community. While the storiedness of the church primarily offers a religious embodiment, the defining character of the church embodies the Christian in a social way, and the church as performance includes both a religious and social embodiment.[60]

---

56. Hauerwas, *The State of the University*.
57. Ibid., 37.
58. Hauerwas refers to Taylor, *Modern Social Imaginaries*.
59. Hauerwas, *The State of the University*, 37.
60. I will explore these overlapping forms of embodiment in the final section on church practices (chapter 12).

PART III

THE CHURCH BY THE SPIRIT: A PNEUMATOLOGICAL RECONSTRUCTION OF HAUERWAS

THIS SECTION OF THE book consists of a critical discussion of Hauerwas's ecclesiology and a pneumatological reconstruction related to the findings of the critical discussion. I consider part III to be this book' constructive contribution, and thus an analytical terminology is employed to a larger degree in order to gain critical distance from the material as well as to offer constructive suggestions on how the big question of the book can be better and more precisely addressed. In the critical discussion I engage some of Hauerwas's most prominent critics for the purpose of outlining the charges of fideism, sectarianism, and pragmatism. Following on what I consider to be the crucial objections against Hauerwas's project, I subsequently provide a pneumatological reconstruction of his ecclesiology by drawing on the work of Amos Yong. Before doing so, I will recap the highlights of the book thus far (see the beginning of chapter 8) with the intention of keeping the argument focused on the big question. First, however, is the critical discussion of Hauerwas's ecclesiology.

7

Engaging Hauerwas's Critics
A Critical Discussion

IN THE PREVIOUS CHAPTERS I outlined the central features of Hauerwas's ecclesiology: the church as a storied, defining, and performative community. The characteristics of the church are centered on the community and its distinctiveness, which is expressed through the particular story, habits, and practices. Faith statements, liturgy, and offices are vital in constituting, conserving, and conveying the church's story and tradition, but their intelligibility is always dependent on the truthful performance of the community. I also attempted to show how Hauerwas's understanding of the church is in accordance with the changes and challenges of a secular age, as presented by Taylor, and this effort can be summarized as follows: 1) church as a storied community navigates the challenge of deconstructed truth; 2) church as a defining community navigates the challenge of the detached self; and 3) church as a performative community navigates the challenge of disembodied beliefs.

Since it is the ecclesiological implications of Hauerwas's project that are under scrutiny here, the critical discussion in this chapter will argue that the most prevalent objections to his work challenge his understanding of the church as outlined in the previous chapter. First, the charge of fideism will be considered in relation to Hauerwas's stressing the importance and truthfulness of the church's story. Second, the critique of the inherent sectarianism of Hauerwas's work raises questions about what his ecclesiological emphasis on the church as a defining community implies about non-Christians and the world as God's creation. Finally, critics have claimed that his focus on the church's performance leads to a pragmatism that is theologically problematic. Against Hauerwas, his opponents insist that the proof of the Christian pudding does not lie in how the church community tastes (at least not primarily), to rephrase a well-known idiom, simply because the empirical church does not often taste like the truthfulness Hauerwas demands of it, and even attributes to it.

These criticisms have been chosen based on both the comprehensiveness of the arguments and their relevance to the big question of the book, which is to consider the contribution of Hauerwas's particularistic ecclesiology in a secular age. All three criticisms have been more or less refuted and discussed by Hauerwas; however, I do not consider his responses to be conclusive in any way that settles the debates (and, presumably, neither does he). The structure of this chapter follows the critiques, starting with the charge of fideism. I will present the main arguments from representative opponents,[1] provide Hauerwas's response, and conclude with a short precursory comment on each topic.

7.1 *The Shortcomings of Story: The Fideism Critique*

Hauerwas, and his theological position, is notorious among feminist theologians.[2] From various perspectives, and with a varying degree of rebuke, feminists have critiqued Hauerwas for cementing patriarchal hierarchies and structures in his emphasis on *the* Christian story and tradition.[3] One of the most adamant critics has been Gloria Albrecht, who clearly articulates concerns that are echoed among other feminist theologians. Pairing her critique with the criticism of James Gustafson I hope to shed light on different shortcomings of Hauerwas's understanding of the church as a storied community.

7.1.1 Albrecht's Feminist Critique of Hauerwas

Although Gloria Albrecht finds that Hauerwas diagnoses the problems of modern liberal society in agreement with her feminist ethics of liberation, she claims his solutions to mend the ailments of mentioned society fail on several accounts.[4] However, starting with what Albrecht assumes to be convergences in diagnosing the problems, she points out that they agree in four important areas: 1) they both understand the self to be constructed socially, which is emphasized by the storied nature of our identity-formation both as individuals and communities; 2) they both critique the understanding

---

1. The number of Hauerwas's critics is far too large for all to be considered in this chapter, and so I have selected representative opponents who I think argue convincingly and who are among the most frequently cited critics.

2. Bennett, "Being 'Stuck' between Stanley and the Feminists," 229.

3. See ibid., 231–34, for a brief overview of some of the feminist critiques of Hauerwas's position.

4. See also Albrecht, *The Character of Our Communities*, where she further develops a detailed critique of Hauerwas's position on various ethical issues.

of the self as isolated and rational; 3) they both critique the liberal myth of separate public and private spheres; and 4) they share an interest in and place an emphasis on the character of community.[5]

However, Albrecht argues that when moving forward with this analysis, Hauerwas fails to acknowledge the politics of location. Therefore, he discards modern liberalism only to replace it with his own universal description of the human condition and the Christian story, as if its terms and meanings are univocal independently of temporal, social, or cultural location.[6] Her point is that Hauerwas tells the Christian story from the particular location of the center, as opposed to the margins, but without conceding that this location determines how he presents the story.[7]

Drawing on Foucault's concept of discursive fields, Albrecht attempts to show how Hauerwas's discourse contributes to a silencing of the many voices located on the margins, due to their race, sex, class, and/or sexual orientation.[8] She goes so far as to say that Hauerwas "attempts to resist the rise of subjugated voices."[9] This charge is based on her critical analysis of what she calls Hauerwas's "claim to unchanging truth," which is evidenced in the way he simply exchanges the rational subject and ahistorical reason with the Christian man and story.[10] By positing the Christian story as timeless, with particular understandings of sin, violence, and redemption, Hauerwas admits no distinctions regarding specific historic conditions or contexts.[11] Thus, Albrecht accuses him of trying to avoid the uncertainty of historical particularity by positing a new form of foundationalism. According to Hauerwas, the Christian story demands of the church that it is committed to peaceful practices, such as non-violence and non-resistance. When presenting such an interpretation as universal, Albrecht argues that Hauerwas

---

5. Albrecht, "Myself and Other Characters," 99. See also Welch, "Communitarian Ethics after Hauerwas," for another feminist critique that agrees with Hauerwas's emphasis on story and community, but disagrees with his claim about the crucial role of *a* truthful story versus Welch's argument for the import of learning from many stories (ibid., 83).

6. Albrecht, "Myself and Other Characters," 114.

7. Ibid., 111. Lydia Harder offers a similar critique, when she accuses Hauerwas of legitimating "practices that favor the dominant in the church community." She argues that he makes several assumptions in the way he employs the term church that "implicitly justify the continued androcentric patriarchal church" (Harder, "Dialogue with Hauerwas," 153).

8. Albrecht, "Myself and Other Characters," 107.

9. Ibid., 110.

10. Ibid., 111.

11. Ibid., 110.

must assume access to unchanging truth.[12] But for Albrecht, terms like sin and violence must be historically and socially located, something Hauerwas's universalizing descriptions do not allow for (e.g., she refers to how he understands sin to be the core of our human need to be in control of our lives).[13] Such a need is, however, experienced differently by a white, affluent man and a poor, abused woman, and so Albrecht counters that it should accordingly be described and interpreted differently.[14]

To sum up Albrecht's critique from a feminist ethics perspective, she claims that Hauerwas, firmly positioned at the center of Christianity, advances an ahistorical approach to the Christian story as universal and timeless, which leaves no room for the church to listen to the marginalized voices and their interpretations of the same story.[15]

7.1.2 Hauerwas's Response to Albrecht's Critique

Hauerwas's opening remarks in his responding article are programmatic for the rest of his reply.[16] He complains that her criticisms resemble the question "When are you going to stop beating your wife?" which per definition implies his guilt if he were to answer on her own terms. He follows this complaint with similar comments throughout the text: "What she thinks I think I do not think";[17] "she continues to misunderstand me precisely because she insists on reading me as saying what only someone who thinks like she thinks can and must think I must think";[18] "I cannot imagine on what basis Albrecht attributes such a view to me";[19] and "Albrecht and I simply seem to live on different plants [sic!]."[20] This selection of quotes displays Hauerwas's

---

12. Albrecht, "Article Review," 224–25.

13. Linda Woodhead argues a similar point in Woodhead, "Can Women Love Stanley Hauerwas?" Utilizing an empirical study of working-class women in Britain, Woodhead offers concrete examples of the importance and dearth of gendered and embodied perspectives in Hauerwas's theology. I think she is correct in her observation about the "embodiedness" of Hauerwas's work: "In arguing for such an embodied theology, I am merely following hints in Hauerwas . . . Hauerwas's theological sensitivity to the embodied and material nature of creaturely existence is thus the cue to which I have been responding in this chapter" (186f.).

14. Albrecht, "Myself and Other Characters," 110.

15. Ibid., 114.

16. Hauerwas, "Failure of Communication," 228.

17. Ibid., 229.

18. Ibid., 230.

19. Ibid., 231.

20. Ibid., 233.

insistence that he is being misinterpreted by Albrecht. In short, his response is that she "profoundly misunderstands me."[21]

On a more substantial note, in responding to Albrecht's claim that he proffers a new form of foundationalism, or a confessionalist position, Hauerwas responds that he is rather a rationalist for arguing that Christian convictions help us to see the world as it is.[22] He also points out that he is critical of the whole foundationalist/anti-foundationalist alternative since that discussion perpetuates the modernist philosophical project.[23] Likewise, his response to her claim that he does not appreciate the implications that his epistemology has for his ecclesiology is that he has no epistemology, and he is still learning "how to think without assuming that I must first have an account of how to think."[24]

He denies Albrecht's assumption that he does not believe Christians can be multi-lingual—quite the opposite, he says: "it is exactly 'resident aliens' who must become adept at being multi-lingual."[25] However, he emphasizes that he does not believe that the language of Christianity is necessarily translatable to other languages, such as the language of liberalism. Instead, it is the task of Christians to bear witness to their first language of Christianity, and this often requires them to learn other languages. Hauerwas's bout, however, is with the way these other languages often subvert Christians' ability to speak the language of Christianity.[26]

Regarding Albrecht's accusation that he does not acknowledge the church's sinfulness, in particular how church practices have been and continue to be oppressive for women, Hauerwas counters that all practices can be perverted. But what is crucial, in his opinion, is that the church has the resources to expose and correct such perversions. Whether we speak of justice or injustice, Hauerwas presses the point that the background for the church's interpretation of what such terms entail must be the *telos* of our community. Thus, he admits that he does not concur with Albrecht's equating difference with injustice, as her notion of justice is of the distributive and egalitarian kind characteristic of liberal political theory. Rather,

21. Ibid., 239.
22. Ibid., 232.
23. Ibid., 233.
24. Ibid., 229–30. While he has consistently been reluctant to offer an account of his epistemological position, he still has ascribed to a form of epistemological realism, which I outlined in chapter 4.3.1. This quote is presented as a contradiction to this former claim.
25. Ibid., 231.
26. Ibid.

Hauerwas claims the church must begin by discovering the differences that are constructive in working toward its *telos*.[27]

7.1.3 Precursory Remarks on Albrecht's Critique

In his response to Albrecht's critique, Hauerwas does not, and perhaps cannot due to his situatedness, acknowledge how his situatedness at the center of Christianity affects his argument. I think one reason for this is the way in which his project is constructed as a protest against liberalism and modernity, which impairs his ability to accommodate Albrecht's valid critiques; in his hunt for traces of liberalism in her way of thinking, he reduces her opposition to an account of them "talk(ing) past one another."[28] Hauerwas assumes one of the main reasons for the communication failure is that Albrecht finds him insufficiently sympathetic to feminist issues.[29] This appears to me to be a reductionist way of treating her argument. In my reading, this is not her main agenda; rather, she uses feminist issues as examples of how Hauerwas's ecclesiology (and epistemology, although he denies he has one) undermines the voices on the margins of the church. Therefore, I will suggest that the problem of communication stems rather from how they answer the following questions: Whose voice(s) should count? And when various voices disagree, which voice, if any, should be the determining voice?

Even though Hauerwas and Albrecht apparently disagree on how to answer these questions, they do share other preconditions, as well as some basic theoretical assumptions, at least according to Albrecht. I do not think the problem primarily lies in Hauerwas's conclusion—that they live on different planets (sic: plants)[30]—but rather the opposite: They live on the exact same planet, and moreover; on the same continent, in the same country, both being white, middle-class, academics –theologians, even, and Christians, but still they make differing conclusions about what they see, or perhaps more accurately; they see differently. However, I will argue that their projects would benefit from a mutually critical discussion, which was not only about critiquing the other, but also about letting the other's perspective enlarge their own views.[31] In order to do so, I will attempt to make explicit some of the implicit

27. Ibid., 235–36.
28. Ibid., 233.
29. Ibid., 234.
30. Ibid., 233.

31. Still, the objective for this critical discussion is not to defend Hauerwas, but to delineate what I find to be convincing points of critique regarding his project. For a more comprehensive consideration of Albrecht's critique, which also offers a clearer defence of Hauerwas, see Wells, *Transforming Fate into Destiny*, 70–73.

criteria driving their arguments and to discuss whether a dialogue might contribute to making both projects more coherent and authentic.[32]

It seems to me that Hauerwas raises some valid points in his response to Albrecht, e.g., when he accuses her of treating Christianity as a "monolithic 'thing' that is unavoidably oppressive."[33] When he claims that she also speaks of "women's experience" as a unified thing, I only partially agree, for while Albrecht does refer to women's experience, she also concretizes how these can be manifold.[34] Another critical point that Hauerwas could have but did not make is that Albrecht too easily designates Hauerwas (and his likes) to be at the center of the Christian community, exercising his "empowering, unified self, as a white, male Texan."[35] This seemingly disregards other factors that can place one at the margins, such as being handicapped, being unemployed, or being married to a mentally ill person (which Hauerwas was for a long period of his working life), and Albrecht polarizes Hauerwas's monolithic experience, allegedly from the center, against "women's typically more complex experiences of multiple and oppressive social definitions."[36] Although I am not trying to, nor do I have reasons to, paint Hauerwas as a voice from the margins of the Christian community, I am questioning the apparent willingness of Albrecht to paint particular voices as being from the center or from the margins with such broad strokes.

Underlying Albrecht's assertion that Christianity is oppressive because the voices from the margins are suppressed seems to lay the implicit presumption that these voices should be more authoritative within the church than the voices from the center. The voices from the center, which I assume to also be those Albrecht refers to as the ones "who have the power to define confessional language," hold an important privilege if Hauerwas is right in claiming that "the confessional language of a tradition is all Christians have to fall back on."[37] Referring to Foucault, she faults Hauerwas for ignoring how power works through trivial practices, thereby failing to show how the

---

32. The criterion of coherence is formal, while the criterion of authenticity is substantial and refers to compliance with the Christian tradition. However, due to the many interpretations of what is most authentically Christian—and this is also part of the disagreement between Hauerwas and Albrecht—it is crucial to be clear about why one particular argument is considered to be more authentic than another.
33. Hauerwas, "Failure of Communication," 236 n. 14.
34. Albrecht, "Myself and Other Characters," 104ff.
35. Ibid., 107.
36. Ibid.
37. Albrecht, "Article Review," 225.

church can be capable of upholding and reenforcing cultural structures that are oppressive.[38]

This brings me to what I find convincing in Albrecht's critique of Hauerwas, namely her claim that his ecclesiology does not make sufficient room for the many, including marginalized, voices.[39] Hauerwas's response to these criticisms assumes what can be seen as an opposite criterion to Albrecht, namely that it is the church's *telos* that should be determining for what is considered to be injustice.[40] From this, he deduces that for example women's complaints against the church are valid insofar as they help to build the church.[41] This is where I find Hauerwas's response to be inadequate regarding Albrecht's concern: if the *telos* of the church, as depicted in the Christian story, is the decisive background against which all Christians' claims to justice are measured, then it becomes crucial how the story is narrated and who narrates it. If throughout the church's history these narrators have been, and still are to an overwhelmingly degree, men, this fact will have an impact on the background against which all claims to justice must supposedly be considered.

I will conclude these precursory remarks on Albrecht's critique by articulating a challenge to Hauerwas's ecclesiology, which is based on her notice regarding whether the church's story can include and acknowledge the voices form the margins of the church community; in particular, *who is narrating and interpreting the church's story?* In my opinion, Albrecht is justified in her concern regarding Hauerwas's proposals of what seems to be a new foundationalism, in which he ignores problematic implications about the agency of truth and rationality related to the questions of who narrates and interprets the church's story.[42] Feminist theology has certainly taught us that it matters who has the power to define the language and tell the story.

---

38. Albrecht, "Myself and Other Characters," 113.

39. Brad J. Kallenberg defends Hauerwas against Albrecht's critique on the grounds of her misunderstanding the importance of intratextuality that Hauerwas presupposes (Kallenberg, *Ethics as Grammar*, 132). However, I do not find his defense to be any more convincing than Hauerwas's own.

40. Hauerwas, "Failure of Communication," 235.

41. Ibid., 236.

42. Linda Woodhead comments on this problem: "From a gendered point of view this begs the question 'Whose Church and which narrative?'" in Woodhead, "Can Women Love Stanley Hauerwas?," 182.

7.1.4 Gustafson's Ecclesiological Critique

James M. Gustafson has also voiced concern regarding the emphasis on story in Hauerwas's work. In the article "The Sectarian Temptation" he offers a threefold critique of what he calls "the theological assumptions made by the new sectarians,"[43] among whom Hauerwas is included. First, Gustafson claims that the sociological assumption that the church can be an isolated tribe, with its own language and character-forming narrative and separated from the wider society, has always been false throughout the history of Christianity.[44] Second, he questions the philosophical distinction made between religious knowing and other ways of knowing. This epistemological assumption results in an isolation of positively given "truths" that prevents them from being subject to correction by other ways of knowing (e.g., science, human experience, or other religious traditions).[45]

The result is that the Christian narrative is given a self-justifying property, but unlike Albrecht, whose concern is mainly with the marginalized voices within the church, Gustafson is more concerned with how the Christian narrative is immunized from correction outside of the community sustaining it.[46] If the only option the church has when questioned about the validity of the Christian faith is to refer to biblical narratives that explicate the historical continuity and context for its beliefs, this appears to be a self-referential response, as it fails to take any authorizing standard or criteria outside the church's story into account.[47]

Finally, Gustafson worries that the theological assumptions that he calls sectarian, will result in theology and Christianity becoming unintelligible. The theological assumption about God as being known only in and through history, and in particular through Christ, not only ignores parts of the biblical witness, but infers that there are "no indication of God's reality from nature, human experience, and so forth."[48] God becomes the Christian God for the Christian church, and since God has made himself known to and through the Christian community it becomes the sole sustainer of that knowledge. Gustafson concludes his critique by countering this sectarian

---

43. Gustafson, "The Sectarian Temptation," 90.
44. Ibid., 91.
45. Ibid., 85, 92.
46. Harder expresses a similar concern when she faults Hauerwas's emphasis on narrative to lopsidedly assert the continuity between God, Bible, and the church, without sufficiently acknowledging the discontinuity (Harder, "Dialogue with Hauerwas," 155).
47. Similar concerns about Hauerwas's project have been raised in a Nordic context by Gregersen in "The Fluid Mission of the Church" and Jan-Olav Henriksen ("Mission").
48. Gustafson, "The Sectarian Temptation," 92.

temptation: "God is the God of Christians, but God is not a Christian God for Christians only."[49]

7.1.5 HAUERWAS'S RESPONSE TO GUSTAFSON'S CRITIQUE

Hauerwas addresses Gustafson's critique in his introduction to *Christian Existence Today*.[50] Although expressing some bafflement over being misunderstood by Gustafson on several counts, he engages his criticisms quite comprehensively, starting with Gustafson's philosophical critique. According to Gustafson, Hauerwas's fideistic stance entails that the language of religion is considered incommensurable with the language of science, thus leaving the Christian story incorrigible by challenges from outside the religious sphere.[51] Against this charge and the related charge of sectarianism, Hauerwas claims that he does not hold that the Christian story and its truth-claims are self-justifying, but that they can and will be challenged. What he finds problematic in Gustafson's approach is that he seems to assign challenges from science, in particular, an *a priori* superior authority over theological claims.[52]

Instead of the fideistic stance Gustafson charges him with, Hauerwas adheres to what he calls a qualified epistemological realism, referring to Sabina Lovibond.[53] Such realism entails the opposite of what Gustafson assumes of Hauerwas and his likes, namely that religious language should not be treated as a self-validating and internally consistent language, since it is expected to refer to reality. Thus, Hauerwas admits there is a sense of self-referentiality to Christian truth, but "the reference is not to propositions

49. Ibid., 94.
50. Hauerwas, *Christian Existence Today*, 3–18.
51. Ibid., 4.
52. Ibid., 9.
53. I outlined Lovibond's position in chapter 4.3.1. Hauerwas's defenders have pointed out that the fideistic charges rest on modern notions that are problematic, such as the premise of translatability. For example, Emmanuel Katongole argues that Gustafson himself presumes a foundationalism, not unlike what he accuses Hauerwas of, but on scientific grounds rather than revelatory. Katongole holds that Hauerwas in fact does not claim that the church's story is foundational, because he refutes the modernist assumption that knowledge can have secure foundations (Katongole, *Beyond Universal Reason*, 184). Also turning to Sabina Lovibond (Lovibond, *Realism and Imagination in Ethics*), Katongole avers that Hauerwas presupposes a form of non-foundationalism which opens "the possibility within a tradition for rational assessment (true/false), for the criticism and revision of one's beliefs, as well as for a dynamic concept of moral objectivity" (Katongole, *Beyond Universal Reason*, 162). I think it is adequate to assume that Hauerwas's followers and interpreters have been more unequivocal about his epistemology than he has himself (cf. above, n. 24).

but to lives."⁵⁴ Underscoring the significance of the church's truthfulness, Hauerwas turns to Gustafson's sociological critique.

Hauerwas responds by questioning the alternatives Gustafson seems to assume: either complete involvement or complete withdrawal from the public affairs of the world, the latter of which he accuses Hauerwas of promoting. Rather, Hauerwas calls for the selective engagement of Christians who have been formed by the church to know when they cannot underwrite their society's agenda without betraying their Christian identity.⁵⁵ This discernment is closely linked to fluency in the Christian language, because only when Christians are thus fluent can they recognize discontinuities, as well as continuities, with the language of the state.⁵⁶ Hauerwas further rejects Gustafson's assumption that his pacifist ecclesiology results in Christians withdrawing from politics. Quite the opposite, he counters, since pacifism demands "strenuous political engagement, because such a commitment forces us to expand our social and political imaginations."⁵⁷

Finally, Hauerwas addresses Gustafson's warrant for a doctrine of creation, particularly in relation to morals and ethics. First, he differentiates between being critiqued for not having a doctrine of creation and for not being able to adequately address moral issues on theological grounds without it. Since he finds that Gustafson is unable to prove the latter, he suspects that his call for a doctrine of creation is grounded in a misguided attempt to justify some form of universal ethics.⁵⁸ To Hauerwas, such an attempt is misguided because he claims there is no "autonomous realm of morality separate from Christ's lordship," and therefore any moral continuities between the world and the church are due to God's kingdom stretching beyond the church and not because there is grounds for a common morality based on the doctrine of creation.⁵⁹

7.1.6 Precursory Remarks on Gustafson's Critique

While Gustafson's main critique is that Hauerwas's ecclesiology promotes a sectarian view of the church, this charge is so closely related by Gustafson to Hauerwas's allegedly fideistic stance that I consider it useful to discuss his criticisms in this first part of the chapter. Since the next topic is the charge

---

54. Hauerwas, *Christian Existence Today*, 10.
55. Ibid., 11.
56. Ibid., 12.
57. Ibid., 15.
58. Ibid., 16.
59. Ibid., 17.

of sectarianism in Hauerwas's project, Gustafson serves as a link to illustrate the overlap between these charges. Also, Gustafson's critique overlaps with Albrecht's, although their concerns differ somewhat, and thus I found it fruitful to juxtapose their arguments.

They both call for a more prominent continuity in Hauerwas's ecclesiology between the church's story and other stories. For Albrecht, these stories can challenge what might be unjust structures of inequality that the church is unable or unwilling to see for itself. For Gustafson, other languages, particularly the language of science, are indispensable with regard to contributing truths that can correct and widen the church's story. His agenda is apologetic in a different way than Albrecht's, as he avers that Hauerwas promotes the unintelligibility of theology through his predominantly Christological emphasis. When Hauerwas grants the church exclusive knowledge of God, primarily through the stories of Israel and Christ, Gustafson avers that he in effect fails to recognize that knowledge of God also can be gained from experience, nature, and the sciences: "knowledge of nature contributes to, but does not finally determine, what can be said about God. Sectarian assumptions seem to deny or underestimate this."[60]

In this I agree with Gustafson; Hauerwas's revaluation of the Jesus story implicitly presumes a devaluation of other ways of knowing about God, and in his emphasis on the import of Christian witness, he explicitly claims that there is no other way that Christianity can be made intelligible.[61] In his response to Gustafson's critique, he also seems to assume that it is largely concerned with how to make arguments in ethics, and thus, whether we need the sciences to agree in order to make a moral argument.[62] Thus, he fails to address Gustafson's theological critique about how we can know what is true about God, which I will relate to Albrecht's critique. While she chides Hauerwas for not recognizing the many voices and stories, Gustafson claims Hauerwas differentiates between the given truths of Christian faith and other corrigible rationalities. In both cases, the Christian story becomes unassailable by either marginalized voices or non-Christian rational activity.

Since another implicit criterion for Gustafson is the intelligibility of Christian faith, the importance of taking other rationalities into consideration becomes crucial, as opposed to Hauerwas, whose project has never been focused on making Christianity intelligible to the world, but rather the exact opposite. His claim is that the church is about making the world and our human existence intelligible to Christians. I would argue, with Gustafson, that

---

60. Gustafson, "The Sectarian Temptation," 92.
61. Hauerwas, *With the Grain of the Universe*, 214.
62. Hauerwas, *Christian Existence Today*, 16–17.

it is imperative for the church and theologians to consider truth-claims from rational activity outside the Christian community, whether it is from the sciences or other religious traditions, in order to make the world intelligible in a truthful manner. Hauerwas's actual work sustains such a claim, by the fact that he avails himself of various sciences and literature to make his arguments, yet his polemic against Gustafson might suggest otherwise.

The shortcomings of Hauerwas's emphasis on story as argued in this chapter can be summarized in the following questions about agency and rationality: *Who is narrating and interpreting the church's story and what are the consequences of that agency for the truthfulness of the story? And is the truth and rationality of the Christian story exclusive or authoritative over non-Christian rational activities or stories that lay claim to truth?* With these concerns in mind, I now turn to the sectarian charges against Hauerwas.

7.2 *The Limits of Human Agency: The Sectarianism Critique*

To articulate the critique of Hauerwas's alleged sectarianism, I will draw on Jeffrey Stout's critical analysis of Hauerwas's traditionalism in *Democracy & Tradition*.[63] Stout is a studious and sympathetic reader who appears to know the work of Hauerwas well, but more importantly, I consider his critique interesting because he, like both Gustafson and Albrecht, shares some fundamental presuppositions with Hauerwas, such as the significance of tradition in a liberal democracy. However, unlike Hauerwas, who is critical of both "liberalism" and "democracy," Stout is devoted to making modern democracy work by allowing the many traditions legitimacy in the public discourse. Moreover, he avers that democracy is a tradition in its own right.[64]

In the presentation of both Stout's critique and Hauerwas's response, I will attempt to frame the debate on sectarianism in relation to Hauerwas's understanding of character and agency. Hopefully, the following rendering of the Stout–Hauerwas dispute can clarify why it is imperative for Hauerwas to maintain the church as *the* defining community for Christians, subverting their allegiances to other institutions, such as liberal democracy, in doing so, and whether this claim needs to be better sustained, or challenged, in light of Stout's critique.

---

63. Stout, *Democracy and Tradition*, chapters 6–7.
64. Ibid., 13.

7.2.1 Stout's Sociopolitical Critique

Preceding Stout's treatment of Hauerwas is his critique of John Rawls' and Richard Rorty's liberalisms on the one hand, and John Milbank's Radical Orthodoxy (RO) and Alasdair MacIntyre's traditionalism on the other hand. Stout charges that Rawls's form of contractarian liberalism distorts democratic values in such a manner that the new traditionalists have felt compelled to reject the whole project.[65] While Rorty's pragmatic approach differs somewhat from Rawls's demand to supplement religious argument with appeals to a free-standing conception of justice, the end result is the same, namely the purgation of religious premises from public life. Stout questions both the underlying moralistic tone and the essentialist understanding of religion in their arguments.[66] Contrary to Rorty, who claims that religious premises *per se* function as conversation stoppers, Stout argues that the pragmatic line should be to consider the use of religious premises in political argument in a manner dependent on the situation and context.[67]

Turning to Milbank and the RO movement,[68] Stout focuses attention on the difference between secularism and secularization, which he chastises Milbank and other RO proponents for blithely ignoring. Rather, they view the secularization of political culture as reflecting the progression of the ideology of secularism.[69] Stout counters that the secularization process is not as ideologically driven as the proponents of RO aver, and by breeding resentment towards all things secular, these theologies are in themselves ideological expressions of the enclave society.[70] Similarly, Stout claims that the most troublesome feature of the traditionalism that MacIntyre and Hauerwas propose is the dismissal of liberal democracy.[71] While he decries their influence, he admits they confront democratic thinkers with a serious challenge, namely "Do we have reason to be happy with the kind of people we have become under the influence of modern ideas, practices, and

---

65. Ibid., 77.
66. Ibid., 86.
67. Ibid., 85–86.
68. Stout does not introduce Radical Orthodoxy (RO) as a movement, but as "currently the hottest topic being debated in seminaries and divinity schools in the United States" (ibid., 92). He does not capitalize RO either, but I have chosen to follow the line of James K. A. Smith, who in his *Introducing Radical Orthodoxy* both capitalizes RO and calls it a movement (26).
69. Stout, *Democracy and Tradition*, 100.
70. Ibid., 115.
71. Ibid., 118.

institutions?"[72] Stout concedes that this is an important question, but he argues that the traditionalists' resounding "no" to that question, decrying the modern lack of commitment to a shared tradition, presupposes a largely false story about modern ethics.[73]

Because Hauerwas relies on MacIntyre in several aspects, Stout's critique of MacIntyre is of particular relevance, and Stout also relates it directly to Hauerwas.[74] Stout avers that MacIntyre presumes modernity to be antitraditional, and consequently, since virtue and tradition are inextricably linked for him, modernity and modern democracy leave us *After Virtue*.[75] In addressing MacIntyre's developing argument throughout his works, Stout points out two main problems: 1) MacIntyre's reductionist understanding of modernity, particularly with regard to liberal democracy, and 2) the dearth of argument on the superiority of his type of traditions in fostering rational discourse.[76] The latter problem is related to his claim that rationality depends on tradition, while offering conflicting views of what a tradition is.

In one version, tradition simply means an ongoing discursive practice regarding the goods constituting the tradition, while in another version MacIntyre emphasizes the requirement that the discursive practice is deferential to authoritative texts. Also, in this second version of tradition, its rationality is dependent on institutionalized practices that ensure agreement on the human good. By staging tradition, thus understood, against the apparent conceptual fragmentation of modern democracy, MacIntyre construes a debate between traditional and modern variations of ethical discourse. Stout counters that the ambiguity of the term tradition proves that the debate is better construed as involving at least two kinds of traditions or strands of modern ethical discourse: one dedicated to a narrow conception of tradition (in the second version), and the other dedicated to loosening that conception democratically.[77] Stout readily admits, however, that proponents of the latter strand of modern ethical discourse have utilized and denounced the term tradition with a fluidity equal to MacIntyre's.[78]

If only MacIntyre had preserved his early appreciation and awareness of the way in which Hegel overcame the dualism between reason and

72. Ibid.

73. Ibid., 119.

74. Ibid.

75. Which is the title of the book by MacIntyre (MacIntyre, *After Virtue*) that Stout calls "the most influential theoretical expression of the new traditionalism" (Stout, *Democracy and Tradition*, 121).

76. Stout, *Democracy and Tradition*, 136.

77. Ibid.

78. Ibid., 137.

tradition, Stout muses that he might have remained conscious of his own dependence on the modern intellectual traditions that he chastises.[79] Stout concludes that MacIntyre is in fact a living proof against his own theory of rationality: "The story of his reasoned movement betwixt and between the various traditions with which he has affiliated himself is itself strong evidence against a theory according to which rationality can be exercised at its best only within highly coherent and 'well-integrated' traditions."[80]

Enter Hauerwas, who is introduced by Stout as having "done more than anyone else to spread the new traditionalism among Christians in the English-speaking world."[81] Stout further claims that "There is no doubt that the main effect of his antiliberal rhetoric . . . is to undercut Christian identification with democracy."[82] In order to argue why and how Hauerwas has gone about this agenda, Stout reads him primarily in light of the influences of Yoder and MacIntyre. He claims that the best critic of the current Hauerwas is actually the early Hauerwas, based on his early critique of Yoder's dualism of faith and unbelief. Stout cites Hauerwas as questioning Yoder's negative assumption about the language of justice as determined by sin, thus suggesting it is unable to have any positive relation to the language of faith.[83]

However, Hauerwas's difficulties with Yoder were seemingly resolved, as he took on the latter's pacifist position during the early 1980s, about the time that he formed his theological position more clearly. This also coincides with his subscription to MacIntyre and his traditionalist framework.[84] Wedding Yoder's ecclesiology, which emphasizes the opposition between faith and unbelief, with MacIntyre's traditionalism, which is thoroughly antiliberal, Stout avers that Hauerwas ends up with a dualism similar to that which he previously critiqued in Yoder: "One cannot stand in a church conceived in Yoder's term, while describing the world surrounding it in the way MacIntyre describes liberal society, without implicitly adopting a stance that is rigidly dualistic. . ."[85]

Consequently, because liberal democracy is pitted against tradition, the church becomes crucial for Hauerwas as the community that is able to

---

79. Stout critiques Hauerwas for similar blind spots regarding his dependence on the history of modern thinking, in general, and Hegel, in particular (ibid., 322 n. 15).

80. Ibid., 138.

81. Ibid., 140.

82. Ibid.

83. Ibid., 144.

84. Ibid.

85. Ibid., 149, italics original.

define and form virtuous people who adhere to the Christian tradition.[86] Stout, however, rejects both the assumption that democracy is void of virtue and that it presupposes the dismissal of tradition. Against Hauerwas, he argues that democratic discourse is in fact a practice that requires and fosters virtues, such as justice, and that rather than simply assuming (or dismissing) any tradition's authority, democracy entails a joint effort in criticizing and renewing traditions.[87] Indeed, it is Stout's larger constructive project to redescribe modern democracy as a tradition in the "Hegelian fashion, as a dialectical argument over goods and virtues in the context of shared social practices that endure over time," attending primarily to the discursive practices of democracy.[88]

A problematic corollary to Hauerwas's adherence to MacIntyre, according to Stout, is that he increasingly turned away from his early interest in the language of justice. Referring to Hauerwas's book *After Christendom*,[89] Stout questions whether it is only the liberal conception of justice that he thinks is a bad idea, and if so, what would be biblical reasons to work for justice?[90] Stout then relates Hauerwas's diminishing interest in the language of justice to Albrecht's feminist critique of his project, and he suggests that her complaint that his ethics reinforce unjust structures is valid and can be explained by his unwillingness to speak about justice.[91]

To summarize, Stout charges that Hauerwas propagates a sectarian dualism between the church and the world, resulting in Christians withdrawing their support for democracy and ceasing to engage in democratic practices. Hauerwas's problematic position, according to Stout, is founded on the fusion of Yoder's pacifist ecclesiology with MacIntyre's animosity toward all things liberal. In his vehement rejection of arguments that risk reducing the gospel to liberal democracy, Hauerwas tends to reduce it to sectarian ecclesiology, but Stout points out that these are not the only alternatives.[92] Rather, he advices Hauerwas that if he "were to stop thrashing his liberal straw man, rediscover the language of justice, and put that language to use in prophetic works of social criticism, his reviewers would surely stop charging him with sectarianism."[93]

86. As argued in chapter 5.2.3.
87. Stout, *Democracy and Tradition*, 152.
88. Ibid., 184–85.
89. Hauerwas, *After Christendom?*
90. Stout, *Democracy and Tradition*, 149.
91. Ibid., 150.
92. Ibid., 158.
93. Ibid., 160.

7.2.2 Hauerwas's Response to Stout's Critique

In a postscript to his book *Performing the Faith: Bonhoeffer and the Practice of Nonviolence*,[94] Hauerwas responds to Stout's critique largely by maintaining his own refutation of liberalism, including the liberal understanding of justice *qua* justice, and by dismissing Stout's claim that the combined influences of Yoder and MacIntyre inevitably lead to a problematic sectarianism. After expressing deep appreciation for Stout's comprehensive and critical treatment of his work, as well as acknowledging Stout's constructive contribution to the discourse on democracy,[95] Hauerwas is quick to reassure his readers that "That does not mean, however, that I am ready to concede every point he makes in criticism of me."[96]

For the purpose of my upcoming critical reconstruction of Hauerwas, I will highlight the most relevant arguments he makes, regarding the dualism between church and world, in his response to Stout.[97] The first of his remarks I will address is concerned with how his worries about liberalism originated. Hauerwas rebuts Stout, who links his ill-will toward all things liberal to MacIntyre's influence, by tracing his first worries back to the realization that liberal theory depended on the separation of action from the agent. The conviction that actions are constituted by our agency, following Aristotle's understanding of activity, was fundamental to his initial skepticism about liberal political theory, ethics, and practice. Hauerwas links the separation of action and agency to the liberal attempt to outline a politics and ethics without memory.[98]

It is the same push to abstraction that he wants to avoid when he refrains from using "the language of justice" that Stout calls for.[99] Hauerwas refers to what he has written on the mentally handicapped as an example of how justice can be thematized without employing the language of justice. He observes that "When people use the language of justice in the abstract in relation to the mentally handicapped, it turns out the mentally handicapped are judged not to have the characteristics to be treated justly."[100] The problem with liberal accounts of justice, according to Hauerwas, is that they tend to

---

94. Hauerwas, *Performing the Faith*.

95. He praises Stout's pragmatic position as "a position with which we Christians not only can, but should want to, do business" (ibid., 219).

96. Ibid., 219.

97. For a consideration of the debate between Stout and Hauerwas, which offers a sympathetic defense of Hauerwas's position, see Cavanaugh, "A Politics of Vulnerability."

98. Hauerwas, *Performing the Faith*, 224.

99. Stout, *Democracy and Tradition*, 160.

100. Hauerwas, *Performing the Faith*, 230 n. 29.

make justice an end in itself, without describing the practices that give content to justice. Thus, he denies the charge that at some point he dismissed the importance of justice on the grounds of furthering the church's sectarian withdrawal from the world.[101]

Against Stout's charges of rigid dualism, Hauerwas insists on the boundary between the church and world being permeable, and here he makes the second remark that I will highlight, claiming that the difference is about agency. He avers that "the duality can only be displayed historically, that is, the grounds of duality constantly require discernment. Such discernment is made possible by the practices of the church acquired by faithful performance."[102] He argues similarly in *Peaceable Kingdom*, where he states that "The only difference between church and world is the difference between agents."[103]

Finally, I will briefly mention Hauerwas's eschatological emphasis in his response to Stout's problematizing the combined influences of Yoder and MacIntyre on his work. While Stout assumes that MacIntyre pushed Hauerwas toward a sectarian position, Hauerwas claims the opposite, referring to the "Constantinian presumptions" of MacIntyre's grand narrative.[104] Following Yoder, Hauerwas instead has tried to do theology "from beginning to end apocalyptic,"[105] entailing a differentiation between the church and the world, which he admits can lead to a complete rejection of the world.[106] It is in an attempt to avoid this that he has employed MacIntyre, in order to "serve my neighbor both in and out of the church by saying what I take to be true given what I have learned from the church."[107]

7.2.3 Precursory Remarks on Stout's Critique

Stout raises a convincing concern about the withdrawal of Christians' engagement in liberal democracy, by contesting Hauerwas's crucial assumption that liberal democracy is unable to inculcate virtues since it is not submissive to a tradition (in MacIntyre's sense of the word). Hauerwas's ecclesiological concept of the church as defining for Christian agency, shaping

---

101. Ibid., 231.

102. Ibid., 231 n. 32. Hauerwas's oft-made reference to the status of faithfully performed practices will be further investigated in chapter 7.3.

103. Hauerwas, *The Peaceable Kingdom*, 101.

104. Hauerwas, *Performing the Faith*, 234.

105. Ibid., 235.

106. Ibid., 237.

107. Ibid., 238.

virtuous character through story and practices, depends on the differentiation between the church and the world, with the latter lacking the means to form people of good character. This is to be expected since the world, which in Hauerwas's rhetoric is largely represented as liberalism, modernism and democracy in various constellations, has no *telos* or understanding of the ultimate good, which leaves it in MacIntyre's state of "after virtue."

The problem with this argument, which Stout argues convincingly in my opinion, is if democracy and democratic discourse in fact contribute to the formation of good citizenry, as well as function as a looser form of tradition. I find Hauerwas's response that liberalism maintains the wrong virtues[108] to be too dismissive, as it does not acknowledge Stout's point about the necessity for the democratic purgation of traditions and their virtues, such as the church's, in order to reveal how they cement oppressive structures and practices.[109] However, given the story told by Hauerwas of the church as a contrasting and defining community, practicing faithfully in an unfaithful world, there is no apparent room for the collaborative democratic efforts that Stout envisions. Still, there are some hints in his story that may open a way forward, as Hauerwas admits that the world is also "those aspects of our individual and social lives where we live untruthfully by continuing to rely on violence to bring order."[110]

Considering Stout's critique of Hauerwas's alleged sectarianism, I find that the following questions are left unsatisfactorily answered by Hauerwas: *What is the theological basis for claiming the church's tradition and practices are exclusive in forming the character of a virtuous Christian? In other words, and related to the fideist critique, who or what is the agent that forms a truthful character?*

---

108. Ibid., 225.

109. This criticism is also argued from a feminist perspective. For example, Lydia Harder says that "The interruptions that come to the dominant narrative do not only come from within the community. At times they come from without, as new experiences are brought into the midst of the community or new interpretations of the church and Bible challenge our own" (Harder, "Dialogue with Hauerwas," 156). While Hauerwas acknowledges that the other can challenge the church, he frames this as reminders of what the church ought to be, and not as new experiences that may bring new understanding and interpretations to the church.

110. Hauerwas, *The Peaceable Kingdom*, 101. From the context, I assume Hauerwas refers to "our" as meaning "our Christian individual and social lives."

7.3 The Imperfect Peace of the Empirical Church: The Pragmatism Critique

One of the changes that Taylor claims characterizes a secular age is that belief becomes disengaged and excarnated. Hauerwas's understanding of the church counters this form of modern disengaged belief with an emphasis on the embodied truthfulness of the Christian story. He argues that the church is a community whose story can only be known as true by referring to the faithful practices of the church, among which peaceable practices are crucial. According to Hauerwas, the church's ability to live peacefully is preconditioned by the realization that we, as created humans, do not control our own destinies, but God does.

Nicholas M. Healy, a professor of theology and religious studies at St. Johns University, New York, recently published a critical introduction to Hauerwas in which he tries to stay clear of topics that have already thoroughly discussed, such as the charges of fideism and sectarianism, and attempts a different line of attack.[111] In brief, he critiques Hauerwas's ecclesiocentricism, which Healy worries has detrimental consequences for the church and its account of Christian doctrine and practice.[112] The following section will focus on his critique of Hauerwas's emphasis on and normative claims about the church as a performative community.

7.3.1 HEALY'S ECCLESIOLOGICAL CRITIQUE

Healy begins his critical introduction by introducing Hauerwas's conception of the church as marked by "a distinctive narrative, a distinctive identity, distinctive practices and, as such, a distinctive people, who constitute an alternative community that is holy and truthful, and as such, embodies and witnesses to the truth in and for the world."[113] He then moves to the critical part, arguing that Hauerwas's method and approach to theology align him, probably unintentionally and unwillingly, with the German theologian Friedrich Schleiermacher.[114] Despite obvious differences, Healy argues that their projects share a sharp methodological turn to the church, and he offers five areas of convergence as proof.[115]

---

111. Healy, *Hauerwas*. Although I think Healy succeeds in bringing fresh perspectives, such as his comparison of Hauerwas and Schleiermacher, it still seems to me that his critique comes down to the classic complaints about fideism, sectarianism, and pragmatism.
112. Ibid., 39–40.
113. Ibid., 38.
114. Ibid., 44.
115. Ibid., 48.

First, they both use non-theological theory instead of biblical analogies when arguing about what the church is.[116] They each start with a non-theological account of community and then consider the church's particularity as such. In doing so, according to Healy, there is a second methodological convergence in that they contrast the church community with similar groups, be it alternative religious or ideological traditions, and argue that the church is the highest form of community. Third, they consider Jesus as constitutive for the church's identity; for Schleiermacher he exemplifies perfect God-consciousness, while for Hauerwas, it is the story of Jesus' life, death and resurrection that makes the difference.[117] Fourth, Healy avers that they share an ecclesiocentric apologetic approach, which relies on the church in order to either display the truthfulness of Christianity (per Hauerwas) or offer a community in which people can achieve higher sensibilities (per Schleiermacher). Finally, their shared turn to the church entails a revision of how to understand doctrine. While Schleiermacher relates doctrine to reflection on religious experience, Hauerwas relates doctrine to practice in a manner that reduces doctrinal discussions to abstractions.[118]

Healy suggests that one of the two most obvious differences, however, is that Schleiermacher views the church and the world as collaborative and symbiotic entities, which directly opposes Hauerwas's previously discussed dualism of the church and the world. The other divergence that Healy points to is Schleiermacher's turn to the subject and her religious experiences, which Hauerwas upends with his rejection of any tendencies that might lead to the subjectivization or spiritualization of Christianity. Instead, he turns to the embodied and material practices of the community as the defining religious formation.[119]

This brings me to Healy's critique of Hauerwas's "pragmatic conception of Christian truth claims in the form of their embodiment in truthful church life."[120] The problem, according to Healy, is that the church's contrast identity, which according to Hauerwas is based on practicing peace truthfully, does not seem to have been manifested in empirical reality. Healy's threefold critique attacks Hauerwas for 1) emphasizing character formed by practices to the degree that he reduces a person to physiology,[121] 2) emphasizing church identity as contrasting to the world while seemingly ignor-

---

116. Ibid., 49.
117. Ibid., 50.
118. Ibid., 51.
119. Ibid., 48.
120. Ibid., 73.
121. Ibid., 95–96.

ing ethnographic descriptions of congregations that imply that the church seems to be "the world that is Christian,"[122] and 3) emphasizing a pragmatic truth concept, which is unable to accommodate the empirical diversity of the church.[123]

In his emphasis on practices as defining for the shaping of Christian character, Hauerwas makes several problematic assumptions. Healy argues that Hauerwas seems to assume that enacting practices is sufficient for character formation, thus ignoring cognitive negotiations, decisions, and discussions as crucial parts of such formation.[124] Another assumption that Healy questions is that particular practices, in and of themselves, are character forming, independent of the agent's understanding and interpretation of the practice.[125] Against this, Healy mentions three ways in which a practice can be enacted ineffectively: First, a practice can be enacted without engagement, merely like a physical rehearsal. For some practices superficial enactment is more problematic than for others, (e.g., Healy avers that the Roman Catholic Rite of Reconciliation requires a genuine remorse if the practice is to be effective and have actual impact on the person's character).[126] Second, a practice can be enacted badly, according to Healy, such as tithing reluctantly or in a tight-fisted manner. Third, and most significantly, is to enact Christian practices incorrectly. Healy adamantly points out that the intention of, and beliefs about, a church practice are crucial if it is to have a formative effect on the agent's character.[127] Hauerwas underestimates the limits on the transformative potential of practices, regardless of whether they are related to belief, intention, or contextual factors, as all are decisive in determining whether a practice reinforces who we already are or transforms us to be more like the ideal Christian.[128]

Healy's complaints that Hauerwas emphasizes the contrast identity of the church and a pragmatic ecclesiocentric concept of truth both rest on an apparent lack of attention to ethnography and the empirical church.

122. Ibid., 98.
123. Ibid., 97.
124. Ibid., 96.
125. Kelly S. Johnson makes a similar point, by arguing that the church's practices are formative in a similar sense to how all human practices are formative, and that the difference that Hauerwas does not sufficiently attend to is pneumatological (Johnson, "Worshiping in Spirit and Truth," 305).
126. Healy, *Hauerwas*, 111.
127. Ibid., 112.
128. Ibid., 113. Harder makes a similar point when she claims Hauerwas ignores the gender factor in relation to Christian character formation. She questions the assumption that the male Christian identity and the female Christian identity that result from church practices are the same (Harder, "Dialogue with Hauerwas," 154).

Hauerwas's concept of the church as a contrast community presupposes the existence of a critical mass, of both saintly individuals and congregations, in order to be more than an abstract and meaningless ideal, says Healy.[129] In preferring anecdotal stories to actual ethnographic studies of congregations, Hauerwas merely demonstrates the power of community-in-general but fails to prove that the church he describes actually exists.[130] Healy, referring to ethnographic studies, claims it does not.[131] Rather, the empirical church turns out to be diverse in its beliefs and practices, even within congregations.[132] Moreover, individual Christians are far from consistent in their beliefs and practices, which can result in living rather incongruently inside and outside of the gathered church community.[133]

Healy also regards the diversity of church communities, including the mixture of more or less holy people, to be a problem for Hauerwas's pragmatic truth concept: If the truth of Christianity is displayed by the church's practices, which church community and whose truth should be preferred? Healy, given the problematic task of discerning what constitutes truthful living in the empirical church, considers the varied practices to be more or less successful experiments in truthful living.[134] Hauerwas's failure to take the "confusingly messy realities of ordinary church life" into account endangers the credibility of his larger theological project.[135]

To summarize, the aspect of Healy's criticism of Hauerwas I have focused on in this discussion is his claim that Hauerwas's normative account of the church, based on the crucial formative role of practices and a correlated pragmatic concept of truth, fails to account for the diversity and mixed nature of the empirical church and its members.[136] The result is that Hauerwas's ecclesiology, quite contrary to his intentions, appears to be an abstract ideal.[137]

---

129. Healy, *Hauerwas*, 81.

130. Ibid., 85.

131. For a substantive argument on the missed opportunity of ethnographic studies in Hauerwas's work, see Scharen and Vigen, *Ethnography as Christian Theology and Ethics*, 50–53.

132. Healy, *Hauerwas*, 91.

133. Ibid., 94.

134. Ibid., 97.

135. Ibid., 98.

136. Healy refers to "church members" seemingly as equivalent to "Christians" (ibid., e.g., 78). Samuel Wells makes similar points of critique, questioning whether Hauerwas is describing or prescribing, and whether it is possible to assess the Christian story pragmatically when there are both many stories and many ways to practice them (Wells, *Transforming Fate into Destiny*, 67).

137. Healy also offers a critical analysis of the theological implications of Hauerwas's

7.3.2 Awaiting Hauerwas's Response

Healy's book was published quite recently, and I am not aware of a published response from Hauerwas. However, based on previous critical discussions about his work, including the charge of pragmatism, I will suggest a few lines of argument that could serve as a hypothetical response to Healy's critique. In other words, it will be a brief consideration of Healy's argument that draws on Hauerwas's previous responses to his critics.

Hauerwas specifically addresses the charge that his ecclesiology portrays an ideal church by claiming that such a church (i.e., the local congregations) does in fact exist. He offers the anecdotal example of a Methodist Church that he previously attended, suggesting that their seemingly common acts have significant theological value.[138] Obviously, such references do not allay Healy's complaints, as he argues that there must be a critical mass of such examples in order for Hauerwas's project to make sense. But for Hauerwas, this empirical example is crucial, as it proves that the church he speaks of is possible.[139] And that it has existed throughout church history, which is why he thinks it is so important that the stories of the many faithful congregations are told in order to teach Christians what it means to be church.[140]

However, he is not denying the unfaithfulness of the historical and contemporary church, but rather insists that the church despite this "must lay claim to being the earnest of God's kingdom and thus able to provide the institutional space for us to rightly understand the disobedient, sinful, but still God-created character of the world."[141] Thus, the failure of the church does not change its *telos*, which is to be the place and community that enables Christians to rightly see the world and enact the story of God.

Finally, I suspect Hauerwas would be sympathetic to Healy's call for further ethnographic research on congregations, though with preconditions. He has previously expressed concern about the sort of social science that precludes theological claims for the church's existence, claiming that the social-scientific use of mechanistic metaphors reflects "the world view of the middle class, ordered by its penchant for management and its convictions that life processes are to be managed according to standards of

---

ecclesiology, but for the purpose of this critical discussion, I found this part of his critique to be sufficient. The critical analysis of the theological implications is mainly outlined in chapter 5 (Healy, *Hauerwas*, 100–136).

138. Hauerwas, *Christian Existence Today*, 112, 123.
139. Ibid., 113.
140. Ibid., 125.
141. Hauerwas, *A Community of Character*, 92.

predictability and lawlike generalizations."[142] But there are other less reductive ways of conducting social science that allow for theological convictions, and I think Hauerwas would agree that ethnographic studies done in such manner would be beneficial both to theology in general and ecclesiology in particular. Certainly that is my conviction.[143]

7.3.4 Precursory Remarks on Healy's Critique

In Healy's claim that Hauerwas's demands on the church are unrealistic, as well as theologically unsustainable, he rightly correlates these with Hauerwas's reluctance to consider how God acts outside, and sometimes in spite of, the church.[144] By insisting that it is church practices that are primarily formative for Christians and decisive for the manifestation of Christianity's truthfulness, Hauerwas fails to sufficiently acknowledge the limitations of the church's embodied truthfulness and the consequences of such limitations. In contrast, Healy proposes that an ecclesiology accommodating the empirical reality of the church must recognize that "What constitutes truthful living is often very difficult to discern in the concrete..."[145] Consequently, such claims from Hauerwas that the church should exhibit the morality that God desires must be avoided, since it displays arrogance and hubris.[146]

While Healy's concerns are understandable and well argued, it seems to me that he adopts a far too polarized position to Hauerwas. Reinhard Hütter describes the theological problem with two such dichotomized poles: "on the one hand, the one-dimensional understanding of 'reality' is oriented toward the tacitly normative facticity of the existing church; on the other hand the explicitly normative ideal of the church always implies a synergistic logic of production or social engineering, the point of which is the 'realization' of this preconceived 'idea' of the church..."[147] In my reading, Healy comes close to the first position by emphasizing the empirical reality of the church to the extent that it becomes one-dimensional, while Hauerwas clearly represents the latter in the way he upholds the social-ethical

---

142. Hauerwas, *Christian Existence Today*, 130 n. 15.

143. For an innovative and instructive argument on the theological use of ethnography, see Scharen and Vigen, *Ethnography as Christian Theology and Ethics*. For their engagement with Hauerwas's critique, see ibid., 50–57.

144. Healy, *Hauerwas*, 75.

145. Ibid., 97.

146. Ibid., 98.

147. Hütter, "Ecclesial Ethics," 439.

nature and ideal of the church. Hütter also refers to Hauerwas as an example of such an ecclesiology.

For the purpose of my upcoming pneumatological reconstruction of Hauerwas's ecclesiology it is also of interest that Hütter argues for the important difference between what he calls "a utopian and a pneumatological eschatology."[148] A utopian eschatology results in an ecclesial ethics that portrays the church as a project of human agency, which is intended to be transformed according to an eschatological ideal. As such, human agency becomes imbued with a redeeming character.[149] Pneumatological eschatology, on the other hand, leads to an understanding of the church as the project of God's agency through the Holy Spirit, who works for the transformation of the world through the transformation of human beings.[150]

Related to Healy's critique, I will argue that the eschatological character, more or less explicitly stated, of Hauerwas's church, might contribute to his ecclesiology presenting less as a display of arrogance and hubris. By explicating the eschatological implications in Hauerwas's work through a pneumatological framework, I intend to address what I consider to be legitimate objections from Healy, as articulated in the following questions: *Is it sufficient, or even required, to be trained in and to perform particular church practices in order to be a Christian? And can the empirical church perform as the truthful witness demanded by Hauerwas's ecclesiology?*

7.4 Chapter Summary

This chapter has addressed three of the common criticisms of Hauerwas's work: fideism, sectarianism, and pragmatism. These –isms serve as shorthands for the objections, but as we have seen, the complaints regarding his use of story include both charges of fideism and sectarianism, and when discussing his emphasis on practices, his critics are concerned with both fideism and sectarianism in addition to the central problem of pragmatism. Thus, in accordance with Hauerwas's own apparently haphazard style, the criticism of his project may as well deserve that label. The goal of the following chapters, however, is to offer a pneumatological reconstruction of Hauerwas's ecclesiology that is less haphazard, and that can gather the various strands of criticism within a pneumatological redemptive effort.

---

148. Ibid., 435.

149. I would add that Hütter's suspicion that Hauerwas's ecclesiology is utopian in this sense is further sustained by my analysis of Hauerwas's strong sense of self-agency (chapter 5.3.1).

150. Hütter, "Ecclesial Ethics," 435.

8

Introducing the Pneumatological Reconstruction

THIS CHAPTER INTENDS TO lay the foundation for the subsequent pneumatological reconstruction by first briefly summarizing the findings thus far and then providing the necessary introductions and preparations for the remaining part of the journey. Starting from the beginning, I recap Taylor's secular challenges, then rehearse how Hauerwas's understanding of church relates to these, and finally restate the most relevant critiques of his critics. Based on this overview, I suggest that a pneumatological turn would be fruitful and introduce Amos Yong as the proponent whose work I intend to utilize.

8.1 Overview

In outlining the central features of Hauerwas's ecclesiology, I have argued that his understanding of the church as a particular community offers insights into the empirical church in a secular age. As previously stated, the secular age presents challenges that must be negotiated by any church that recognizes the secular conditions for religious belief and practice as part of its context.

8.1.1 Taylor's Secular Age

The challenges of a secular age, according to Taylor and here briefly recapitulated, are related to:

1. *The deconstruction of truth*: With the rise of natural science, the priority relations of epistemology changed, and human reason became the starting point and precipitator in the knowing process. Knowledge was no longer viewed as grounded in or predicated on transcendent ideas, whether these were Platonic or Christian. Instead knowledge was to be discovered as humanity subtracted religious superstition and gained intellectual boldness in seeking truth, without any transcendent agent considered necessary as some sort of revered guardian of truth.

2. *The detachment of self:* The secular construction of the self is conditioned by what Taylor refers to as "the modern subtraction story" and the related "maturation story." Both of these narratives construe human agency as maturing into adulthood with the coming of modernity and scientific discoveries, and the related riddance of religion and superstition. With the modern image of individual identity developing as a lone hero, the concept of the self leaves the communal arena of social spaces and becomes detached both horizontally and vertically.

3. *The disembodiment of belief:* Due to the modern reliance on reason and thought, belief was gradually disconnected from experience and practice. Truth became overwhelmingly propositional and intellectualized, and following this, apologetics became a theoretical endeavor which resulted in an overall undermining of Christian practice. Taylor calls this the excarnation of religion, and I argued that this disembodiment of belief poses a challenge for the church in a secular age.

8.1.2 Hauerwas's Church Community

By insisting on the church as *a storied community*, Hauerwas argues that people come to know truth and the meaning of truthfulness based on the story they find their lives to be a part of, and for the church, this story is the Gospel story. To confess Jesus as Lord is only intelligible, and can only be known to be true, in the context of the Gospel story and the church's performance. The truthfulness and content of Christian claims are thus made intelligible and convincing when Christians live truthful lives faithful to the church's story. Hauerwas's notion of the church as a storied community primarily navigates the challenge of deconstructed truth in its insistence on truth being dependent on narrative, community, and performance.

The second central feature of Hauerwas's church is that it is *a defining community*. To be defining, both in the sense of being important and determining, entails for Hauerwas that the church is a community that constructs human agency and moral good theologically, and in so doing also defines what the world is. He claims that even though theological constructs of agency and moral good may not seem relevant to the world, the church—simply by being the church—in fact defines what the world is: lost without God. I argued that this ecclesiological feature navigates the detachment of self, as it reclaims the importance of social spaces and community, on theological terms, for the defining of self.

Third and closely related to his understanding of the church as a storied and defining community, I traced in Hauerwas's ecclesiology the feature of church as *a performative community*. This entails understanding the church as a practice community that seeks to perform faithfully according to Christian convictions and theory. Performing the liturgy is the most central church practice, according to Hauerwas, partly because it enables peaceable living by reminding the church that peace can never be attained through violence. In this respect, the liturgical practices he emphasizes are preaching the Gospel of peace, regular confessions, which both prevent and expose self-deceptions, and celebrating the Eucharist, which reminds the church of how Christ responded to the violence to which he was subjected. By stressing the crucial import of the church as performance, Hauerwas counters the secular challenge of disembodied belief.

8.1.3 Critique of Hauerwas's Ecclesiology

In the previous chapter I outlined some convincing and overlapping criticisms of Hauerwas that are related to these ecclesiological features. Albrecht questions whose voice is heard in the story that Hauerwas emphasizes as crucial to how the church understands truth and truthfulness. Gustafson's critique also addresses Hauerwas's emphasis on story, as he charges him with both fideism and sectarianism in his lack of recognition of the truth outside the church and the church's story. Important questions thus seem to be left unanswered by Hauerwas: *Who is narrating and interpreting the church's story and what are the consequences of that agency for the truthfulness of the story? And is the truth and rationality of the Christian story exclusive or authoritative over non-Christian rational activities or stories that lay claim to truth?*

Further, based on Hauerwas's continued emphasis on the church as a defining community, and the development of Christian character by cultivating habits, the charge of sectarianism has been made by several critics, most forcibly by Stout. By refuting Hauerwas's central premise that the church is the principle (or even exclusive) community of character for the Christian, Stout problematizes the sectarianism inherent in such a claim. His critique is motivated by his defense of democracy as a tradition with its own virtues and formative qualities however, since my agenda is theological, my summary questions reflect this approach: *What is the theological basis for claiming the church's tradition and practices are exclusive in forming the character of a virtuous Christian? In other words, and related to the fideist critique, who or what is the agent that forms a truthful character?*

Finally, the following questions related to Hauerwas's understanding of the church as a performing community, were asked: Who or what makes the Christian a Christian? According to Hauerwas, the answer is practice. However, critics ask whether it is sufficient, or even required, to be part of a community and trained in particular practices in order to be Christian? Healy argues that there are several reasons why this is not so, and he claims that Hauerwas's ecclesiology is weakened by his idealistic picture of the church's ability to practice peace and perform truthfully. The empirical church's performance of the Christian story is partially successful, at best, much in the same way as for people not affiliated with church, which leaves us with the following questions: *Is it sufficient, or even required, to be trained in and to perform particular church practices in order to be a Christian? And can the empirical church perform as the truthful witness demanded by Hauerwas's ecclesiology?*

8.2 A Pneumatological Turn

In my opinion, Hauerwas's lopsidedly communitarian way of constructing Christian agency is one of the most foundational shortcomings of his work, as it also affects the other problems flagged by his critics, which I intend to argue. Healy critiques what he calls Hauerwas's sharp turn to community and compares his work to Schleiermacher, although they obviously take different angles. Where Schleiermacher turns to the subject, Hauerwas turns to the community. However, Healy finds it problematic that they both similarly disallow the importance of the logic of belief for Christian living and church life. But whereas Healy suggests a focal shift of *loci* for church practices, from ecclesiocentric to theocentric, I will argue that a focal shift of agency is more fruitful.[1] In doing so, I am drawing on the work of the Pentecostal theologian Amos Yong to reconstruct Hauerwas's ecclesiology, addressing both the challenges of a secular age and the critical questions outlined in the previous chapter. My central hypothesis is that by developing the agency of the Spirit in relation to Hauerwas's ecclesiology, his emphasis on Christian particularity can be retained, while arguing for a pneumatological continuity between the church community, the world as creation, and the promised kingdom.[2]

With regard to Yong and his work, I will also address concerns about the compatibility of Yong and Hauerwas. However, it is my contention that there are pneumatological intuitions in Hauerwas's ecclesiology that are in

---

1. Healy also acknowledges the unrecognized agency of the Spirit in Hauerwas, e.g., Healy, *Hauerwas*, 131f, 68.

2. Several other theologians have previously pointed out the lack of pneumatological reflection in Hauerwas's work. E.g., Rasmusson, *The Church as Polis*, 179.

accordance with Yong's foundational pneumatology.³ Thus, the presumption substantiating the overall reconstruction is that Hauerwas's underdeveloped pneumatology is the central crux of his project. Without the explicit agency of the Spirit, he is left with the disputed ability of the community to act upon (and perhaps through) individual Christians in order for them to be witnesses to the world through truthful performance.

8.2.1 Reconstruction Movements

The pneumatological reconstruction will proceed according to the three features of Hauerwas's ecclesiology—the church as storied, church as defining, and church as performance—and along three recurring movements:

1. The restating of the main questions from the critical discussion of the ecclesiological feature at hand, which where articulated in the precursory comments in the previous chapters.

2. Yong's pneumatological contribution to the considered question is explicated, following his own conceptual categories of the Spirit as rationality, relationality, and *dunamis*. In presenting the categories, I have rearranged Yong's order in line with the systematic argument of the book as a whole. As such, no descending or increasing theological importance is intended in the sequence of the pneumatological categories.

3. Finally, I return to the ecclesiological feature and attempt to reconstruct it by developing an explicit pneumatological agency in relation to Hauerwas's understanding of the church.

Since Hauerwas does not speak much about the Spirit's agency in relation to the church, and barely makes references to the Spirit whatsoever in his most-read works, my approach will be to read him through the pneumatological categories provided by Yong, allowing his implicit pneumatological intuitions to gain credence and content from Yong's work. However, where such pneumatological references are absent in Hauerwas's work, or misplaced, critical corrections will be in order. Thus, it is my working assumption that the most promising avenue for reconstructing Hauerwas's ecclesiology, in a manner that engages both the critical charges against it and the challenges of a secular age, is to explore the Spirit's agency in relation to

---

3. E.g., Hauerwas, *With the Grain of the Universe*, 210–14, where he clearly states the crucial agency of the Spirit, although not unpacking what it entails concretely in relation to the church.

the ecclesiological features previously outlined. Whether this assumption is correct will best be proven by the actual work ahead.

The final reconstructive movement entails a loosening of my commitment to Hauerwas's and Yong's initial concepts, as I attempt to articulate the features of a pneumatological ecclesiology while also negotiating the challenges of a secular age. As such, the intention is not to amend Hauerwas's ecclesiology *per se* but to draw from his work, in dialogue with Yong, to answer the big question of this book, which is concerned with how an understanding of the church as a particular community can navigate the CWS of a secular age. Thus, the resulting ecclesiological contribution attempts to argue how the church's particularity, which Hauerwas asserts, is better equipped to navigate the CWS when acknowledging the Spirit's work of continuity between the church, creation, and the kingdom.

When the Spirit is the decisive agent, enabling both the will and the ability to do good, then it is not the communal formation or habits in themselves that are sanctifying, but rather the work of the Spirit through these habits and virtues. The Spirit also holds together the temporal events of creation, salvation, and eschaton, and thus reminds the church of the promise of God's kingdom. This implies that while there is an "already" aspect to God's peace being made present to the church by the Spirit, the inability of the church to live perfectly peaceable is a manifestation of the "not yet" aspect.[4]

8.2.2 Pneumatology, Pneumatological Ecclesiology, and Pentecostal Theology

It is not within the scope of this book to offer a survey of pneumatology as such, or even pneumatological ecclesiology, but a brief introduction to the theological landscape of pneumatology will provide a helpful context for the work ahead. Pneumatology has traditionally not been considered as a separate *locus* in theological treatises, as pneumatological issues have been addressed as part of soteriology or ecclesiology.[5] However, prominent modern theologians across the denominational specter, such as Wolfhart Pannenberg,[6] John Zizioulas,[7] and Yves Congar,[8] have contributed to the development of a more comprehensive pneumatological approach in

---

4. With Yong's help I must clearly develop *how* the agency of the Spirit works in and through the church.
5. Kärkkäinen, *Pneumatology*, 19.
6. Pannenberg, *Systematic Theology*.
7. Zizioulas, *Being as Communion*.
8. Congar, *I Believe in the Holy Spirit*.

theological work, allowing the Spirit a central role in relation to the other systematic topics.[9]

Particularly relevant for this project is the increased focus on pneumatology being crucial for ecclesiology. According to Zizioulas, the content of both Christology and pneumatology must for several reasons be present when considering the foundation of the church.[10] While he emphasizes that God's activity is one and indivisible, he points out that the contributions of the Son and the Spirit are different in several ways. Central to the pneumatological aspects are eschatology and communion.[11] These are pneumatological characteristics that I explore in Yong's work, through the categories of *dunamis* (cf. eschatology) and relationality (cf. communion).

Parallel to this pneumatological awakening in systematic theology, Pentecostal theology has slowly emerged as a corollary to the global Pentecostal movement.[12] The inherent anti-academic leaning of the movement contributes to the inertia of Pentecostal theology. Pentecostal ecclesiology has been described as having an ad hoc nature, allowing for improvisation.[13] However, the landscape is shifting, and in the forefront of these developments in Pentecostal theology is the Asian-American Pentecostal scholar, Amos Yong.[14]

8.3 Amos Yong's Pneumatology

In this section, I introduce Amos Yong and his work, as well as comment upon why I think he is a constructive interlocutor with regard to Hauerwas's ecclesiology and my project.

8.3.1 Yong, the Pentecostal Scholar of Pneumatology

With my Pentecostal church background, I readily recognized the experience described by Amos Yong in his autobiographical essay "Between the

---

9. Kärkkäinen, *Pneumatology*, 20.

10. Zizioulas, *Being as Communion*, 129.

11. Ibid., 130.

12. For more on the massive growth of Pentecostalism, particularly in the global south, see Jenkins, *The New Faces of Christianity*. For Pentecostal theology in the Norwegian context, see Sæther and Tangen, *Pentekostale Perspektiver*.

13. Kärkkäinen, *An Introduction to Ecclesiology*, 73.

14. Oliverio presents Yong as a pioneering Pentecostal theologian, who has "expanded the palette of Pentecostal theology" (Oliverio, "An Interpretive Review Essay," 302).

Local and the Global,"[15] which is about entering academia and approaching the theological task: "I was convinced that part of my vocation involved a stance of critical loyalty toward the denomination and movement which had nurtured my Christian faith."[16] Moreover, I also share his ecumenical intuitions and convictions that contemporary theological work must engage in dialogue with global perspectives and concerns, as well as interdisciplinary discourses,[17] without undermining the importance of doing contextual theology and theology in and for the local church.[18] Although these shared intuitions about the contemporary theological task contributed to my initial interest in Yong's work, it was his creative ethos and pneumatological vision that convinced me his project could offer a purposive contribution to the forthcoming reconstruction.[19]

Yong is considered to be the leading Pentecostal constructive theologian, and his work is for many a gateway to Pentecostal scholarship.[20] However, he has not been chosen primarily as a Pentecostal scholar but as a scholar of pneumatology, since the intent of this reconstruction is not to make a particularly Pentecostal turn, but a pneumatological turn. Yong is a prolific writer, engaging with a wide array of topics, but the undercurrent is thoroughly pneumatological. From the outset, going back to his doctoral thesis, *Discerning the Spirit(s)*,[21] he addressed theology of religion- issues through a pneumatological lens. By developing a foundational pneumatology, he attempted to open up a new passage for inter-religious dialogue, postponing the Christological question in order to clear some theological space for working on the tension between Christianity's particularity and its universality.[22] He has continued this endeavor with several subsequent contributions to a Pentecostal theology of religions, as well as by pursuing the possibility of a pneumatologically driven world theology.[23]

---

15. Marks, *Shaping a Global Theological Mind*, 187–94.

16. Ibid., 188.

17. Ibid., 194.

18. Ibid., 192.

19. However, I am not the first to employ Yong in constructive efforts in ecclesiology, see e.g., Lord, *Network Church*, and Smith, "The Church Militant."

20. Vondey and Mittelstadt, *The Theology of Amos Yong*.

21. Yong, *Discerning the Spirit(s)*.

22. Ibid., 58.

23. For a more comprehensive presentation of Yong's work and a contextualization of it as Pentecostal theology, see Vondey and Mittelstadt, *The Theology of Amos Yong*, 1–19, and for a critical assessment, see Stephenson, *Types of Pentecostal Theology Method, System, Spirit*, 82–110.

8.3.2 Yong and Hauerwas: A Constructive Engagement?

Rather than offering a broad introduction to Yong's work at this point, I will, during the reconstruction, focus on the perspectives most helpful in infusing Hauerwas's ecclesiology with a well-developed pneumatological consciousness. However, before forging ahead, concerns with the commensurability of the projects of Hauerwas and Yong must be addressed. While Yong has worked extensively with foundational questions in theology, Hauerwas has eschewed concepts like epistemology and metaphysics for cementing the modernist approach to knowledge as abstract and theoretical. Likewise, he has refused the notion of doing systematic theology on similar grounds, and his works are primarily essayistic in form, which contrasts with Yong's systematic approach and structure. And while Yong pursues a global theology that accounts for the many perspectives and experiences, Hauerwas insists on primarily[24] addressing church and theologians in his local context, with its particular adversaries (e.g., liberalism and Constantinianism) and challenges.

These differing interests might be construed as signifying an incommensurability of a more critical kind. What if Hauerwas and Yong, when it all comes down to it, fundamentally disagree about what theology—and even truth—is, and should be done? For Hauerwas, it is actually accurate to speak of truth as something to be done and displayed, however, as a critical realist he certainly would not reduce truth to pragmatics. So my reading of these two thinkers is that while Hauerwas's starting point is the concrete, the pragmatics, the ethics, the church as a living community, Yong often times (not always!) start at the other end of the scale, with the theoretical arguments. But as I will argue, Yong's way of doing theology is dynamic—or infused by *dunamis*, and therefore never remains within the realm of theorems, but always presses toward theological embodiment and incarnation.

This means that while Hauerwas starts with the importance of the church's story as praxis, and then might deduce how that story demands of the church hospitality and generosity towards the stranger, Yong starts out with a theological and biblical consideration of hospitality, and then deduces that the church should be hospitable towards the stranger. Likewise, Hauerwas in essayform might start out by portraying how the church community is more truly Christlike when the disabled are part of it, and then offer some brief theological reflections on disability theology, anthropology, or suffering. Yong, on the other hand, offers a systematic theological

---

24. I write "primarily" because his work has been translated into several languages, which is a testimony to the cross-cultural relevance of a highly contextually developed theology (Hauerwas, *The Hauerwas Reader*, 4).

INTRODUCING THE PNEUMATOLOGICAL RECONSTRUCTION   135

treatise on disability theology, but always with reference to lived practices and embodied realities.

My understanding is therefore that while they certainly differ on method and style, they are actually quite attuned when it comes to what theology—and truth—is, and they might not even disagree as to how it should be done. Hauerwas has certainly paid dues to systematic thinkers, though claiming himself not to be one. And Yong, the obvious systematic theologian, has never to my knowledge disavowed the value of various theological approaches and methods. They both argues theology should serve the church, however, again their emphases are slightly differently put: Hauerwas stresses that the primary task of theology is to make the Christian faith intelligible for the church, while Yong certainly would agree that is one of theology's tasks, but at the same time, strives to make Christian faith intelligible to a wider and more multiple communities. Could Yong's emphasis then undermine Hauerwas's, so to speak? In my opinion, the answer is a resounding no. Rather, these different emphases makes the conversation even more potent, and contributes important perspectives that each on its own does not.

Additionally, there are several shared topical and theoretical convergences, that also justify bringing these theologians together on the same stage: 1) Their shared departure from modernist assumptions about truth,[25] 2) their shared theological heritage of Methodism's holiness movement, 3) their shared interest in church as a particular and political community,[26] including 4) an emphasis on the embodied nature of Christian life. However, these are merely a few theoretical reflections on their compatibility, while the real proof of the setup is in the actual reconstruction.[27] The final

---

25. And, I might add, their shared subscription to a critical realist position, see Yong, *Spirit-Word-Community*, 83, and Hauerwas, *Christian Existence Today*, 10.

26. See Yong, *In the Days of Caesar*, 186–90, for Yong's largely appreciative reading of Hauerwas's post-Christendom ecclesiology.

27. Another relevant discussion is to what degree reconstructive work of this kind demands commensurability between the different thinkers whose theories are on the table. It can be argued that the important thing is to lay out the premises for the reconstruction, which may not comply fully with either of the thinkers, but merely be sufficiently in agreement for a reconstruction to make sense. Obviously, for any interdisciplinary work to be possible, such a sufficiency will have to be sufficient. Disciplines such as theology and sociology of religion certainly differ in both methods and theoretical grounds, but may very well offer constructive findings when crossing borders and working together—on what is considered in each case by the researcher to be sufficiently common thereotical ground. This is my position on this matter, but since I do not find the works of Hauerwas and Yong to be incommensurable on this scale, I will not explore this line of argument further.

preparatory task is to briefly introduce Yong's foundational pneumatology, as it is vital to the reconstructive effort.

8.3.3 Introducing Yong's Foundational Pneumatology

In one of Yong's earliest books, he presents what he calls a pneumatological-trinitarian hermeneutic, which is described as a theological hermeneutic based on the agency of the Holy Spirit.[28] Yong introduces his "pneumatology of quest"[29] by proposing that a pneumatological approach to theology offers a more robust trinitarianism than theology from a Christological starting point.[30] Such claims have led others to consider Yong's work to be thoroughly pneumatological in shape. Christopher A. Stephenson avers that "The primacy of pneumatology owes to Yong's contention that the 'Holy Spirit' is the most fundamental symbol of, and therefore, most appropriate category for referring to God's agency in the world."[31] Thus, Yong's foundational pneumatology is an account of the relationship between God and the world.[32]

Yong's ambitious project in *Spirit-Word-Community*[33] is to develop a triadic construct of reality, knowledge, and hermeneutics, which he calls a "trinitarian *Weltanschauung*."[34] For the purpose of my reconstruction, however, it is the first part of Yong's project that is of particular relevance. Here he outlines the biblical, theological, and metaphysical aspects of a foundational pneumatology that is structured around three categories: relationality, rationality, and *dunamis*.[35] Since Yong avers that theology cannot be divorced from methodology, he notes that the theological discussion will also reflect and encroach upon the final part of the book, which is his focus throughout the journey, where he explicates the hermeneutical assumptions of his project.[36]

---

28. Yong, *Spirit-Word-Community*, 19.

29. Ibid., 8.

30. Ibid., 9.

31. Vondey and Mittelstadt, *The Theology of Amos Yong*, 64.

32. On the difference between systematic pneumatology and foundational pneumatology, see Yong, "On Divine Presence and Divine Agency," 178–79.

33. Yong, *Spirit-Word-Community*.

34. Ibid., 21.

35. He notes that the categories are not intended to constitute a comprehensive biblical pneumatology, but should rather be considered as pneumatological trails that can be followed in order to explore their theological implications (ibid., 115).

36. Ibid., 25–27.

Still, I find that the first part offers in itself a concise and potent pneumatological contribution, which I will employ in an ecclesiological effort as opposed to Yong's hermeneutical application. The differing purposes of our pneumatological enterprises also determine the varied procedures: while Yong advances from a biblical pneumatology to a pneumatological theology and then to a pneumatological metaphysics, I have chosen to structure Yong's contribution according to his pneumatological categories of rationality, relationality, and *dunamis*. The primary intent is to relate the pneumatological categories to Hauerwas's ecclesiological features, the corresponding points of criticism, and finally, to the challenges of a secular age. Before forging ahead, however, I will make a short comment on Yong's concept of S/spirit.

8.3.4 Yong's Spirit

Yong has elsewhere outlined his understanding of the Holy Spirit through an exegesis of Luke and Acts.[37] In accordance with the biblical material, he focuses on the works of the Spirit rather than offering a theological description of the Spirit *per se*. For the following reconstruction, however, it may be useful to make a few observations about Yong's use of the concept of the Spirit.

First, he differentiates between Spirit and spirit.[38] Spirit in the initial sense (with a capital S) refers to the Holy Spirit, and this is Yong's sole qualifier for the term in this context.[39] However, spirit in the latter sense (with a lowercase s) receives far more attention: as a metaphor, it can refer to manifold concepts such as atmosphere, tradition, and intentionality. As such, it is an anthropological category: "the relationality that provides the contexts of our human life and interactions in the world."[40] However, since my main interest is in his understanding of Spirit, I will not attend further to his explication of the various categories of spirit.[41]

37. Yong, *Who Is the Holy Spirit?*
38. Yong, *Spirit-Word-Community*, 14.
39. Ibid., 15. It is worth noting, however, that Yong subscribes to a Pentecostal understanding of the Spirit as encountering and manifesting not only in the church as a gathered community, but also in the individual lives of Christians (*The Spirit Poured out on All Flesh*, 136). This is probably a point about which Hauerwas would be more reluctant, but to my knowledge he has not denied that the Spirit can so manifest, though he is critical of the subjectivity that he relates to such views. Following Hauerwas's ecclesiology, I am not focusing on such individual manifestations of the Spirit in this book, but I am noting that it would be a constructive inquiry related to the emphasis on the church's liturgical life.
40. Yong, *Spirit-Word-Community*, 15.
41. It has been argued that Yong's notion of the spirit shares connotations with Hegel's *Geist* (Oliverio, "An Interpretive Review Essay," 307 n. 14). Yong himself

Second, I have not been able to find a treatise where Yong addresses the issue of gendered language about the Spirit. While he refers to the Spirit both as female[42] and male[43] in his various works, the selected gender is not explained or discussed explicitly, at least in the works here cited. Since my focus in the following reconstruction is mainly on the pneumatological categories and the capacities of the Spirit, and since Yong does not discuss these in gendered terms, I will not do so either. However, I will follow his use of the female pronoun in *Spirit-Word- Community*, although I am aware of the contentious issues related to this discussion.[44]

Finally, who and what characterizes Yong's notion of the Spirit is the objective of the following exploration, so I will now turn to this. Starting with his claim about the Spirit as the source of rationality, as well as the communicator of rationality, I relate this pneumatological category to Hauerwas's conception of church as a storied community. Then, in the subsequent chapter, I move on to the category of relationality, attempting to overcome the charges of sectarianism by arguing that Hauerwas's emphasis on the church as a defining community can be seen in continuity with the Spirit working to form virtuous character through communities other than the church. Finally, the Spirit as *dunamis* offers a theological basis for reconstructing Hauerwas's focus on the church's performance as part of the eschatological promise, which the Spirit both animates and reminds the church of.

---

carefully distinguishes his trialectic from Hegel's synthesis, arguing that the latter objectifies a new thesis, while his trialectic process preserves the radical differences of thesis and antithesis (Yong, *Spirit-Word-Community*, 107).

42. I.e., he refers to the Spirit as "she" throughout *Spirit-Word-Community*.

43. I.e., he refers to the Spirit as "he" consistently in *Who Is the Holy Spirit?*

44. For a critical discussion of the feminine naming of the Spirit, see Parsons, *The Cambridge Companion to Feminist Theology*, 171–89. I would add that Yong does not attempt to present a feminist pneumatology. By referring to the Spirit as "she," however, he does not essentialize "stereotypes of the feminine which is variously identified with mothering, affectivity, darkness, or virginity" (ibid., 183). Rather, he does the opposite by arguing for pneumatological categories—rationality, relationality, and *dunamis*—that do not particularly pertain to these stereotypes.

9

The Church as a Storied Community by the Spirit of Rationality

9.1 Whose Story? Which Rationality?

IN THE CRITICAL DISCUSSION (cf. chapter 7), I concurred with Albrecht and Gustafson in questioning whether Hauerwas's emphasis on the church being a storied community because of the particular Christian story could accommodate the potential truthfulness of other stories and of marginal voices within the church community. In terms of reconstructing Hauerwas pneumatologically, the first task is to argue how an explication of pneumatological agency can supersede the discontinuity between Hauerwas's alleged fideism and the rationality extrinsic to, or at the margins of, the church's story.

9.2 Yong: The Spirit of Rationality

9.2.1 Biblical Testimony to the Spirit as Rationality

When Yong suggests that the Spirit as rationality is a fundamental pneumatological motif, he refers to rationality understood as intelligibility.[1] In order to unpack the contents of this motif, Yong guides his readers through the biblical warrant for claiming the Spirit as the divine mind, understanding, and intelligence.[2] Starting literally with the beginning, Genesis, the Spirit enters the creation story as the divine breath and medium for God's creative word.[3] Grounding the creative property of the Spirit in the sapiential tradi-

---

1. As opposed to some form of Enlightenment rationalism (Yong, *Spirit-Word-Community*, 35). Regarding the references to the Spirit *of* and *as* rationality, Yong uses both interchangeably. This seems to reflect his claim that the Spirit is both the source and the mediator of rationality (ibid., 35).

2. Yong makes continual biblical references in the text. I have chosen to merely refer to Yong, for readability and because it is the (systematic) argument that is of primary interest for my reconstruction.

3. Yong, *Spirit-Word-Community*, 35.

tion, Yong argues that already, in what constitutes the backdrop to theological reflections in early Jewish Christianity, the link between the Spirit and rationality is emphasized. The Spirit gives the creation meaning, purpose, and intelligibility relative to its creator.[4]

Navigating through Pauline claims of Christ as God's wisdom, Yong highlights the tension between the Word and the Spirit, contending that while Jesus is the content of wisdom, the Word incarnated, it is out of the convergence of the Spirit and the Word that truth must be understood. Jesus is the truth, yet the truth that the Spirit communicates is not limited to Jesus' teachings.[5] Rather, the Spirit of truth expands, illuminates, applies, and communicates the truth that Jesus incarnated.[6]

Further, Yong claims that any attempt to recover truth and meaning in times of postmodern lack thereof must presume the recovery of the Spirit and of the self as a spiritual being.[7] After all, Yong contends that "Human beings are rational precisely because they are spiritually created in the image of God."[8] As the divine agent of intelligibility, the Spirit is the presupposition for the human understanding and interpretation of divine life.[9] This leads to Yong concluding that theological rationality is thoroughly pneumatological.[10] However, pneumatological rationality motors not only theological endeavors, but also Christian faith and practice.[11] This correlation will be further explored in chapter 11, when Yong's notion of Spirit as *dunamis* is considered.

While Yong in his book moves on from biblical testimony to a theological explication of two Trinitarian models[12] to make a case for the trialectic movement of the hermeneutical method he anticipates, I will instead focus on his discussion of the metaphysical aspects of pneumatological rationality

---

4. Ibid., 37.

5. In this claim I think there is an intimation of how Yong differentiates between the terms rationality and truth. Although they overlap, and he depicts them often in similar ways (e.g., he speaks seemingly interchangeably about the "Spirit of truth" and "the Spirit of rationality"), I will suggest that the difference lies in the truth having been incarnated in Jesus, in whom the Word and Spirit converge perfectly, while rationality is what (or who) makes truth intelligible, including the truth beyond the incarnated Christ (ibid., 41).

6. Ibid., 41.
7. Ibid., 42.
8. Ibid., 41.
9. Ibid., 42.
10. Ibid., 43.
11. Ibid., 76.

12. I.e., the model of the Spirit and the Word as the two hands of the Father, and the model of the Spirit as the mutual love between Father and Son (ibid., 50ff, 59ff).

in order to make my case for the reconstruction of the church as storied by the Spirit of rationality.

9.2.2 Metaphysical Implications of the Spirit as Rationality

In the following, I cannot pretend to do justice to Yong's careful interweaving of biblical, theological, and metaphysical concerns regarding the Spirit as rationality, all while pointing toward his trialectically driven hermeneutics.[13] Even so, I will do my best to adequately convey Yong's argument, although my reading is guided by a quest for the ecclesiological implications of pneumatological rationality.

Even though rationality is closely correlated to epistemology, Yong avers that it is possible to investigate one without the other. Since rationality describes the state or quality of being intelligible, it concerns the way we think, while epistemology examines how we know: the nature of knowledge, and its warrants and limits.[14] Following Yong, I will start with his discussion of the foundational issues of rationality and then consider related epistemological concerns.

Assuming that all rationalities and epistemologies are foundational in the sense that foundations are equivalent to warrants, Yong sketches out three features of the foundational pneumatology he proposes:

1. It is fallibilistic, which indicates that there are no incorrigible grounds for it, but it is a "shifting foundationalism" marked by an openness to the expanding data of experience.[15] Even though it serves as a theoretical guide to inquiry, it is to be considered a speculative hypothesis and thus revisable according to others' experiences and corrections.

2. The communal aspect of inquiry is the second feature of Yong's foundational pneumatology. An important point here is that a collaborative effort safeguards against the totalitarian exercise of power, even if the product is a metanarrative, such as the church's story.

3. Yong aims for a universal application of the foundational pneumatology he outlines. As demonstrated by the two first features, he is not thinking of universal in an incorrigible or totalitarian sense, but rather he argues that if theology concerns God's relationship to all of creation

---

13. This disclaimer also applies to the upcoming presentation of Yong's other two categories.

14. Yong, *Spirit-Word-Community*, 96.

15. Ibid., 100.

then theology is accountable to all other forms of human knowledge and experience.[16]

Based on these presuppositions, Yong envisions pneumatological rationality as the only "sufficiently dynamic, historical and eschatological [rationality] to drive the dialectical movement of thought."[17] Any Trinitarian theology is inherently dialectic, since it must account for both hands of the Father—the Word and the Spirit—in the process of inquiry.[18] However, it is also trialectic, considering the mediational structure of the movement back and forth between the two and keeping in mind the dynamic nature of rationality.[19] He is careful to distance his understanding of the trialectic movement from Hegel's synthesis, as the latter negates the thesis and antithesis to itself become a new thesis, establishing a new dialectic. In contrast, Yong argues that the pneumatological rationality maintains the particularity of both thesis and antithesis, and thus it preserves both plurality and difference.[20]

To explore this claim further, he offers examples in which the Spirit enables us to transcend theological dualisms, such as the church and the world, and creation and eschaton. Yong emphasizes that the Spirit's role should be considered crucial not merely in eschatological terms but also in the past and present, as she is necessary for the relationality of the Trinity.[21] Presuming such theological and metaphysical claims in all three temporal modes for the Spirit, Yong considers that a central theological contribution of pneumatological rationality is to hold together the notions of God as the creator, sustainer, and consummator of the world.[22] Circumventing the dialectical drive toward synthesis, pneumatological rationality drives the ongoing pursuit of truth, preserving the importance of both thesis and antithesis.[23]

To summarize, Yong's exploration of the Spirit as rationality offers biblical, theological, and metaphysical perspectives that suggest that

---

16. This comes close to Wolfhart Pannenberg's view of theology-as-universal-science. He claims that "The question of the truth of Christianity can be discussed only within the framework of a science whose study includes not merely Christianity, but also the reality of God on which the Christian faith rests" (Pannenberg, *Theology and the Philosophy of Science*, 298).

17. Yong, *Spirit-Word-Community*, 105.

18. Ibid., 50ff, 105.

19. Ibid., 59ff, 105.

20. Ibid., 105.

21. Ibid., 107. Yong's concept of the Spirit as relational will be explored in chapter 10.2.

22. Ibid.

23. Ibid., 108.

pneumatological rationality is crucial for the human understanding and interpretation of divine truth and life. The Spirit provides intelligibility by driving the dialectics of thought and reality while holding together theological dualisms and preserving the truth of both sides rather than subordinating one of them, or sublating the two positions into a synthesis. How does this understanding of the Spirit's crucial role in relation to truth and intelligibility resonate with Hauerwas's pneumatological intuitions, and what are the consequences for a pneumatological reconstruction of the ecclesiological feature of the church as a storied community? These are the questions that will be pursued next.

9.3 *Church as Storied by the Spirit of Rationality*

9.3.1 Reading Hauerwas through the Pneumatological Category of Rationality

When reading Hauerwas's ecclesiology through the pneumatological category of rationality, it is "the story"[24] that emerges as the agent of rationality, actuating what Yong assigns to the Spirit of rationality. In the following, I will further argue this claim and then suggest how and why the ecclesiological feature of the church as a storied community should be pneumatologically reconstructed in order to address both the charge of fideism and the challenge from the deconstructed truth of a secular age.

For Hauerwas, "the story" is the fundamental category through which the church comes to know God, the self, and the world. In other words, reality-making claims have a narrative form, and stories are not mere illustrations of "some deeper truth."[25] Liturgy and doctrine are, for Hauerwas, tools that can help the church hear, tell, and live God's story. Polemicizing against viewing principle or doctrine as more fundamental than narrative, he claims "the story" is necessary for the human understanding and knowledge of God.[26] He rightly points out how knowledge of God, the self, and the world is intertwined, and he again avers that it is "the story" that teaches us who we are, namely God's creatures.[27] Recalling Yong's pneumatological category of rationality, the knowledge that Hauerwas subscribes to the story is made intelligible by the Spirit.

---

24. Quotation marks are employed in the following when the story is referred to as an agent.
25. Hauerwas, *The Peaceable Kingdom*, 25.
26. Ibid., 26.
27. Ibid., 27.

In his essay "Story and Theology,"[28] Hauerwas offers a more formal account of the term story (in a theological context) by listing the following characteristics:[29] 1) story involves a pattern of events that elicit the question "what happens next?"; 2) story connects contingent events and demonstrates their significance by narrating their interrelatedness; and 3) story makes human actions and responses intelligible by displaying the agent's intentionality. Hauerwas thus concludes that "A story is a narrative account that binds events and agents together in an intelligible pattern."[30] As such, story is an indispensable form of understanding that does not merely symbolize meaning but embodies it.[31]

Applying this concept of story theologically, Hauerwas argues that God as an agent can only be known through his story, which is similar to any other self.[32] Embarking on the issue of how to discern which stories are authoritative in offering a truthful understanding of God and ourselves, Hauerwas refers to practical criteria rather than the notion of truthfulness being dependant on accurate descriptions.[33] He claims that a truthful story helps us to go on, even when facing what is unknown and foreign. However, Hauerwas readily admits that since peoples' lives consist of many stories, it may be that the story that was truthful yesterday will be abused in order to sustain false accounts of life today. To prevent this, he points out the importance of tradition and the examples of saints.[34] I think Yong's pneumatology offers a crucial contribution to Hauerwas's argument in this regard, as it emphasizes that the Spirit drives the dynamic that tradition depends on. Thus, it is neither tradition nor story in and of themselves that ensure the church's truthfulness. Rather, the Spirit as rationality preserves insights (and, I might add, stories) from different positions, seeking to hold together theological dualisms in the church's search for truthfulness.

Such a pneumatological move is not without resonance in Hauerwas's work as he acknowledges the agency of the Spirit, however, his neglect in explicating the agency of the Spirit in relation to the church's story, considering the comprehensive case he makes for the church as storied, leads to

28. Hauerwas, Bondi, and Burrell, *Truthfulness and Tragedy*, 71–81.
29. Ibid., 75.
30. Ibid., 76.
31. Ibid., 77.
32. Ibid., 79.
33. Hauerwas does not find it sufficient to merely refer to the stories found in the Scripture, since they are many and various (ibid., 79). I would add that the interpretations of the scriptural stories are even more manifold and varied, which underlines the difficulty of such an argument.
34. Ibid., 80.

the charge that the pneumatology in his work is underdeveloped. As seen in chapter 5.1.1, Hauerwas states that the church was created by the Spirit, and that by the Spirit the church is enabled to hear the word rightly.[35] However, he subsequently refers to Frei, who equivocates the presence of the Spirit with the church,[36] thus undermining the Spirit as a separate agent from the church. When Hauerwas then claims that the story "creates a people capable of being the continuation of the narrative by witnessing to the world that all creation is ordered to God's good end,"[37] he further cements the charge that he collapses the agency of the Spirit into the agency of "the story." Thus, to the pneumatological reconstruction of church as a storied community I will proceed.

9.3.2 Pneumatological Reconstruction of the Church as Storied

Even though I find Hauerwas's understanding of the church as a storied community both convincing and important, my contention, as outlined above, is that the absence of pneumatological references related to his concept of story as a decisive category for theological understanding results in a problematic bestowal of agency upon the story itself. As briefly demonstrated, "the story" is for Hauerwas the indispensable category for the human understanding and interpretation of God, the self, and how to live life truthfully (i.e., how "to go on"). However, my claim is that "the story" is not merely referred to as a hermeneutical category but rather—given the emphasis Hauerwas puts on the irreplaceability of story, as well as the active role of "the story" in teaching and displaying the rationality and intelligibility of the Christian faith—it emerges as the crucial agent for conveying truth and developing truthfulness in the church.

By conceptualizing the church's story as the agent of rationality and intelligibility, Hauerwas is hard pressed to defend his position against critics like Albrecht and Gustafson, who charge him with fideism. What about the other stories? And which of the manifold stories within the church's many congregations and varied denominations should be considered authoritative? If the tradition is the reference for truthfulness and authority, what then of marginalized stories and voices? In order to address these concerns, while still maintaining the importance of the church as a storied community, I suggest that Yong's pneumatological category of rationality offers

---

35. Hauerwas, *Christian Existence Today*, 47, 60.
36. Ibid., 59.
37. Ibid., 61.

theological and constructive input. By transferring agency from the story to the Spirit, it is not the church's story, or even stories,[38] that should be considered indispensable for the human understanding of God and the self, but rather the Spirit of truth.

Yong avers that even though Jesus is the truth, the Spirit is not limited to his teaching and life. Rather, the Spirit works dynamically in order to expand, illuminate, and apply the truth of God, which was incarnated in Christ.[39] The tension between the church's story and other stories, whether marginalized within the church or coming from outside the church, can thus be approached through the perspective of continuity rather than competition. Yong claims that this same Spirit of rationality is one of the persons in the Trinitarian God-life, who also anointed Jesus and who continues to communicate truth to and through creation. Because all truth is God's truth, all people can reflect aspects of truth in their lives and convictions, as they are created in the image of God.[40]

Applied to the ecclesiological question at hand, we therefore should understand the truthfulness of the church's story in continuity with the truth of other witnesses and stories. By reconstructing Hauerwas's understanding of the church as a storied community with the Spirit in a decisive role, as the one who reveals and guides us to the truth of any story, the apparent opposition between Albrecht's concern for the many voices and Hauerwas's concern for the church's *telos* as authoritative may be overcome. Because the Spirit is the one who works through the church's *telos*, as well as speaks through the voices from the margins, the narrators of the church's story should understand it in continuity with the truth and rationality furthered by the Spirit, wherever and whenever she is at work.

However, such a claim should not undermine the particularity of the church's story in conveying the intelligibility of God's truth. Following Yong, the pneumatological rationality, grounded thoroughly in Trinitarian theology, holds together the notions of God as the creator, sustainer, and consummator of the world. This entails that the Spirit drives and mediates an ongoing pursuit for truth that is not limited in time or space, circumventing the drive toward synthesis by preserving the truth of both thesis and antithesis. With regard to the pneumatological reconstruction of the church as a storied community, Yong's insight thus offers a path that preserves the distinctiveness of the church's story (the position of thesis, if you will) while

---

38. As previously noted, Hauerwas is not consistent in referring to the story in the singular, as he occasionally refers to stories in the plural, e.g., *A Community of Character*, 91–92.

39. Yong, *Spirit-Word-Community*, 41.

40. Ibid., 305–6.

simultaneously acknowledging the Spirit of truth at work in the world and in other stories (the antithesis), which Gustafson rightly demands.

In this section I have argued that when the agency of the story is replaced by the agency of the Spirit, the church cannot take a fideistic stance and remain Trinitarian, at least in Yong's sense. The pneumatological agency supersedes the discontinuity between the church's story and the rationality extrinsic to, or at the margins of, this story. Before moving on to the next reconstructive effort, I will briefly look at how understanding the church as a storied community by the Spirit may challenge the first CWS of a secular age, as outlined in the beginning of this thesis.[41]

9.3.3 Church as Storied by the Spirit Challenges the Modern Epistemology of ASA

In Taylor's critical overturning of modern epistemology, the secular notion of truth was problematized and exposed as depending on stories that legitimize particular premises. Rather than uncritically embracing these modern premises that delimit truth to theoretical propositions restricted by scientific validations, Taylor rightly argues for the necessity of exploring truth as a more comprehensive and embodied category than the CWS allows for. Along these lines, I argued that Hauerwas's understanding of the church as a storied community offers a narrative approach toward truth and truthfulness that is closely related to the community's tradition and practices. Hauerwas shares Taylor's concern for an embodied truthfulness that challenges modern epistemology, and he argues that the church's storiedness is crucial for the intelligibility of Christian truth claims.

However, critics of Hauerwas point to the fideistic problem of referring to the church's story as the agent of truth and rationality. Acknowledging this problem, I have pneumatologically reconstructed the ecclesiological feature of the church as a storied community, by casting the Spirit as the agent of truth, working within and through the church's story, but not being limited by it. Related to Taylor's deconstructed epistemology of truth, the church as a storied community by the Spirit challenges the modern epistemology by offering a storied and embodied truthfulness that depends on the transcendent agency of the Spirit of truth. Thus, the church should, following Yong's pneumatological argument that the Spirit is rationality, seek to preserve both thesis and antithesis in its pneumatologically motored drive toward truth and truthfulness. This entails that the church cannot close the doors and be content with its own story, as it must practice hospitality and

---

41. See chapter 3.1.

critically engage with the many stories and witnesses of our secular age, realizing that the Spirit works toward the church's truth and truthfulness in continuity with creation as a whole.

To conclude, while Hauerwas's notion of the church as a storied community navigates the modern epistemology by emphasizing the narrative aspect of rationality and truth, the pneumatological agency points to the continuity of truth provided by the Spirit, which in turn challenges the immanentistic premise of the deconstructed truth.

10

The Church as a Defining Community by the Spirit of Relationality

10.1 How Is the Church Defining for Christian Character?

IN THE SECOND PART of the critical discussion (cf. chapter 7.2), I traced Stout's charge of sectarianism in Hauerwas's project. Although Stout does not have a theological agenda, his critique has theological implications that I attempted to articulate in the following summary questions: What is the theological basis for claiming that the church's tradition and practices are exclusive in forming the character of a virtuous Christian? In other words, and related to the fideist critique, who or what is the agent forming a truthful character? Following my proposed direction of reconstructing Hauerwas pneumatologically, the next step is to argue how the relational agency of the Spirit is pertinent to the understanding of the church as a defining community.

10.2 Yong: The Spirit of Relationality

10.2.1 BIBLICAL TESTIMONY TO THE SPIRIT AS RELATIONALITY

When reading the pneumatological narratives in Scripture through the category of relationality, Yong starts with the incarnation and the Gospel stories. This starting point is chosen because the Gospel stories are primarily about God relating to the world, obviously centered on the person of Jesus, but Yong argues that the Spirit has an equally important role as the agent working through Jesus' life and deeds.[1] From descending upon Mary to inspiring the prophecies of Jesus' mission, working the growth of wisdom in Jesus' youth, manifesting in the form of a dove at his baptism, and anointing Jesus for ministry, the role of the Spirit is a central motif in the gospel narratives in general and in the Lukan account in particular.[2]

---

1. Yong, *Spirit-Word-Community*, 28.
2. Ibid., 29.

It is, however, in the paschal events that the triune mystery is most fully manifested in the life and ministry of Jesus. Yong understands the cross and resurrection as trinitarian events between the Father, Son and Spirit, notably when Jesus surrenders his spirit to the Father. Also, it was the Spirit who resurrected Jesus, whose ascension was required for the Pentecost event of Jesus sending the Spirit upon those who believe in him. Yong avers that the Gospel stories demonstrate the crucial relational role of the Spirit, which made the incarnation possible.[3]

According to Yong, Pentecost still provides the ultimate image of how the Spirit bridges the gap between God and humanity. The Pentecostal outpouring of the Spirit is the fulfilment of Jesus' promise and mission statement to baptize believers with the Spirit.[4] Yong emphasizes the various aspects of the Spirit's relational actions: turning hearts back to the creator, deepening the relationship with God, and anticipating the parousia of Jesus as well as the restoration of all things. He thus understands the Spirit as the agent who brings about what is traditionally termed justification, sanctification, and glorification.[5] Particularly relevant to the reconstruction at hand is Yong's consideration of the Spirit's role in the continuing sanctification of believers. The Spirit produces perseverance, character, and hope even through sufferings, and enables believers to follow in Jesus' footsteps.[6]

10.2.2 Theological and Metaphysical Implications of the Spirit as Relationality

Turning to the theological exploration of the Spirit's relationality, Yong argues that both the Trinitarian models of two hands and mutual love depend on a robust pneumatology that avoids consigning the Spirit to theological oblivion.[7] Rather, the Spirit is essential to the complex and dynamic interrelationality of Trinitarian life, which provides the eternal model of relational accounts and of divine life *ad extra*.[8] Yong thus claims that creation itself is relationally, and thereby pneumatologically, constituted. To understand reality in relational terms presupposes a real-

3. Ibid., 30.

4. Yong differentiates between baptism in the Holy Spirit and the Spirit's work of baptizing believers into the body of Christ (ibid., 30). For the purpose of this reconstruction, however, it is the agential role of the Spirit (in both events) that is the main point of interest.

5. Ibid., 31.

6. Ibid., 32.

7. Ibid., 59, 75–76.

8. Ibid., 78–79.

ity that is dynamically evolving, which brings Yong to the metaphysical implications of pneumatological relationality.[9]

I will not go into Yong's discussion of various philosophical perspectives on the concept of relationality,[10] but suffice it to say that he adheres to a process-oriented and relational metaphysics that views relationships, processes, and interactions as being more fundamental than the categories of being, essence, and substance.[11] As seen in the previous presentation of the Spirit as rationality, the trialectic movement toward intelligibility implies the relationality of the Spirit, which holds together and preserves dualistic theses as well as the *tempora* of the past, the present, and the promised future. Thus, the pneumatological categories of rationality and relationality are both necessary in Yong's dynamic epistemology, which itself is predicated on a dynamic metaphysics.

Before turning to the third and final pneumatological category, I will highlight Yong's application of the Spirit's relationality in lived experience, as this is particularly relevant to the issue of this chapter, namely how Christian character is defined. Developing on John Zizioulas's notion of the church as a community constituted by the relationality of God, Yong suggests that human life as a whole is constituted by the same divine relationality.[12] Thus, he concretizes his earlier claim about creation being pneumatologically constituted.[13]

Yong's argument presupposes that human life exists and is experienced in various overlapping social environments. If it is the Spirit who engenders relationality and community, then it is the mutual love between the Father and Son that, by the gifting of the Spirit, is expressed in the establishment of fellowship. Consequently, it is pneumatological relationality that brings healing and reconciliation to people in and through their social environments.[14] Yong does not limit the Spirit's relational agency to the church

---

9. Ibid., 79.

10. Yong has particular sympathy for the work of the logician and philosopher Charles S. Peirce's work, and he adheres to his form of critical realism, which is based on three moments of inquiry: 1) the phenomenological investigation of experience; 2) the normative inquiry into various sciences in order to categorize experiences; and 3) the metaphysical judgements regarding the character of reality based on the previous two moments. Related to Peirce's epistemology is his triadic metaphysics, which Yong develops theologically in order to explicate divine experience (ibid., 92, 94f).

11. Ibid., 116.
12. Ibid., 112.
13. Ibid., 79.
14. Ibid., 112.

community, as he explores how pneumatological relationality is fundamental to the social constitution of reality as a whole.[15]

Summing up Yong's investigation into the various aspects of pneumatological relationality, he argues that the Gospels and the Book of Acts, in particular, offer demonstrations of how Trinitarian relationality is crucial to God's agency. By expounding on the theological models of two hands and mutual love, he shows how the Spirit is crucial not only to Trinitarian relational dynamics but also to all created relationality. Thus, it becomes clear that pneumatological rationality and relationality are co-dependent, since the how of pneumatological rationality predicates the relational dynamics between thesis and antithesis as well as between the *tempora* and various social environments. With this correlation of the Spirit as rationality and relationality in mind, I will turn to the pneumatological reconstruction of the church as a defining community by the Spirit.

10.3 Church as Defining by the Spirit of Relationality

10.3.1 READING HAUERWAS THROUGH THE PNEUMATOLOGICAL CATEGORY OF RELATIONALITY

The notion of the story as crucial to the church's understanding of God's truth was recently recounted when considering Hauerwas's emphasis on the church as a storied community. However, he also attributes to the church's story the ability to challenge Christians' self-righteousness and teach them why they need to be reborn and transformed.[16] Further, he claims that "The Christian story trains us to see that in most of our life we act as if this is not God's world..."[17] and that the story "exposes the unwelcome fact that I am a sinner."[18] Not only does the narrative provide the Christian with the skill to reveal her rebellion against God,[19] but it also forms and defines the church as a distinct community.[20]

In his essay "A Story-Formed Community,"[21] Hauerwas also argues for the significance of narrative and tradition in Christian life.[22] Starting

---

15. Ibid., 114.
16. Hauerwas, *The Peaceable Kingdom*, 29.
17. Ibid., 30.
18. Ibid., 31.
19. Ibid., 31.
20. Ibid., 60.
21. Hauerwas, *A Community of Character*, 9–35.
22. While I focused on the role of tradition as defining when referring to this essay

by presenting ten theses for reforming Christian ethics, he continues to "practice what he preaches" by re-narrating and re-appropriating a novel by Richard Adams in order to show what the theses entail in practice. While his primary intent in this essay is to challenge modern thinking on Christian social ethics, he also makes assumptions and claims about the church that I consider representative of his ecclesiology in general. Reading his argument through the pneumatological category of relationality it is primarily the particular story and tradition that define the church and its relation to the world. However, this relationship is described in rather ambiguous terms (e.g., as represented by the stranger): "The Christian story teaches us to regard truthfulness more as a gift than a possession and thus requires that we be willing to face both the possibilities and threats a stranger represents."[23]

The ambiguous relationship between the church and the world is further entrenched in PK when Hauerwas affronts the natural-law assumption that Christian ethics are human ethics, and thus he underwrites the possibility that "there might be a radical discontinuity between Christians and their culture."[24] Arguing for the necessity of the church as a peaceful and truthful community in a world of war and lies, Hauerwas simultaneously assumes the ability of the church and the inability of the world to achieve peace and truthfulness.[25] Based on this foundational assumption about the radical difference between the church and the world, he continues to prescribe how this difference is essential in understanding both the church and the world. They are relational concepts, which means their intelligibility is mutually dependent.[26] As previously noted, Hauerwas intermittently switches between descriptive and normative modes when he admits that the church's disunity reflects its sinfulness, while in the next paragraph he proclaims that the church should help the world understand its sinful distortedness. He is careful to clarify that the world is not an ontological category, but it is descriptive of those who—out of free will—oppose God,

---

previously (chapter 5.2.3), I will here focus on the role of tradition related to church-world issues.

23. Hauerwas, *A Community of Character*, 10.
24. Hauerwas, *The Peaceable Kingdom*, 59.
25. Ibid., 100.
26. Ibid., 101.

and Hauerwas, in yet another descriptive moment, allows the inclusion of Christians[27] when they live untruthfully.[28]

In summary, the defining relations for the church are, for Hauerwas, primarily the church's formative story and its ambiguous and complex relation to the world. He also makes the connection between the church rightly understanding and rightly relating to the world.[29] This observation is relevant to how Yong connects the pneumatological categories of rationality and relationality. I will now turn to the pneumatological reconstruction of the church as a defining community.

10.3.2 Pneumatological Reconstruction of the Church as Defining

One of the most pertinent questions raised in the critical discussion is concerned with how Hauerwas argues that the church community is exclusive in defining Christian character and virtues. Stout avers that democracy, with its values and practices, presupposes virtues and practices that may be defining for the character of its citizenry, including Christian citizens. When reconstructing the feature of the church as a defining community, I will develop on Hauerwas's intimation of the unlimited reach of God's kingdom.[30] While this acknowledgement concurs with his insistence that the church is not anti-world, since the world is "God's good creation," it is not explicated with regard to the possible implications for his dominatingly antagonistic portrayal of the relationship between the church and the world, which he recounts in the following manner: "Our task as church is . . . to understand rightly the world as world, to face realistically what the world is with its madness and irrationality."[31] I will, however, emphasize Hauerwas's push for the import of understanding the world rightly, because together with his admission about the world being present in Christians and the kingdom being present in the world, my claim is that his argument is ripe for a pneumatological reconstruction.

---

27. Or so I must assume, even though his actual phrasing is ". . . the world consists of those, including *ourselves,* who have chosen not to make the story of God their story. The world in *us* refuses to affirm that this is God's world and that, as loving Lord, God's care for creation is greater than our illusion of control" (ibid., 101, italics mine). Given the context of this argument, I consider it obvious that "us" refers to Christians.

28. Ibid., 101.

29. Ibid., 102.

30. Ibid., 101.

31. Ibid., 102.

According to Yong, the Spirit works relationally in order to make God's truth intelligible and to provide humans with a truthful understanding of God, the self, and the world. While Hauerwas points to the virtues and their particular content in the church's tradition in order to explain how the church community differs from "natural virtues" manifested in any defining human community, Yong's pneumatological category of relationality argues that it is the Spirit who defines humans, through their relationships with God and with each other.[32] Because the Spirit of relationality is not limited to the church community, she can define Christian character and develop virtues through any truthful relationships.

Following such a line of argument, the Spirit also provides a defining continuity for the Christian character, since the various stories and engagements in, with, and for the world are enabled by her agency, and not by the particular story or virtues of the church. Thus, Stout's concern is addressed, as the Spirit can define Christian character through democratic practices and moreover, a Christian can define and critically engage with democratic practices by insisting on faithful adherence to Christian convictions. This dynamic engagement is called for by Stout, and I would argue, that it is in line with Hauerwas's intuition about the world as an integral part of Christian living –and even of the Christian believer. Emphasizing that the Spirit is the agent who defines Christian character, instead of the community or the story, picks up on the single direct reference in PK to the Spirit, which is found in a quotation from Yoder: "Christian ethics calls for behaviour which is impossible except by the miracle of the Holy Spirit."[33]

While Hauerwas seems content to leave the Spirit to the realm of unspecified miracles, Yong helps us to acknowledge the relational agency of the Spirit, which together with the pneumatological rationality constitutes a pneumatological approach to the church as a defining community. Let me briefly unpack this on two fronts: first, according to Hauerwas, the church is a real and concrete community, a "natural institution," but nature does not determine its character because the church is able to exist peacefully in the world, without resorting to violence. As previously noted, this ability is rather questionable, precisely because of what Hauerwas admits about the church's natural character. However, when realizing that it is the Spirit who is the able agent, and who enables the church to live peacefully, the church is no longer limited to a particular story in order to be defining and to define

---

32. For a constructive proposal of a pneumatological understanding of the Christian tradition's self-exceeding and self-critical properties, see Svenungsson, "Transcending Tradition."

33. Hauerwas, *The Peaceable Kingdom*, 106.

each other virtuously. I will return to this point when outlining the practice of encountering the other in the next part of the book.[34]

10.3.3 Church as Defining by the Spirit Challenges the Constructions of Human Agency in *ASA*

According to Taylor, several of the CWS rely on a particular understanding of human agency as a result of individual rational choices, which has become part of the unquestioned background for how we interpret human existence. This concept of moral agency is interwoven with the notion of human progress and the construction of human good as entirely immanentistic. Together they comprise a powerful narrative about the maturation of humanity: after achieving independence from religion and freedom from superstition, humanity emerged with the noble goal of human welfare. Taylor problematizes this maturation narrative and claims that we have replaced theistic constructions of the self and human agency with atheistic ones without becoming better or more moral, and perhaps even the opposite.

Hauerwas adamantly argues that the only way to be moral is to be part of a community in which the story makes virtues intelligible and in which the practices form character in its members. While this (re)turn to community offers a challenge to the secular notion of individual moral agency, I agree with Stout that Hauerwas's understanding of the church as a defining community raises questions about the significance of other communities in defining Christian character and engagement. Thus, with the help of Yong's pneumatological category of relationality, I argued that if it is the Spirit who is the agent of definition, then she provides continuity for the Christian self who is part of several communities that are potentially defining.

How, then, does the pneumatological reconstruction challenge the secular construction of human agency, with its many and previously discussed immanentistic implications? The Spirit of relationality not only work through human horizontal relationships, but is also incessantly going back and forth between the Father, Son, and creation, making God's truth intelligible to humanity, and in so doing, she also restores peaceful relations and enables truthful living. The relational agency of the Spirit thus challenges the secular notion of a buffered and detached self, which is characterized by

---

34. Both Hauerwas and Yong have worked with the theology of disability and suggested that communities with mental disabilities, such as Down syndrome, practice several of the virtues Hauerwas emphasizes as important to the church, such as patience and truthful friendships. In the next part of the book, I will argue why this is an excellent example of how the Spirit defines a Christian's character through partaking in communities other than the church.

being unapproachable and inaccessible to any transcendent agency outside oneself. By claiming that the agency of God's Spirit is crucial for a person to discover herself, in relation to God and her neighbor through the pneumatological category of relationality, the church challenges the secular and immanentistic maturation narrative of human agency.[35]

---

35. I would add that such a pneumatological reconstruction places an emphasis on the relational reciprocity, and the importance of the agencies of both the Spirit and the self, thus providing a buffer against charges of the Spirit acting unilaterally.

11

The Church as a Performative Community by the Spirit of *Dunamis*

11.1 What Is the Promise of Performance?

HAUERWAS'S EMPHASIS ON THE performative character of the Christian community can be viewed as a constructive engagement with the secular emphasis on beliefs over practices. However, the third and final part of the critical discussion (cf. chapter 7.3) raised questions about the pragmatism inherent in some of Hauerwas's claims about the church's practices. Healy argued that the empirical church's limited truthfulness proves the problem of tying the church's performance too closely to the promise of the eternal and peaceable kingdom of God. In order to address this concern in my pneumatological reconstruction of Hauerwas's understanding of the church as performance, I will now turn to Yong and his notion of the Spirit as the *dunamis* (dynamic power) who performs through the church's practices, and thus reminds humanity of the promised kingdom of God.[1]

11.2 Yong: The Spirit of Dunamis

11.2.1 BIBLICAL TESTIMONY TO THE SPIRIT AS *DUNAMIS*

Yong posits the Spirit as the power of life in creation, in humanity specifically, and in the cosmic and historical movements toward the eschaton.[2] Referring to the various natural symbols in the Scriptures, he claims they all witness to

---

1. I think it is important to emphasize Hauerwas's eschatological argument in relation to the church's performance, especially the nonviolence and peacemaking efforts that he adamantly promotes as crucial. Peace is not merely a promise, according to Hauerwas, but a part of the overlapping history present to the church (see chapter 6.4). Where this argument stops short is in extrapolating how the overlapping ages are made present in and through the church's performance, and so this is the inquiry I will make in the pneumatological reconstruction.

2. Yong, *Spirit-Word-Community*, 43.

the Spirit being the divine life breath in and for creation.³ Moreover, the present work of the Spirit is of a proleptic nature, anticipating the eschatological recreation of the world. By working to complete all that is presently incomplete and continuing to renew life in the world, the Spirit is the agent of the power that was manifested in Jesus' life, death, and resurrection.⁴

The power of the Spirit is not limited to the church community, emphasizes Yong, but she works teleologically toward the purposes of God both for humanity, specifically, and for creation as a whole.⁵ Thus, the Pentecostal outpouring demonstrates the universal reach of the Spirit's work, including the cosmic perspective of God answering creation's longing for redemption. In the midst of a fallen creation, the Spirit's dynamic presence counters the effects of sin and death, reminding us that natural processes and existence in historical time do not have the final word but that life will finally trump death in the consummated eschatological kingdom.⁶

Holding together the Spirit's rational, relational, and dynamic works, Yong claims human activities in these areas, directed toward the teleological fulfilment of life, are done by and through the Spirit. Human practices in themselves, including the church's performance (this concretizing assumption is my own), are limited both by the contingency of creation and by historical finitude. To undermine the provisional character of human thoughts and actions entails a claim for ultimacy that rightly belongs to God, Yong warns before turning to the theological and metaphysical aspects of pneumatological *dunamis*.⁷

11.2.2 THEOLOGICAL AND METAPHYSICAL IMPLICATIONS OF THE SPIRIT AS *DUNAMIS*

Once again, by attending to Yong's exegesis of the trinitarian models of the Spirit and the Word as the two hands of the Father[8] and of the Spirit as the mutual love between Father and Son,[9] the theological implications of the pneumatological category of *dunamis* can be traced. The dynamic of the Spirit is not only constitutive of the mutuality between Father and Son, but also of the movements of the two hands back and forth to the Father.

3. Ibid., 44.
4. Ibid., 47.
5. Ibid.
6. Ibid., 48.
7. Ibid.
8. Ibid., 50ff.
9. Ibid., 59ff.

As previously noted, the relational and dynamic work of the Spirit is not limited to the interior Trinitarian movements, as it is also constitutive of divine engagement in the world.[10]

Yong avers that the dynamics of history itself, culminating in the promised eschatological kingdom, is motored by the power of the Spirit.[11] Relating the pneumatological *dunamis* to the category of rationality, he suggests that the Spirit as dynamic life also motors human drive for meaning and intelligibility.[12] It is exactly the pneumatological *dunamis*, holding together the *tempora* of the past, the present, and the promised future, that enables the Spirit to drive the dialectical movement of thought.[13] The metaphysical implication of the pneumatological category of *dunamis* is manifest in the understanding of reality as an ongoing and interactive social process, where societies are the fields of the Spirit's activity.[14] If reality is thus dynamic and temporal, this means that knowledge cannot be seen as static, as it is an investigative process with eschatological anticipation.[15]

To provide a brief summary, the pneumatological category of *dunamis* refers to the Spirit as the divine and creative life-breath, encountered already in the Genesis story of God creating all that is. Working throughout history, most notably in Jesus' life, death, and resurrection, the Spirit always points to the eschatological promised kingdom. She is thus the powerful life breath, constitutive for both the interior Trinitarian dynamics and for the divine ongoing renewal and healing of creation.

Having explored Yong's three pneumatological categories of rationality, relationality, and *dunamis*, the following observations should be noted: 1) understanding the Spirit in such concrete categories entails metaphysical implications and a form of critical realism, the latter of which Yong seems to share with Hauerwas; 2) the three categories are deeply interrelated and interdependent, which entails that none can be conceived of as isolated from the other two; and 3) Yong's exploration of the Spirit, by following these three categories, is grounded in, as well as grounds, the Trinitarian divine life, which is always engaging with creation, moving it toward the promised eschatological kingdom.

---

10. Ibid., 78.
11. Ibid., 115.
12. Ibid., 77.
13. Ibid., 105.
14. Ibid., 113, 116.
15. Ibid., 117.

11.3 Church as Performance by the Spirit of Dunamis

11.3.1 Reading Hauerwas through the Pneumatological Category of *Dunamis*

In a previously mentioned essay in which Hauerwas offers pneumatological reflections on the church's status, he claims that the Spirit makes Jesus present to the church, and the church becomes part of God's new time.[16] Hauerwas indeed emphasizes the power of the Spirit, or the Spirit as *dunamis*: "For this new creation aborning through the power of the Spirit does not make irrelevant all that has gone before nor make indifferent all that comes after."[17] He continues to describe the Spirit as "a wild and powerful presence creating a new people where there was no people . . ."[18] Reading Hauerwas through the pneumatological category of *dunamis*, it becomes obvious that he recognizes the church's existential dependence on the power of the Spirit.

Perhaps most explicit is this pneumatological recognition in the final chapter of *With the Grain of the Universe*,[19] in which he correlates the agency of the Spirit to the church's witness.[20] Repeatedly, he refers to the work of the Spirit; in the church's witness and argument, in God's enactment of the story, and through the confession of sins.[21] Yet, a few pages later, he makes the now familiar turn and claims that the truth of Christian convictions depends on the church's ability to live faithfully and non-violently. The Spirit is again on the wing, and Hauerwas concludes that "The problem for Christians and non-Christians alike is the Christian inability to live in a way that enables us to articulate what difference it makes that we are or are not Christian."[22] Recalling Healy's critique, it is right about here that Hauerwas's ecclesiological feature of the church as performance runs into the problem of pragmatism. As Healy points out, the church is a rather flawed referent of God's story, and thus he argues that the church should acknowledge this while continually striving to offer better glimpses of the eschatological peace of God's kingdom.

In PK, Hauerwas connects God's *dunamis* in Jesus' life and the eschatological promise of peace, but he does this without explicit references to the

---

16. Hauerwas, *Christian Existence Today*, 52.
17. Ibid., 51.
18. Ibid., 51–52.
19. Hauerwas, *With the Grain of the Universe*, 205–41.
20. Ibid., e.g., 210.
21. Ibid., 210–12.
22. Ibid., 231.

Spirit as the power being referred to.[23] Jesus was possessed by God's truthful power, which does not use force or violence but calls upon the other to freely be faithful and obedient to the covenant with God.[24] The message of Jesus was to announce the coming kingdom, and in doing so he affirmed the eschatological view of the world held by Israel. When Hauerwas explicates how Israel's journey with God is decisive for the church's understanding of the kingdom's presence, he makes an important comment about God's effective power: "Rather he [Jesus] proclaims that the kingdom is *present* insofar as his life reveals the effective power of God to create a transformed people capable of living peaceably in a violent world."[25] Reading this through the pneumatological category of *dunamis*, Hauerwas's claim can be understood implicitly to affirm the Spirit as the agent transforming the church to live peaceably in a violent world. Building on these pneumatological intuitions: how can a pneumatological reconstruction of the ecclesiological concept of the church as performance address the charge of pragmatism? To this endeavour I now will turn.

11.3.2 Pneumatological Reconstruction of the Church as Performance

Both Yong and Hauerwas are adamant about the pragmatic aspect of truthfulness. Hauerwas uses the example of the crusader exclaiming "Jesus is Lord!" as he beheads the infidel. Yong refers to the performative understanding of the words "I do" at the altar. However, their shared interest in the performative importance of truth statements leads them down somewhat different paths. As previously recounted, Hauerwas holds that the church is the performance that demonstrates the truthfulness of God's story, and thus he ends up wedged into a corner by his ecclesiocentrism.[26] Yong, on the other hand, stresses the "pneumatological component whereby truth is not an abstract relation between a proposition and certain facts or states of affairs, but is a personal, affective, existential and embodied relation whereby to know the truth both implicitly and explicitly demands and, in some sense, brings about conformity of life to it."[27]

While Yong in this quotation, and in the section it is extracted from, intends to expand on his particular notion of truth, the pneumatological

---

23. Hauerwas, *The Peaceable Kingdom*, 80ff.
24. Ibid., 81.
25. Ibid., 83, italics original.
26. Healy, *Hauerwas*, 67.
27. Yong, *Spirit-Word-Community*, 175.

claims are relevant to the task at hand. He argues that it is the Spirit of truth who brings about the character that Hauerwas claims the story forms in and through the church's performative practices. Yong clearly states that the agency of the Spirit is what brings humans to truthful living, as it is the transformative truth directed toward eschatological fulfillment.[28] Wedding this pneumatological agency to Hauerwas's eschatological perspective on the church's performance, it is possible to counter the charges of pragmatism.[29] Instead of being the proof of the peaceable kingdom, the church's occasionally and partially peaceable performances are signs or glimpses of the eschatological life and promise, which is made possible by the Spirit of *dunamis*, who holds together the events of creation, salvation, and eschaton.

The *dunamis* of the church's performance is the *dunamis* of incarnation; it is concrete and embodied, and thus makes present what might otherwise remain abstract. However, performance and incarnation share the weakness of being limited by time and humanity. It is here that the Spirit comes to the church's rescue, like Jesus aforementioned, because she holds together the testimony of God through all times and reminds the church of creation and eschatology in the face of its inability to perform perfectly. Thus, the Spirit brings the church in continuity with God's eschatological timeline and holds forth the promise that the church's performance once will become perfectly truthful and peaceable.

11.3.3 Church as Performance by the Spirit Challenges the Excarnation of Religion in *ASA*

Taylor claims that the secular obsession with belief as a cognitive enterprise has pushed religion, in general, and the church, in particular, toward what he terms excarnation. The notion of religion has thus turned into systems of proper beliefs rather than being considered as embodied lifestyles that are expressed through liturgy, ritual, and practices. Together with the Cartesian ideal of the disengaged and rational self, the excarnation of religion has led the church to be more concerned about ortho-doxy (right belief) than ortho-praxy (right worship).

As part of a more comprehensive academic turn toward the embodiedness of religion and knowledge in general, Hauerwas's project seeks to retrieve the incarnational thrust of the church that Taylor laments the loss of in a secular age. However, critics claim that, in doing so, Hauerwas makes too sharp a turn to the embodied performance of the church and thus fails

---

28. Ibid., 175.
29. I attended to Hauerwas's eschatological underpinnings in chapter 6.3.

to acknowledge the tentative character of the church's ability to perform truthfully. By pneumatologically reconstructing the church's performance as offering glimpses of the eschatological kingdom through the *dunamis* of the Spirit, Yong's insight was utilized in order to make explicit the pneumatological agency implicit in Hauerwas's eschatological claims.

Returning to Taylor's concern about the religious excarnation of a secular age, my claim is that the church as performance by the Spirit not only retrieves the embodiedness of the church's story and liturgy, but the pneumatological category of *dunamis* also holds together the events of creation, salvation, and eschaton, and thus it challenges the secularization of time. As outlined in the beginning of the book, a corollary to the CWS of the subtraction story is that human experiences are severed from any transcendent agency or intention. Together with the secularization of time the subtraction story leaves humans with thoroughly immanentistic and limited notions of time and existence. The Spirit, understood as the divine power that holds together the *tempora* and ushers the world toward the promised eschaton, challenges the secular notion of the present being all that is present.

The church's performance is made possible by the Spirit's promise of a peaceable kingdom. However, that kingdom is yet to come in full, and therefore the church's performance will persist in offering imperfect glimpses of the eschatological promised peace. *Pace* Hauerwas, this pneumatological reconstruction of the church's performance does not demand that the church community "must be capable of being peaceable among themselves and with the world, so that the world sees what it means to hope for God's kingdom."[30] Rather, it is the Spirit who is the rationality that makes God's kingdom intelligible, and she is the relationality that defines the church through engagement with the other, empowering the church to perform eschatologically motivated practices. It is to these practices that I will turn in the next section, with the intent of exploring how the pneumatological reconstruction might inform such concrete practices for the church in a secular age.

11.3.4 Summarizing the Pneumatological Reconstruction

The pneumatological reconstruction of Hauerwas's ecclesiology shows that the particularity of the church community must be related to the agency of the Spirit. Only when the particularistic ecclesiology is pneumatologically grounded is it possible to make sense of the church's simultaneous ability

---

30. Hauerwas, *The Peaceable Kingdom*, 103.

and inability to live truthfully while engaging the challenges of a secular age. When the Spirit as rationality, relationality, and *dunamis* is acknowledged as the agent who makes God's truth intelligible through the church's story, as well as through other stories, and who defines virtuous character through human relations with both God and neighbour, and makes God's promise present through the church's performance, then the tension between the church, creation, and coming kingdom is appended by the continuity that the Spirit represents and reinforces. However, allowing the continuity of the Spirit's work does not undermine that the particularity of the church community can and should challenge the characteristics of the wider society it is part of, such as the CWS of a secular age.

Returning to my hypothesis at the beginning of the pneumatological reconstruction, the preliminary conclusion is that developing the agency of the Spirit in relation to Hauerwas's ecclesiology has allowed me to retain his emphasis on Christian particularity while arguing for a pneumatological continuity between the church community, the world as creation, and the promised kingdom. While the reconstructive endeavor has focused on the systematic task of the argument, I will in the next and final part of the book explore the concrete implications of the pneumatological ecclesiology attempted here in relation to the practices of religious dialogue, meeting the marginalized, and liturgical living.

PART IV
EXPLORATIVE PROPOSAL: CRUCIAL PRACTICES

12

Practicing Church in a Secular Age

IN THE PREVIOUS CHAPTERS, I have argued how a pneumatological reconstruction of the central features of Hauerwas's ecclesiology preserves his insight about the church as a storied, defining, and performing community, while also developing more convincing theological grounds by extrapolating the work of Yong, in order to address both the critical charges against Hauerwas's project and the CWS of a secular age. The overall question for this final chapter is as follows: What are crucial practices for the church in a secular age in terms of understanding itself as a storied, defining, and performing community by the Spirit? As such, the following conversation is intended to be an explorative venture to identify topics for further investigation. In this endeavor, I continue to draw on the works of Hauerwas and Yong, but I also bring other voices into the exchange.[1]

The suggestions are not intended to be comprehensive with regard to the practical implications of a pneumatological ecclesiology, but I consider them to be central practices that embody the ecclesiological features from the preceding pneumatological reconstruction. Consequently, the present chapter is structured around the three church practices of *religious dialogue* (which is related to the church as storied by the Spirit of truth), *meeting the marginalized* (which is related to the church as defining by the Spirit of relationality), and *liturgical living* (which is related to the church as performance by the Spirit of *dunamis*). The explorative work in this chapter does not include comparative considerations of other potential practices, but the criteria for selection are as follows: 1) the practices are particularly relevant for the church in a secular age;[2] 2) the practices are related to the pneumato-

---

1. It could be argued that a more obvious and cleaner approach would be to simply stick to and follow Yong and Hauerwas through here. However, bringing other voices into the conversation is as much a performative point, in the sense that I am a firm supporter of striving for refreshing takes on traditional problems by putting together thinkers and theorists that normally frequent different worlds. Which is a rehearsal I think Hauerwas, Taylor, and Yong all perform brilliantly.

2. As such, they are overlapping with regard to what challenges they address and relate to. E.g., I will argue that all three practices demonstrate a substantial and consistent

logical reconstruction in previous chapters, as noted; 3) Yong and/or Hauerwas have treated the topic quite extensively; and 4) there is great potential in cross-fertilization with perspectives from other disciplines.

In order to answer the overall question, the practices are approached with two explorative questions: How do Hauerwas and Yong understand these practices? How can an interdisciplinary perspective relating to the practice prove to be instructive for the church's performance? The selection of extra-theological perspectives was done in an ad-hoc manner; however, the main criteria are that they offer a relevant theory with practical implications for the topic discussed, and that they are related to the thinking of Hauerwas and/or Yong. The preliminary summaries will revisit the criteria for selection, particularly with regard to why the practice is relevant for the church in a secular age and how it is related to the pneumatologically reconstructed ecclesial feature, since criteria 3) and 4) are most directly addressed in the explorative efforts.

12.1 Religious Dialogue Practiced by a Storied Community

Not surprisingly perhaps, Hauerwas has not been much of a religious-dialogue theologian,[3] though, not (stated, at least) for the distinctiveness reason, but for reasons that I will look more closely at in the following. Yong, on the other hand, has worked extensively with religious dialogue (RD), but with the intent of preserving the church's *telos* and identity throughout the practice. In fact, he argues it is an imperative practice for the church if it is to follow in the footsteps of the One who became man in order to commune with us.[4] On this premise, Jesus is portrayed as the protagonist of the RD metaphor of hospitality, which Yong develops in *Hospitality & the Other*.[5]

12.1.1 HAUERWAS AND YONG ON THE CHURCH'S RELIGIOUS DIALOGUE

As I concur with Yong's claim that "Christian faith is distinctive . . . but not absolutely so,"[6] part of my pneumatological reconstruction of the church as a storied community by the Spirit of truth entails holding the particularity

---

movement toward embodiment, which characterizes Hauerwas's understanding of the church.

3. Hauerwas on relativism, see Hauerwas, *A Community of Character*, 94ff, 105.
4. Yong, *Spirit-Word-Community*, 304.
5. Yong, *Hospitality and the Other*, 101ff.
6. Yong, *Spirit-Word-Community*, 301.

of the church's story together with the potential truthfulness of other stories. Concretely, this conviction implies the practice of dialoguing with religious others, but before making further inquiry into Yong's theology of religions, I will introduce Hauerwas's friend, David B. Burrell, C.S.C., to the scene. According to Hauerwas, Burrell's engagement with Jews in Jerusalem and Muslims in Bangladesh taught him that "they recognize in Christians who pray something of their own lives."[7] Hauerwas argues that Burrell was drawn into the lives of these religious others because he is a Catholic but not the Constantinian kind of Catholic. By making this distinction, Hauerwas substantiates his overall claim in this essay[8] that Christians need no theory in order to talk with religious others, but rather they need to rid themselves of the coercive and colonial character of the Constantinian understanding of the church, so pervasive in the wider Western discourse on religious pluralism.[9]

Hauerwas frames the terminology of dialogue, religion, and pluralism within this problematic Constantinian understanding of the church and Christendom. He avers that pluralism is merely a term pushed by Protestant liberals who are determined to keep control of America's future. The same goes for religion, which, according to Hauerwas, is intended to privatize convictions and thus render them harmless for democracies that allegedly flourish on difference.[10] In familiar Hauerwas style, he attempts to recast the conversation by questioning its terms and conditions. However, after dismissing the petition for a theory or policy of RD, he offers the example of Burrell, who certainly engages religious others with what I would call an imitable openness and interest.[11] Drawing on Yong's work, I will in the following attempt to argue why the example of David Burrell offers policy implications for a church understood as a storied community by the Spirit.

Yong's theology of religions rests on epistemological convictions inherited from the American pragmatist Charles Sanders Peirce, further developed and appropriated theologically by Yong.[12] From his doctoral thesis[13] onward, Yong has offered creative and pneumatologically grounded contributions to the increasingly important field of the Christian theology of religions.[14] Central to his argument has been that Christological questions

---

7. Hauerwas, *The State of the University*, 74.
8. Hauerwas, "The End of 'Religious Pluralism.'"
9. Ibid., 64.
10. Ibid., 60.
11. Ibid., 72ff.
12. E.g., Yong, "The Demise of Foundationalism."
13. Amended version published as *Discerning the Spirit(s)*.
14. Kärkkäinen, *An Introduction to the Theology of Religions*, 17–29.

may intentionally be postponed in the dialogical setting while emphasizing the interdependence of Christ and the Spirit.[15] However, for my purpose here, I must focus on Yong's contribution to answering the why question: Why is RD of such importance for the contemporary church?[16]

While Yong certainly speaks of the theological work that needs to be done in the field of RD, which I will return to shortly, he has also done considerable work outlining what this might entail for the church.[17] Of particular interest to the conversation at hand is his reference to Yoder's work, as it substantiates my claim that Hauerwas's ecclesiology is more amenable to a robust pneumatological theology of religion than his work evidences. Yong briefly refers to Yoder's contribution to the Jewish–Christian dialogue, and he suggests that the church might follow up on Yoder's envisioning of how it could be of service to other religions through a genuine dialogue, challenging religious others to be true to their original commitments and enabling the reform of corrupting elements.[18]

Hauerwas refers to the same Yoder text, but he does this to demonstrate the essentially local, ad hoc, and fragmentary nature of the kind of conversations Yoder encouraged the church to pursue.[19] Again, his point is that Yoder does not outline general policies or abstract theories but thoroughly grounds his engagement in a "concrete encounter with the neighbour who is different from me."[20] Hauerwas's anti-Constantinian thrust, which he shares with Yoder, undergirds his assumption that to query the truth content of another religion is a Constantinian endeavour, as it fails to attend adequately to the dignity of the religious other as a person.[21] However, it is my contention that Yong's pneumatologically informed theology of religion allows for truthful content to be queried while preserving the importance of engaging locally with religious others.

Returning to Yong's theological argument, he claims that if Western theologians are to take their contemporary context seriously, they need to engage dialogically, and not merely polemically, with the truth claims of

---

15. Yong, *Beyond the Impasse*, 135.

16. For an instructive overview of the discipline of theology of religions, see Kärkkäinen, *An Introduction to the Theology of Religions*.

17. Convinced as he is, that interfaith engagement is not a luxury but mandatory for the contemporary church living in a pluralistic world (Yong, *Hospitality and the Other*, 12).

18. Yong, *The Spirit Poured out on All Flesh*, 266.

19. Hauerwas, *The State of the University*, 69–70.

20. Ibid., 70.

21. Ibid.

religious others.²² His description of "the postmodern global village" resembles Taylor's notion of the "cross-pressures" that the secular age exposes us to, as we become familiar with several traditions and narratives, and even those to which we are outsiders still affect us.²³ Thus, it is a matter of acknowledging and examining the contemporary context of our theological enterprise; moreover, Yong avers that RD will result in Christians discovering divine truth, goodness, and beauty in the other, as well as a renewed appreciation of their own tradition.²⁴ These assumptions are mirrored in Hauerwas's claim that the existence of other religious traditions should be considered a gift to the church.²⁵

Having established why RD should be considered a pertinent practice for the church in a secular age, as a storied community by the Spirit, who is also working in and through the religious other, I will explore one aspect of how such an engagement can be performed, although in a brief and piecemeal manner. Both Hauerwas and Yong are concerned with the metaphor of vision, although they unpack it differently. How we see determines how we live, Hauerwas argues, in his emphasis on the correlation of vision and virtue.²⁶ Our imagination, pneumatologically conceived, bridges the orders of knowing and being, says Yong.²⁷ They both agree that the point of imagination and vision is to discern what is true and thus be enabled to live truthfully.²⁸

Precisely because these metaphors are decisive for how Hauerwas and Yong explicate the human understanding of truth, I will argue that they are also relevant to a fruitful approach to RD, since at the end of the day it is the truth that is at stake when engaging with religious others.²⁹ Therefore, a brief recapitulation of Hauerwas's vision and an introduction to Yong's imagination are required in order to display the correlation to the extrapolated work of the French philosopher Paul Ricoeur on the role of the imagination in the process of metaphorization, and its relevance for the practice of RD.

Starting with Hauerwas and his emphasis on the ethical importance of vision, he links our seeing inextricably to our being. His initial undertaking as an ethicist was to replace decision ethics with virtue ethics, and part of

22. Yong, *Spirit-Word-Community*, 303–4.
23. Ibid., 303, and Taylor, *ASA*, 592–93.
24. Yong, *Spirit-Word-Community*, 304.
25. Hauerwas, *The State of the University*, 71.
26. Hauerwas, *Vision and Virtue*, 46.
27. Yong, *Spirit-Word-Community*, 120.
28. Hauerwas also uses the term imagination, and in function it seems to be interchangeable with vision, e.g., Hauerwas, *The Hauerwas Reader*, 422–23.
29. Hauerwas discusses the challenge of relativism related to religious dialogue in the essay "The Church in a Divided World."

this effort consisted of arguing that ethics should focus on the character of the self rather than obsessing over moral choices. A good person acts accordingly, and it is her vision that determines her actions. Such vision is not the mere product of looking, however, as it requires the kind of trained vision enabled by a community of saints who with their lives embody the result of seeing through the metaphors and symbols constituting their central convictions.[30]

For Yong, the metaphor of imagination is what structures his pneumatological epistemology, after moving on from the foundational pneumatology in *SWC*.[31] Tracing the concept of imagination from Plato to postmodern thinkers like Sartre, he highlights its relational, integrative, and normative character.[32] These characteristics are similar to Hauerwas's description of vision. Metaphors and stories teach us particular ways of seeing the world and our existence in it. When arguing this point, Hauerwas *inter alia* refers to the importance of poetry in how we perceive the world. The ability to not only intimate what moral life is about but to reveal "dimensions of the unknown that make the known seem unfamiliar," makes poetic imagery irreducible to prose or principles.[33] I would argue that the concept of vision in Hauerwas's argument shares fundamental premises with Yong's imagination, with regard to this particular point about ethics as poetics and also in more general terms.

For my purpose here, I will have to limit the comparison to a few relevant points: 1) both Hauerwas's vision and Yong's imagination enable us to make sense of our existence by bridging meaning and reality; 2) both concepts are understood as decisive for ethical valuation by distinguishing truth from falsity; and 3) they are dependent on communal enculturation. While both vision and imagination are experienced and exercised individually, Hauerwas and Yong are equally adamant about the role of community in the hermeneutical and pedagogical processes.[34] Moving on to the focused exploration of Ricoeur's metaphorization process, I will further develop the term imagination in concurrence with Ricoeur's terminology, all the while assuming its convergence with Hauerwas's vision.

---

30. Variations of this argument are presented in several of Hauerwas's essays, e.g., "The Significance of Vision," and "Vision, Stories, and Character."
31. Yong, *Spirit-Word-Community*, 123.
32. Ibid., 132.
33. Hauerwas, *The Hauerwas Reader*, 167.
34. However, Yong displays a balancing concern for the individual's autonomy and integrity, e.g., Yong, *Spirit-Word-Community*, 148.

12.1.2 Religious Dialogue and Ricoeur's Imagination

Ricoeur's wide-ranging work is frequently applied in theological deliberations, particularly in the field of theological hermeneutics; but also in the theology of religions. Recently, his claim that linguistic translation demands the ethical attitude of hospitality has been applied to the inter-RD, following the theoretical presupposition that religious language is translatable.[35] Putting the question of translatability on pause, and presupposing the ethical necessity of a hospitable attitude, I will in the following explore how metaphors might offer a fruitful alternative entry point to the doctrinal discussions that tend to become stranded on irreconcilable (or untranslatable) truth claims. Drawing on imagination, feeling, and (re)cognition, metaphors bring aspects of the human experience into the dialogue other than competing arguments and propositions.[36] Attempting to sustain this contention, I will turn to Ricoeur in search of methodological resources that may prove instructive for an approach to practicing RD that utilizes the potential of metaphors, with particular regard to the role of imagination.[37]

In *The Rule of Metaphor*, Ricoeur argues that metaphor is not merely about substituting and displacing tropes or figures, with the word as its basic unit, but rather he argues that metaphor is also the rhetorical process of redescribing reality, with the sentence as its smallest unit.[38] Thus, metaphorization is a discursive method for producing new meanings by simultaneously recognizing the conventional meaning and use of a term, and circumventing these conventionalities in the pursuit of possible meanings. This process entails a semantic innovation in which the imagination plays a crucial—and underestimated—role, according to Ricoeur.[39] In order to better account for the psychology of imagination related to the semantics of metaphor, Ricoeur offers three steps of adjustment, which are of particular interest because he thereby emphasizes dimensions of the imagination that I will argue are relevant to the practice of RD.[40]

---

35. Moyaert, *In Response to the Religious Other*.

36. An example of how this can be done is found in Jeannine H. Fletcher's project, which explores the potential of the metaphor of motherhood and women experiences as data for interreligious dialogue (Fletcher, *Motherhood as Metaphor*, xii).

37. It is not possible to present Ricoeur's theory of metaphor in any detailed manner within the limits and intent of this section, and so in the following I offer a focused glimpse of the parts that are relevant to my argument.

38. Ricoeur, *The Rule of Metaphor*, 5.

39. Ricoeur, "The Metaphorical Process," 146.

40. Ibid., 147.

The first step is to consider imagination as seeing, which entails insight into the likeness and difference of terms that are initially remote from each other.[41] Ricoeur emphasizes that seeing a likeness is to see sameness in spite of, and through, the differences. Imagination is thus the ability to grasp the combinatory possibilities of, and consequently effect rapprochement between, terms that remain in tension.[42] An important aspect of the seeing is to account for the frame/focus interplay, with the frame being the context for the term that causes the potential change of meaning.[43] Pertaining to the practice of RD, imaginative seeing entails insight into the likeness and difference of terms that are initially far apart (i.e., from different religious traditions) but yet with the potential of fruitful rapprochement. I would add that such seeing does not predicate a particular religious identification on part of the one who sees; however, it does not preclude it either. In any case, it demands familiarizing with the terms, ideas, and their initial contexts and uses (i.e., the frame/focus interplay).

Second, Ricoeur argues that the pictorial dimension of imagination should be incorporated into the semantics of metaphor.[44] In so doing, he refers to Wittgenstein's concept "seeing as," and avers that picturing as "seeing as" is not about having a mental picture of something but rather about displaying relations in a depicting mode.[45] This mode is limited to the concrete representations triggered by the verbal entity, and as such it is not a dreamlike foray into the unknown. The "seeing as" dimension of imagination rather rejuvenates traces of sensorial experiences, and invokes the qualities, situations, locations, and feelings related to the depicted icon.[46]

What I would highlight, with regard to methodological reflections on RD, is the intuitive grasp of predicative connections, which Ricoeur emphasizes as determinative for our imaginative "seeing as." His understanding of metaphors as dependent on intuitions, imagination, and feelings (which he distinguishes from emotions) offers valuable insight into the power of

---

41. Ibid., 147–48. Partly pertaining to this argument, I also consider Ricoeur's use of the metaphor space to be relevant for the discourse on religious dialogue. Similar to how he applies it when explaining resemblance as the changing of distance between ideas that initially are remote from each other; we might explain the project of religious dialogue as the process of obtaining proximity between terms and ideas in spite of their initial remoteness.

42. Ibid., 148.
43. Ibid., 149.
44. Ibid.
45. Ibid., 150.
46. Ibid., 151.

religious metaphors.⁴⁷ While imagination as "seeing" and as "seeing as" are closely related, with both relying on the intuitive schematization and picturing that occurs during metaphorization, the third dimension of imagination, which Ricoeur calls the suspension, demands the opposite of positive conjuring.⁴⁸

This third step is what he explains as the negative condition for remaking and redescribing reality.⁴⁹ Through suspension of ordinary references, new ways of imagining the world are made possible. However, such suspension does not abolish but rather maintains the original reference in tension with the new one, leading to a stereoscopic vision; or, alternatively, ambiguity in reference. The ability to simultaneously entertain two points of view is thus indebted to the imagination insofar as it presupposes the moment of suspension.⁵⁰ Ricoeur then summarizes the role of imagination in the metaphorization process: 1) *schematizing* predicative assimilations between terms (seeing); 2) *picturing* the generated relations and experiences (seeing as); and 3) *projecting* new possible descriptions of the world (suspension in order to see anew).⁵¹

While it is easier to see the relevance of the metaphorization process, and the role of imagination, in relation to theological language and biblical imagery,⁵² what it can yield to the practice of RD may not be as obvious. Therefore, in conclusion I will offer some concrete proposals by way of summarizing the dimensions of imagination, drawing on Wittgenstein's concept of "seeing as," which will be open to further assessment by those currently engaged in RD:

1. Corresponding to the first dimension of imagination, the *seeing* consists of exposure to the other's faith, story, and meaning. This can be maintained on two levels: on the executive level in terms of approaching the religious discourse of the other, but also when considering sentences and stories within that discourse. Imagination (and based on Yong, I would add *pneumatological* imagination) is vital for our ability to envision constructive potential in the rapprochement between terms initially far apart, and drawing on Ricoeur's analysis, such seeing

---

47. An example of how these insights from Ricoeur can be extrapolated with regard to religious metaphors can be found in Baumann, *Love and Violence*, 33ff.

48. Ricoeur, "The Metaphorical Process," 151.

49. Ibid., 152–54.

50. Ibid., 154.

51. Ibid.

52. Ricoeur's most pertinent essays in this regard are gathered in Ricoeur, *Figuring the Sacred*, see in particular chapter 8: "The Bible and the Imagination."

also entails *feeling* the sameness and the difference that constitute likeness between terms.[53]

2. The seeing must then expand into *seeing* the term *as* the flow of images and sensorial experiences related to the term. I think this is especially important in a secular age, where the excarnation of religion necessarily affects not only how we relate to our own religious beliefs, or lack thereof, but to other's beliefs as well. Therefore, I contend that in the Wittgensteinian term "seeing as" several strands converge that together clarify the importance of engaging the religious other with imagination enabling us to see as: Ricoeur's picturing of the flow of images related to a term, Hauerwas's conception of vision as the seeing which defines our character, and Yong's understanding of imagination as bridging human knowing and being. I suggest all describe some aspect of what it means to see as. To employ our imagination in order to explore how religious others see as is not merely a cognitive performance, as it involves feelings in the Ricoeurian sense as well as the willingness to suspend our own references, which is the third and final dimension.

3. The moment of suspension enables the possibility of *seeing as something more*. Suspending the references of ordinary descriptive language by way of imagination opens up the possibility of a remaking, not only of the terms but, following Ricoeur, of how we perceive the world.[54] My claim is that this negative moment of imagination is also crucial for the practice of RD, because it enables us to develop a stereoscopic vision: maintaining our own religious convictions and practices while fully engaging the other by suspending our initially held references. Hopefully, the result is that we can see both ourselves and the other as something more than we were able to see before our imaginative journey began.

Before concluding this section, I will reflect briefly on the limitations of imagination in relation to RD. Imagination is not in and of itself a sufficient guide for the discernment of good and evil in religious traditions, including the Christian tradition in all its diversity. Yong, who has done extensive and constructive work within the theology of religions, argues that a pneumatological approach to the theology of religions offers important

---

53. Ricoeur differentiates between "feeling" and "emotion," ascribing a complex kind of intentionality to the first (Ricoeur, "The Metaphorical Process," 156).

54. Ibid., 154.

perspectives on our contemporary globalized situation.[55] Part of this argument concerns the Spirit as enabling imagination and discernment, which goes beyond the intellectual exercise of evaluating doctrinal texts.[56]

Without entering the complex field of demonology and discernment of spirits, I will make note of the convergence between Yong's determination of the demonic and what H. Richard Niebuhr termed the "evil imagination."[57] They both attempt to draw a line in the sand with regard to God's presence and absence in and through religions, again including Christianity, and while it is a difficult and at times blurry line to clearly define, it functions minimally as a reminder for the church of the existence of "a destructive field of force," which attempts to "influence the course of things and events so that destructive outcomes ensue."[58] Thus, although I am convinced of the crucial significance of RD for the church in a secular age, I think it equally important to not be naïve about the challenges it also entails, including a continuous reflection on how to discern and reveal the evil imagination at work both in our own tradition and in others'.[59]

12.1.3 Preliminary Summary

With this brief exploration of the performative role of imagination, in relation to metaphors as potential conversation starters for RDs, I am painfully aware of the dearth of examples and empirical references. However, I hope to partake in the ongoing work on the methodological aspect of the theology of religions by further pursuing the preliminary proposal I have

---

55. Yong also addresses concerns about the importance and intention of religious dialogue, as previously mentioned, and these are just some of the many issues related to this topic that I have not touched upon in this brief engagement. However, I am highly sympathetic to his theological understanding of the role of religions, and the way he argues for the significance of religious dialogue, e.g., in Yong, *The Spirit Poured out on All Flesh*, 235ff. See also his more recent *Dialogical Spirit*, which argues for dialogue not only with other religions, but with science and society as constituting a larger contextual situation for the church and theology. For (more and less) critical assessments of Yong's theology of religions, see Miles, *A God of Many Understandings?*, chapter 6, and Vondey and Mittelstadt, *The Theology of Amos Yong*, chapters 5–6.

56. Yong, *The Spirit Poured out on All Flesh*, 254.

57. E.g., they both ascribe racism and other more structural injustices to this demonic, or evil, imagination (Niebuhr, *The Meaning of Revelation*, 54, and Yong, *The Spirit Poured out on All Flesh*, 253).

58. Yong, *Beyond the Impasse*, 138.

59. Yong admits the risks and challenges are many for the church when encountering other faiths today, but these challenges must all the more be embraced if we want to allow our understanding of other faiths to be shaped by the other's religious life and tradition ("Performing Global Pentecostal Theology," 320).

sketched out here. For such a purpose, it would be interesting to explore the central metaphors of selected religious traditions, emphasizing the proposed steps of imagination, in search for how the metaphors shape various ways of "seeing as." Drawing on Yong's conceptualization of the pneumatological imagination, which assumes God's universal presence by the Spirit working also in religions for divine purposes;[60] it is my contention that the church has been offered an alternative starting point for RD that allows for the religionists to be heard on their own terms.[61]

Returning to Hauerwas's concern about the terminology of RD as simply blanketing a Constantinian understanding of the church and Christendom, I would respond to that by emphasizing the pneumatological imagination, which converges with Hauerwas's vision; while acknowledging the particularity of religions (cf. "being heard on their own terms"), Hauerwas's reference to the example of Burrell is given a theological framework. On the other hand, I do think that the Christological thrust of Hauerwas's work in general represents a challenge to Yong's call for suspending Christological issues in favour of a pneumatological approach to RD, but these are challenges Yong acknowledges and engages.[62]

Next, what does the notion of the church as a storied community by the Spirit of rationality yield to the practice of RD? My contention is that the pneumatological category of rationality offers a theological understanding of how meaning and truth are mediated by the Spirit through the church's practice of RD. Also, by emphasizing the importance of imagination and metaphors in the practice of RD, I believe the church is presented with an approach that could be particularly fruitful in a secular age. Conversely, the practice of RD might expand on the notion of the church as storied. Appreciating the critical arguments of both Albrecht and Gustafson, the practice of RD depends on a fundamental recognition of the many stories. Thus, in this chapter, I have suggested that the method of suspending our own stories when engaging with the other could contribute to expanding our vision and ways of understanding, which in turn, following Taylor, shapes how we experience our existence.

Finally, in relation to the secular challenge of a deconstructed truth, part of Taylor's argument is precisely that the modern and secular hailing of propositional truths, without regard for how humans experience their existence, is an insufficient form of truth. Subsequently, I would argue

---

60. Yong, *The Spirit Poured Out on All Flesh*, 250.

61. Yong, *Beyond the Impasse*, 29.

62. E.g., in *Hospitality and the Other*, 168ff. For a sympathetic review of the Christological critique against Yong's work, see Vondey and Mittelstadt, *The Theology of Amos Yong*, 111–12.

that RD should no longer consider comparative discussions of dogma, or propositional truths, to be its primary method. Rather, the call for storied, as well as embodied, truth must be recognized by the church; in addition, when engaging the subject of RD, and in my brief engagement with Ricoeur above, I have ventured to push in such a direction by exploring approaches to RD that focus on metaphors, and pneumatological imagination as argued by Yong. Turning now to the practice of meeting the marginalized, I will continue to push for fresh perspectives on old practices, this time by exploring how a theological anthropology might challenge the church's notion of the status of the marginalized.

12.2 Meeting the Marginalized as a Defining Community

While RD is about how the church engages with the religious other, the practice of meeting the marginalized is concerned with how the church should relate to and include the marginalized of our society. About as varied as the religious other might be, is just about how varied the marginalized other might be. However, presupposing that the church as a defining community should meet the marginalized based on the church's theological anthropology,[63] I will make several delimitations: first, I will focus on the marginalized group of the mentally disabled, mainly because both Hauerwas and Yong have dedicated considerable theological attention to this group;[64] second, I will not go into the larger field of the theology of disability but confine myself to reconstructing some of the central arguments from Hauerwas and Yong; and third, while the sociological perspective is selected on the basis of the mentioned criteria (in the chapter's introductory comments), I am fully aware that *inter alia* psychological theories of self and identity could have proven equally relevant. However, I have preferred Smith because of the convergence of sources and concepts with Yong and Hauerwas, as I suspect this will facilitate a more productive conversation.

---

63. For reflections on the relationship between various anthropologies and approaches to prenatal diagnosis (predominantly aimed at detecting Down syndrome) in a Norwegian context, see Heiene and Torbjørnsen, *Kristen Etikk*, 103–8.

64. For Hauerwas's work on disability theology, see Hauerwas, *Suffering Presence*; Hauerwas and Swinton, *Critical Reflections on Stanley Hauerwas' Theology of Disability*; and Hauerwas and Vanier, *Living Gently in a Violent World*. For Yong's work on disability theology, see Yong, *Theology and Down Syndrome*, and *The Bible, Disability, and the Church*.

12.2.1 Hauerwas and Yong on the Church and the Mentally Disabled

True to the differences of their overall style and method, Hauerwas and Yong approach the topic of how the church should think about and practice the inclusion of the mentally disabled differently. While Hauerwas addresses the issue in essayistic form and dialogical style,[65] Yong offers a comprehensive and systematic treatment of the relationship between theology and disability. From Hauerwas, I will select some central tenets regarding the church's understanding of mental disability, while Yong will contribute the theological anthropology that I think necessary to sustain Hauerwas's claims.[66]

It could be argued that one of the most distinctive trait of the mentally disabled, as emphasized by Hauerwas, is their fundamental interdependence. They're often viewed by society merely as dependent on their caretakers, but Hauerwas argues that society, and the community of the church in particular, is also dependent on the mentally disabled.[67] Not only do they offer the gift of difference to the community, but they also teach us not to consider ourselves primarily as victims.[68] Hauerwas avers that it is the mentally disabled's reliance on others that really complicates matters for the rest of us, because their dependence reminds us that human identity is deeply interdependent, contrary to the modern notion of the self-possessed and self-reliant individual.[69]

Acknowledging, on the one hand, the peril of claiming the normalization of the mentally disabled in the form of equality and rights, only to end up with unjust politics, and, on the other hand, the peril of exercising oppressive and disabling care, Hauerwas cautions against the sympathy and compassion that seek to eliminate all suffering, even if it demands eliminating the subject who suffers.[70] By analyzing the concept of suffering in relation to the mentally disabled, he argues that suffering is part of human existence in general, and it should not merely be attempted eliminated,

---

65. By "dialogical" I mean that some of the relevant essays are written as speeches, e.g., "Community and Diversity" in *Suffering Presence*.

66. Obviously, Yong presents several claims of his own, but I have chosen to focus on their common agenda and theological presuppositions. The following is therefore not an attempt to survey either Hauerwas or Yong's theologies of disability in a comprehensive manner.

67. This is the main thrust of his essay "Community and Diversity" in *Suffering Presence*, 211–17.

68. Ibid., 214.

69. Ibid., 169–70.

70. Ibid., 160–62.

but sometimes endured and always shared, both as a community and with God.[71] Hauerwas recognizes the danger of wrongly justifying and accepting injustices and sufferings that the church should fight fiercely against, but he warns against distancing ourselves from those whose sufferings we cannot alleviate or war against.[72]

Maintaining that it is our human condition of incompleteness that causes our sufferings, Hauerwas attempts to explain why we have such difficulties relating to the mentally disabled.[73] His argument can be summarized as follows:

1. Suffering is causally related to our interdependence as human beings. We are who we are to the extent that we sustain the existence of others, and the others include creation as a whole, not just humans.

2. Suffering threatens our identity as self-reliant and self-made, and it makes us insecure of who we are because of our inability to integrate suffering into our ongoing projects.[74]

3. Experiencing and understanding suffering in these terms, we cannot but attribute suffering and unhappiness to the mentally disabled, since they are unable to cover up their neediness and dependence on others. And this is where it all goes wrong, according to Hauerwas, for in our inability to see like the mentally disabled, we attribute to them our suffering and thus rob them of the common human experience of enduring and sharing our individual sufferings.[75]

Reading Hauerwas on this topic leaves me with an unsettling impression that his argument does not sufficiently engage the actual suffering of the mentally disabled in his eagerness to reveal our (*inter alia* society, church, and the "normal") inability to accept suffering as part of the human condition. Also, he praises the mentally disabled as a prophetic sign of our human nature as being created and utterly dependent on God and one another, but in so doing he *de facto* bestows them with an *extra*ordinary role rather than argue for their value simply by virtue of being human.[76] While I heartily agree with his good intentions to critique the modern view

---

71. Ibid., 179.
72. Ibid., 176–78.
73. Ibid., 169.
74. Ibid., 175.
75. Ibid., 174–75. Note that this detrimental inability to see like the mentally disabled causes the church to exhibit a similar alienation from the disabled as from religious others.
76. Ibid., 179.

of individual independence by recasting our understanding of the mentally disabled as enabling and revealing our interdependence, I suspect my reservations are grounded in the absence of a clearly stated theological anthropology undergirding Hauerwas's argument.[77] In search for this, I now turn to Yong's theology of disability, and in particular his outline of a theological anthropology.

According to Yong, two main questions must be addressed in order to lay out a theological anthropology: First, what constitutes the image of God (*imago Dei*)? And second, what defines human nature?[78] Starting with the latter, Yong discards both trichotomist (spirit, soul, and body) and dichotomist (body and soul) views of the human being in favor of the more recent emergentist view.[79] The theory of emergence recognizes human identity as constituted by both body and brain, substantiating a view of the soul as an emergent set of features dependent on bodily parts but not reducible to them.[80] Similarly, our mental properties cannot be fully explicated by brain properties, even though they are dependent on them. Emergentism thus emphasizes the holism of human character, and in so doing Yong argues it is convincingly compatible with Christian anthropology.

Before sustaining this claim theologically, Yong makes the following points with regard to emergentism from a disability perspective: 1) since embodiment is constitutive of personhood in the emergentist view, severe mental disability cannot be considered the sole measure of determining personhood; 2) claiming that human beings are constituted by webs of significance (but not reducible to any one of them) entails the need for a multidisciplinary approach (e.g., biology, sociology, political science, and economics) to better understand mental disability; and 3) the emergentist view allows the transcendent value of human life insofar as personhood includes a reality that resists positivistic quantification.[81]

---

77. In the article "Why Stanley Hauerwas Needs Blaise Pascal," Lexi Eikelboom argues that Hauerwas's ethics would benefit from a better developed theological anthropology, and attempts to show why Pascal offers a good fit in that respect.

78. Yong, *Theology and Down Syndrome*, 169.

79. Ibid., 170.

80. The sociologist Christian Smith, whom I will return to in the next section, explains emergence as "the process of constituting a new [and unified] entity with its own particular characteristics through the interactive combination of other, different entities that are necessary to create the new entity but that do not contain the characteristics present in the new entity" (Smith, *What Is a Person?*, 26). While Smith also applies the theory of emergence in his anthropological project, he offers several examples of other useful applications of the process of emergence, as well (ibid., 27–31).

81. Yong, *Theology and Down Syndrome*, 171–72.

In line with Yong's larger pneumatological project, he contends that a pneumatological framework highlights how the theory of emergence is conducive to a theological anthropology of interrelationality.[82] Concurring with the emergentist view of the human soul as levels of experience constituted but not reducible to the body, Yong suggests that the Genesis account of God breathing life into the dust of the ground can be read on emergentist terms.[83] Furthermore, our interactions and relations are similarly embodied, yet they are not reducible to the sum of the engaging parties. The relationship between God and human can then be understood as a defining emergent level of experience that is constituted not only by our embodiment but also by our interactions with other humans and the world.[84] Remembering Yong's pneumatological category of relationality,[85] the role of the Spirit as enabling both human relationships with God and with each other is further substantiated.[86]

What then defines human personhood is the creative enabling of the Holy Spirit in relation to our embodied selves, to each other, and to God. This pneumatologically driven anthropology presumes human nature as an ongoing, or emerging, reality that anticipates the promised eschaton. Such a relational and dynamic understanding of personhood does not require subjective self-consciousness, which mentally disabled people might possess to a varied degree. Thus, Yong claims self-consciousness is neither a crucial criterion for personhood nor the image of God, as it is relationality that is defining for both.[87] This brings me back to Yong's second question of theological anthropological relevance, namely what constitutes the image of God (*imago Dei*)?

Acknowledging that both human *being* and *doing* may inform a theological anthropology, Yong insists that it is human *relationality* that should be considered constitutive for the *imago Dei*.[88] From a disability perspective the emphasis on the inherent human capacity of being in the divine image is problematic insofar as it has been closely correlated to particular features, such as rationality, morality, responsibility, the aptitude for feeling guilt and shame, or spirituality.[89] Also, the understanding of *imago Dei* as constituted

---

82. Ibid., 186.
83. Ibid., 188.
84. Ibid., 189.
85. See chapter 10.2.
86. Yong, *Theology and Down Syndrome*, 190.
87. Ibid., 191.
88. Ibid., 173.
89. Ibid., 172.

through function (doing) presupposes the capacity to exercise dominion over the created order (ref Genesis story), which again centers on human responsibility.

Yong avers that in order to include the mentally disabled in such a functionalistic approach, we should understand the responsibility of ruling as a cooperative effort rather than a dominating one.[90] Thus, the *imago Dei* consists of the human relationship with God—including the cooperative effort to care for creation—interrelationality with other persons, and embodied interdependence with the world. Such a view of the *imago Dei* contributes, together with the pneumatologically informed anthropology above, to a theological anthropology that is fully in line with the emergentist view of personhood and that also accounts for the disability perspective.[91]

Before turning to the sociological perspective on personhood, I will summarize both Hauerwas's and Yong's theologies of disability with some Christological reflections from Yong that are representative of their common agenda regarding disability theology: The life and cross of Christ means that we are never alone in embracing the suffering that is part of all human existence.[92] And as surely as the cross of Christ means that he has experienced human suffering, the resurrection means that he is present with us in our sufferings.[93] Moreover, the life of Jesus demonstrates how friendship with one another and with God entails participation in God's life. Through the mutual appreciation and commitment that friendship fosters, the Spirit transforms the relationship for the glory of God in ways that overcome dichotomies like us/them, and abled/disabled.[94]

This common emphasis on friendship by Hauerwas and Yong dovetails with their understanding of suffering as a fundamentally human experience that is to be shared and endured as friends in community. By framing friendship within a pneumatologically informed theological anthropology, the argument for meeting the marginalized, *inter alia* the mentally disabled, as relationally constituted persons has been made. For further exploration of the interdependence constituting personhood, I will now turn to the sociological work of Christian Smith.

---

90. Ibid., 173.
91. Ibid., 174.
92. Ibid., 179.
93. Ibid.
94. Ibid., 187.

12.2.2 Smith's Sociological Perspective on Personhood

North American sociologist Christian Smith argues that it is important to inquire about the human person in order for the social sciences to better understand and explain the social.[95] Such inquiry needs to be sufficiently complex, *pace* the principle of parsimony enforced by the social scientists' indiscriminate use of Occam's razor, which is what Smith sets out to offer in his *What is a Person?*[96] Shunning the reductionism of sociological models like social constructivism[97] (taken too far) and network structuralism,[98] Smith critically engages these models as part of his construction of a sufficiently complex anthropology that takes into account the moral and teleological character of the human person, which is manifest in the capacity for relationships of self-giving.[99]

Adjoining several prominent sociologists, Smith adheres to the concept of emergence as crucial for understanding personhood, much as Yong does (as outlined above).[100] Due to its significance in Smith's argument, I think it worth revisiting, and Smith also offers a more detailed explanation of the components of emergence. According to Smith, emergence involves the following four events: 1) two or more entities interact or combine; 2) the interaction functions as the basis for a new entity existing at a "higher" level; 3) the higher-level entity is fully dependent on the interaction of the lower-level entities; and 4) the new entity still possesses characteristics irreducible to the lower-level entities.[101] Emergence, as explicated, happens everywhere, from the molecular level of water (H_2O) to the composition of a computer.[102] Indeed, social systems can be explained by the concept of emergence.[103]

Proceeding to explicate what might qualify as a sufficiently complex model of personhood, Smith lists 30 causal capacities that interact and

---

95. Smith, *What Is a Person?*, 2.

96. Ibid.

97. Smith engages social constructivism both critically and appreciatively in chapter 3 (ibid., 119–206).

98. His engagement with network structuralism is found in chapter 4 (ibid., 220–73). Note also his critique of how some proponents of network structuralism misunderstand and misuse religion and theology in order to make their case against atomistic social theories (ibid., 273–76).

99. Ibid., 71–73.

100. Ibid., 25.

101. Ibid., 26.

102. Ibid., 27, 29.

103. Ibid., 30.

emerge as personhood.[104] While his exposition of these capacities and how they interact on various levels is fascinating reading, I will in the following focus on his concluding discussion of human dignity related to personhood, as I think it is most pertinent to the task at hand, which is to suggest how Smith's project can prove instructive for the church in meeting the marginalized. The first benefit drawn from Smith is that he clarifies what is at stake in the question of human dignity. He outlines three positions: those who ground human dignity in capacities, such as rationality or purposive agency; those who ground dignity theistically; and those who abandon the notion of dignity on the grounds that there is no convincing warrant for claiming such a particular dignity for humans.[105]

In relation to the disability perspective, as well as other marginalized groups, both the first and third positions are highly problematic, which Smith also argues. He problematizes the first position of capacity-based dignity, questioning how the logic of such accounts can discern who qualifies for dignity. Newborns, mentally disabled, the severely sick, or even people who are simply asleep, are all arguably lacking dignity according to the capacity-based position. However, Smith avers that this position is held by many as more promising than the theistic position, since dignity grounded in humanity rather than God can be universally accepted.[106] Turning to the third position, Smith is quick to dismiss it on ontological grounds. All who are convinced of the existence of human dignity agree that the challenge is to better explain it, regardless of whether one holds the first or second position. Smith claims he cannot give credence to the third position, which he refers to as skepticism, simply because it is not true to reality.[107]

Stating that his agenda is to address the impasse of the first two positions, Smith swiftly leaves the skeptics behind. However, for the church that wants to meet the marginalized of secular societies, I think it is necessary to consider the force of the position of skepticism. While the most controversial arguments from this position (e.g., promoting infanticide, cf. Peter Singer[108]) might seem to be extreme and unacceptable to the majority

---

104. Ibid., 54.
105. Ibid., 447.
106. Ibid., 450.
107. Ibid., 451.

108. Singer's argument for infanticide is relevant to the topic at hand, because it rests on his understanding of what constitutes a "person." Since infants lack personhood, which according to Singer includes the ability to desire life, their parents' preferences are decisive, and in instances where they would prefer to kill the infant, they should be allowed to. After all, he rhetorically asks, how is it different from the practice of abortion? (Singer, *Practical Ethics*, see chapters 6–7.) Arguably, Singer could

population even in secular societies, their logic should be scrutinized by theologians contributing to the practice of the church. Acknowledging that such engagement, even when highly critical, may confer legitimacy to the argument under scrutiny, I still think it necessary because the peril of the unexamined impact of the logic of skepticism is greater.

However, it is not within the scope of this rather brief exploration of personhood to pursue the task of scrutinizing Singer and his followers, so I will return to Smith and his attempt to mediate between the humanistic and theistic grounds for human dignity. While he acknowledges that his own reasons for believing in the existence of human dignity are "at rock bottom theistic," he also argues for the importance of "a defensible account of dignity that bridges across as many people of good will as possible, one that includes as many discussion partners as it is able who believe in and want to protect human dignity."[109] As an example of how this has been done historically, he offers the 1948 Human Rights Declaration.[110]

Having already clarified the problems of both the capacity-based and theistic positions, Smith returns to his model of personhood as emerging from a list of lower-level capacities and suggests that dignity should be considered as an emergent property.[111] Rather than tying dignity to the empirical observation of certain lower-level capacities, be it rational decision making or intentional agency, dignity is emerging as a reality on a higher level. Similarly, the wetness of water exists as a reality on the higher level of H_2O, but not on the lower level of individual H_2O molecules. Dignity is thus inextricably linked to the emergence of personhood and not to any particular capacity on the lower level. However, following the emergence theory, will not personhood and dignity be reliant on the existing function of the lower level capacities (cf. how the interaction of multiple H_2O molecules is necessary for the properties of water to emerge)?

Smith addresses this issue with some reflections that are highly relevant to the consideration of the dignity of the mentally disabled as well as other marginalized groups: First, dignity and personhood are not scalable properties; either you have it or you do not.[112] Smith argues that personhood adheres in each human from the start, and thus does not emerge responsively (e.g., like H_2O) but proactively, with the potential to develop and

---

be qualified for Smith's first position emphasizing capacities; however, not attributing any particularity to human dignity, I think his position to be more accurately placed within Smith's skeptics category.

109. Smith, *What Is a Person?*, 452.
110. Ibid., 452 n. 39.
111. Ibid., 453.
112. Ibid., 457.

unfold.[113] Second, Smith emphasizes that there is no exact number for how many (or which) lower-level capacities are required for the ontological reality of personhood to emerge, and therefore personhood and dignity are attributed even though several of the lower-level capacities may be lacking or functioning weakly.[114] Indeed, all persons go through periods with varying degrees of lower-level capacities functioning, and as Smith avers, different persons will be stronger in certain capacities and weaker in others without this fact threatening their personhood or dignity. Thus, he concludes, we rightly protect the dignity of people even in conditions where they are not empirically functioning like persons.[115]

In explaining how the emergence of dignity and personhood operates, Smith admits that it is not fully intelligible (yet), but he insists that the value of accepting partial mystery is far greater than the positivist empiricism that makes it difficult to profess anything about what is most real and important about human beings.[116] From Smith's insistence on the partial mystery of human personhood, I will draw a line to Yong's theological anthropology and his point about human relatedness to God being constitutive for personhood. Within Smith's model, human relatedness to God could be viewed as constitutive for human dignity. While I would hesitate to ascribe it as a lower-level capacity, human relatedness to God seems in my reading to qualify as the partial mystery operating on the higher-level as an ontological reality correlating to the existence of human dignity and personhood.

Before summarizing the practical implications of this exploration in terms of the church meeting the marginalized, I would like to make a final observation regarding Smith's understanding of human brokenness. After admitting that his model of personhood portrays an ideal representation of the capable person, he suggests that the empirical reality of the "downright awful" part of human living can be called "brokenness"; "Humans seem

---

113. Smith explains in greater detail the difference between responsive and proactive emergence, and he suggests that another way to describe the proactive operation of emergence is "immanentist," entailing that there is no external agent who arranges the lower-level entities in order that the higher-level properties may emerge, but rather the higher-level property is nascent and may or may not develop its expression. Relating to the emergent property of human dignity, it means that together with personhood it is nascent in every human being, and works as the causal agent towards its own development (ibid., 86–88). However, as Smith points out, this development and expression of dignity and personhood may vary vastly from person to person, independent of disabilities (ibid., 458).

114. Ibid., 458.

115. Ibid., 459.

116. Ibid., 457.

broken and the world seems broken."[117] Smith's point is neither to argue for whether brokenness is essential or accidental to human reality[118] nor to enter philosophical or religious discussions, but rather to acknowledge that the brokenness of persons and the world must be considered relevant to sociological theory. Only then, he claims, can sociological scholarship hope to understand persons and their social life and structures.[119]

This observation from Smith brings me back to where this exploration started out, namely with Hauerwas's claims about suffering being an inevitable part of human existence, and thus this should also be acknowledged as such, and even perhaps particularly, in the lives of the disabled. The crucial difference between Smith's concept of brokenness, which is all bad,[120] and Hauerwas's suffering is that for Hauerwas suffering must not be avoided at all cost. This means that even though suffering might very well be pointless, the willingness and ability to make it our own is part of human personhood—and, may I add, dignity.[121] Thus, what Smith observes as an empirical and regrettable reality of brokenness, Hauerwas and Yong reimagine as suffering within the eschatological context of the church's story, and thus as something Christians should be willing and enabled, by the Spirit, to own and share as part of human existence.[122]

12.2.3 Preliminary Summary

By presenting Hauerwas's and Yong's works on disability theology, I started out "on the ground" with the reality of disability and questions about suffering and marginalization. With their differing approaches, Hauerwas and Yong contribute perspectives that reimagine personhood, disability, and suffering within the eschatological story of the church. From a disability perspective, Hauerwas warns the church about defining suffering as extrinsic to a meaningful existence. Even though suffering certainly can be experienced as meaningless, a life entailing suffering is still meaningful for

---

117. Ibid., 75.
118. Ibid., 76.
119. Ibid., 78.
120. See his descriptive list of the depressing diversity of brokenness in ibid., 77 n. 78.
121. Hauerwas, *Suffering Presence*, 33–34.
122. As previously mentioned, both Hauerwas and Yong are adamant about not arguing for the uncritical acceptance of all suffering and injustices; rather, the church must vigorously oppose this. However, in relation to mental disability (and other irredeemable conditions), they both make it clear that suffering is neither dehumanizing nor should it be eliminated at any cost, including the cost of taking lives.

the Christian. Yong's theological anthropology goes a long way in explaining why it is so. Because human personhood is theologically constituted by relationships with God, each other, and creation, mental disability does not preclude anyone from personhood.

Extending the exploration of personhood, I found that sociologist Smith adheres to the theory of emergence, like Yong, and offers reflection on how all people vary in their strengths and weaknesses with regard to the many capacities that interact in order for personhood to emerge. Also, he claims another property emerges on the level of personhood, namely dignity. From a disability perspective, I think Smith, together with Yong, offer another argument for a theological anthropology that insists on the value of human beings grounded in relationality rather than capacities. According to Smith, human dignity is a brute fact and an irreducible attribute of persons;[123] I would add that the experience of dignity is relational. Only in meeting the other can both my own and the other's dignity be confirmed or contradicted. Thus, Hauerwas's emphasis on the church as a defining community is further substantiated by Smith's relationally grounded anthropology.

The practical implications for the church in meeting the marginalized can be summarized in the following points:

1. According to a theological anthropology based on the theory of emergence, all humans are at times, and in varying degree, marginalized, suffering, and broken, both in relation to God and one another. Therefore, marginalization is not a static condition or experience.[124]

2. The church community translates theological anthropology into practice by way of meeting the marginalized as being imbued with a dignity that is divinely instituted and relationally constituted.

3. In order to reimagine the role and identity of the marginalized (e.g., the disabled), the church is dependent on the imaginative act of suspending society's views of suffering and other misguided perceptions of the marginalized (*inter alia* the lopsided victim status).

Recognizing that the fluid status of being marginalized also affects how we understand the church as being defining, it becomes impossible for the

---

123. Smith, *What Is a Person?*, 453.

124. In no way is this claim intended to underestimate the extraordinary experiences of marginalization that some groups historically have been, and contemporarily are, victims of. However, I think Hauerwas's work, in particular, helps us to both realize and accept the marginalization that suffering, which is an inevitable part of existence, entails, and in doing so, exhorts the church to meet, include, and learn from the marginalized. E.g., he argues that the mentally disabled teach the church how to be patient and peaceable (Hauerwas and Vanier, *Living Gently in a Violent World*, 45–47).

church to be sectarian considering the mutual defining that meeting with the marginalized inevitably entails. The Spirit of relationality defines the Christian character through these encounters, which the church should foster if it is to be defining. Following Hauerwas, the church learns the virtue of patience from the mentally disabled. I think the practice of meeting the marginalized is particularly important for the church in a secular age, as it is challenged by the detachment of the self. Against the secular notion of the lone hero who has matured away from transcendent notions of good and fullness (and I would add, human dignity), as portrayed by Taylor, the church offers a community of anti-heroes, who recognize that to be marginalized is part of the human condition, without underestimating that some groups, such as the mentally disabled, are marginalized in more obvious ways.

Thus, I would suggest that the practice of meeting the marginalized leads to a re-attachment of the self, that depends on the previously mentioned imaginative act of suspending misguided perceptions of both the self and the other. Recalling the foundational pneumatology of Yong, I will argue that the church should expect that the Spirit of relationality enables and empowers both the church's understanding and practice of meeting the marginalized.[125] Arguably, the primary site for the Spirit to thus expand and train the church's imagination is through liturgy, and so it is to this final practice that I now turn.

12.3 *Liturgical Living as a Performative Community*

While the concrete practices of RD and meeting the marginalized, in and of themselves, can be performed by anyone of good will more or less adequately, the practice of liturgical living is distinctly Christian, in the sense that it is not existentially intelligible to non-Christians. The following exploration is partly based on the presupposition that the particular and peculiar Christian way of ordering life through liturgy makes Christian existence and practices intelligible, as well as enables them. Liturgical living is the overall term denoting any intentional practice with worship of God as its *telos*, while *liturgical worship* is employed as a narrower term that refers to the structured worship of God by the gathered church, which most often (but not necessarily) occurs on Sundays. Liturgical worship thus motivates and enables liturgical living.

Following the presupposition about liturgical living as a particular Christian performance, I will examine the intuition that the church's liturgical worship is the heart of its performance, not only as public worship but

125. Yong, *Theology and Down Syndrome*, 14.

also—and equally importantly—as a formative practice for the character and faith of Christians. Continuing to draw on the foundational pneumatology of Yong, I suggest that the Spirit of rationality, relationality, and *dunamis* makes liturgical living an imaginative and powerful performance, by holding together the *tempora* and events of creation, salvation, and eschatological redemption. Thus, the following inquiry addresses how Hauerwas and Yong approach the topic of liturgy; subsequently, I will turn to the classic work of Aristotle, whose poetic perspective contributes to the emphasis on liturgy as *performative action* in a secular age.

Before surveying the relevant arguments of Hauerwas and Yong, two further distinctions must be made. First, there is the differentiation between the "theology of liturgy" and "liturgical theology," which is made clear by the Orthodox theologian Alexander Schmemann, who was central to the liturgical movement of the twentieth century.[126] While the theology of liturgy has liturgy as the object of study being governed by theology, liturgical theology has as its final goal to "explain how the Church expresses and fulfils herself in this act [of worship]."[127] I will proceed along the latter lines in this section, assuming that the liturgy is the central expression, or performance, of the church. It is thus not a matter of theologizing about the importance of the various liturgical elements but rather a matter of seeing theology and the church as interdependent with liturgical practice.[128]

Schmemann recognized the confessional varieties within liturgical theology, and he worked out his liturgical theology in dialogue with the Orthodox Ordo, but he insisted that the shared substance of the liturgical movement was the discovery of "worship as the life of the Church, the public act which eternally actualizes the nature of the Church as the Body of Christ . . ."[129] It is based upon this fundamental conviction, which I would add is fundamental to the Christian church, that I continue to address the variety of denominations that recognize the CWS of a secular age, even when discussing such a confessionally dependent matter like the liturgy. I do so in the hope that the crucial conviction that worship is the life of the

---

126. See Schmemann and Moorhouse, *Introduction to Liturgical Theology*, for Schmemann's reflections on the liturgical movement post–First World War (13ff) and his definition of "liturgical theology" (16ff). For a more comprehensive review of the liturgical movement, see Fenwick and Spinks, *Worship in Transition*.

127. Schmemann and Moorhouse, *Introduction to Liturgical Theology*, 17.

128. From a methodological perspective, this can be considered to be the dialectic between first- and second- order Christian theology, with the liturgy as first-order and liturgical theology as second-order. See Frei, Hunsinger, and Placher, *Types of Christian Theology*, particularly 20–21. Also, developing on Frei's typology, see Gregersen, "Dogmatik som samtidsteologi," 308.

129. Schmemann and Moorhouse, *Introduction to Liturgical Theology*, 14.

church, which is all the more exigent in navigating the disembodiment of belief, constitutes sufficient common ground and *telos* to explore the role of liturgy in a manner that might prove relevant to more than one specific denominational branch of the church.

Second, there is the differentiation between "ritual" and "liturgy." While sociological investigations of how rituals work as symbolic activities, ranging from recurring everyday practices such as sleeping and eating to particular religious acts of worship, are relevant to the present exploration of liturgy, the latter term is preferred due to its explicit relation to a theological narrative, with its etymology referring to public worship.[130] My use of the term liturgy thus refers to the collective and (per)formative practices grounded in the church's narrative and *telos*. As such, it focuses on the worship of the gathered community with particular liturgical elements, though Christian worship in a wider sense can include everyday practices, such as prayer, Bible-groups, and meditations. However, I am not addressing these everyday practices, nor do I include any "thick" practice with arguable liturgical function (e.g., public citizenry practiced properly according to a particular *telos*).[131] In order to delimit this exploration, I will focus on liturgical worship, as defined above, but with a continuing view to liturgical living.

12.3.1 Hauerwas and Yong on the Church's Liturgical Life

Neither Hauerwas nor Yong have worked comprehensively with liturgical theology *per se*, but they have both certainly made considerable efforts to spell out what the contemporary church's life must look like; in fact, in Hauerwas's case, I would consider it his main agenda. Starting there, I will recap the main points of how Hauerwas understands the role and intent of liturgy (i.e., liturgical worship as previously differentiated from liturgical living) as a church practice.[132] Not surprising given the shape of his work in theological ethics, he argues that liturgy is integral to Christian ethics, insisting that the call for Christians to be holy (not simply do the "right thing") depends

---

130. For a sociological consideration of the concept "ritual" and its genealogy, see Asad, *Genealogies of Religion*, 55–62. For a theological reasoning about liturgy versus ritual, see Smith, *Desiring the Kingdom*, 86–88. However, I concur with Jennifer Herdt's observation that Smith's juxtaposition of Christian and secular liturgies implicitly suggests engagement with the latter is idolatrous and antithetical to the first (Herdt, "The Virtue of the Liturgy," 538).

131. For such a wider use of the term liturgy in recent work, see Mathewes, *A Theology of Public Life*, 26.

132. See chapter 6.1 for my consideration of the role of liturgy in Hauerwas's work.

on liturgical formation.[133] Taken together with the claims made with Samuel Wells—"ethics begins and ends with God"[134] and "nothing is more basic [for the church] than the worship of God"[135]—it is clear that Hauerwas thinks it impossible to get one without the other. Therefore, he also structured his ethics courses at the Divinity School at Duke around the organizing focus of liturgy, attempting to embody the presumption that worship and ethics are integrally related.[136]

To the fundamental assumptions that 1) liturgy is worship of God, and 2) liturgy is ethically forming for the Christian character, I will add a third notion, inspired by Hauerwas, about liturgy: 3) through worship and liturgy the church serves the world.[137] As previously pointed out,[138] Hauerwas considers that the first task of the church is not to make the world a better place but to make it realize that it is the world. This task depends on the church worshipping God, because only by being liturgically shaped can it rightly see the world, including how the church continues to be possessed by it.[139] Based on these and similar foundational claims about the church's liturgy, several theologians have argued that the liturgy of the church is inevitably a political practice.[140] Yong also develops his argument about the role of liturgy along these lines, albeit with a pneumatological twist.[141] As is his custom, Yong makes his case in three installments: biblical engagement, dialoguing with liturgical theologies of the political, and a theological outline of the church as counter-cosmopolis. For my purpose here, I will focus on the last

---

133. Hauerwas, *In Good Company*, 155. He makes an almost identical argument in Willimon, Hauerwas, and Saye, *Lord, Teach Us*, 47.

134. Hauerwas and Wells, *The Blackwell Companion to Christian Ethics*, 14.

135. Ibid., 49.

136. Hauerwas, *In Good Company*, 154. He refers to worship and liturgy interchangeably; however, worship seems to be the broader term, covering liturgy, while the latter is the more precise term for the ordered worship of the gathered church community.

137. Ibid., 163.

138. I presented Hauerwas's understanding of liturgy and the sacraments in chapter 6.1.

139. Hauerwas, *In Good Company*, 156. Remember that Hauerwas considers the world to be all in creation that do not believe, and not an ontological reference (*The Peaceable Kingdom*, 100f), although at times offering contradictory claims (see my consideration of this inconsistency in chapter 5.2).

140. Among the most prominent is Hauerwas's former student William Cavanaugh, who has argued that all politics are acts of imagination, and as such the liturgy is the church's act of political imagination (Cavanaugh, *Theopolitical Imagination*).

141. Yong, *In the Days of Caesar*, 151–65.

part that is Yong's constructive and pneumatologically shaped suggestion for the liturgical imagination, which builds on the first two steps.

Aligned with Hauerwas on this point, Yong makes the basic claim that the church's worship (i.e., liturgical worship as previously differentiated from liturgical living) is that which "nurtures the proper stance toward God, the powers, and the political."[142] For Yong, the proper stance entails both respecting the principalities and powers, and taking responsibility in the political domain.[143] Through the liturgical imagination at work in the liturgy, the Spirit empowers the church to resist political systems and powers that are corrupted.[144] Attempting to mediate between the materialistic reductionism of modernity and the premodern fantastic cosmology, Yong suggests an apophatic theology of the powers that embraces a re-enchanted cosmopolis.[145] Part of Yong's conception of the re-enchantment of the cosmopolitical is to expound the demonic as an emergent reality, which only exists as perverted and parasitic configurations of the good.[146] I think his effort to reintroduce ritual space and time for the renunciation and exorcism of principalities and destructive powers to the church's liturgical life is important to this exploration, both as a pneumatological perspective and as a direct response to the secular condition of disenchantment.[147]

A final comment regarding Yong's notion of the liturgical imagination is that it focuses the liturgical worship on the lordship of Jesus and the majesty of God. Thus, there is no legitimation of violence or of making enemies of people in the church's liturgy.[148] Rather, the church's liturgical practices empower non-violent engagement directed to redeem the powers of this world.[149] In this, Yong resonates with Hauerwas's emphasis on the church's

---

142. Ibid., 161.

143. Ibid. For Yong's attempt to redeem the Pentecostal notion of deliverance from principalities and powers, see ibid., 134–45.

144. Ibid., 162.

145. "Apophatic" in this context is explicated by Yong as knowing enough only to know what it is not (ibid., 164).

146. For Yong's understanding and use of the theory of emergence, see (as previously referred to) *Theology and Down Syndrome*, 170–72. For further elaboration of the emergence theory, see my previous reference to Smith, *What Is a Person?*, 25.

147. Yong, *In the Days of Caesar*, 160. However, Yong is adamant about not giving the destructive powers "more 'air time' than they deserve," and he also suggests that the church should consider whether rites of exorcism may serve to purify the public square, referring to *inter alia* Alexander Schmemann's understanding of the cosmic implications of the baptismal renunciation of the devil (ibid., 160). Regarding the disenchantment of the secular age, see Taylor, *ASA*, 25–27.

148. Yong, *In the Days of Caesar*, 165.

149. Ibid., 165.

pacifism as a crucial part of its performance. I would also add, as a reflection on Yong's suggestion, that the Spirit of *dunamis* holds together the moments of creation, Christ's victory, and the eschatological promise of peace in and through the liturgy of the church. Ensuing from the pneumatologically motivated imaginative suspension of allegiances and powers in this world, the church is empowered to continue living liturgically after being sent out from the Eucharistic table. With these considerations of the role and intent of the church's liturgy in mind, I will turn to the question of what Aristotle might offer to this exploration of what the church's liturgical worship entails in a secular age.[150]

12.3.2 Liturgical Worship and Aristotle's Enactment

As previously noted, the work of Aristotle has been followed by Hauerwas from the beginning of his career, but he primarily refers to Aristotle's ethical project. In the following, it is Aristotle's *Poetics* that is approached in the interest of exploring what it might mean for the church to live liturgically in a secular age. In offering useful distinctions and terminology that enable us to view the church's liturgy through a different lens than the theological, I will argue that Aristotle's analysis of *tragedy* can contribute to the conversation about liturgy as the embodiment of the church's belief.[151] The procedure will be to start with a bounded performance within the particular time and space of the worship service (i.e., liturgical worship) and then widen the focus to include inferences for a broader understanding of liturgical living.[152]

Aristotle defines tragedy as "the imitation of an action that is serious and also, as having magnitude, complete in itself; in language with pleasurable accessories, each kind brought in separately in the parts of the work; in dramatic not in a narrative form; with incidents arousing pity and fear,

---

150. Although choosing the work of Aristotle, I do believe it would be fruitful to explore contemporary works in performance theory or theatre studies, as well. However, this must be the task for another research project. Aristotle has already been introduced in this book as an important influence on the virtue ethics of Hauerwas, and being the place where Hauerwas started his academic journey, I thought it fitting to end this book with a return to Aristotle, although attending to a different part of his work.

151. It is not implied that the liturgy can be reduced to a ritual drama or tragedy of the Aristotelian kind; however, I do think it is fruitful to approach the practice of liturgy from various angles and perspectives. Hopefully, the following analysis proves that assumption.

152. In the following, I will draw on Richard D. McCall's work on liturgy as performance (McCall, *Do This*). References to particular arguments of his are clearly stated, in order to make transparent when my argument rests largely on McCall's analysis.

wherewith to accomplish its catharsis of such emotions."[153] He emphasizes that it is an *action,* and not a person or character, that is to be imitated in the tragedy, since action is the end for which we live, as opposed to a given quality.[154] Similarly, I would argue that it is the *action* of worship that is the focus of liturgy. While the liturgy is not intended to imitate the biblical narrative *per se*, although the narrative is invoked, the liturgy is rather an *enactment* intended to accomplish and make present what is proclaimed and promised in the biblical narrative.[155] Enactment is here understood as a repeatable embodied performance of acts that are set apart from the ordinary everyday life by certain marks.[156] These liturgical acts are structured by the *plot*.

The plot, understood by Aristotle as the combination of incidents, is the "life and soul" of tragedy.[157] According to Aristotle, the plot is the most important thing for the success of a tragedy, and keeping in mind his emphasis on actions over characters, it follows that he argues the import of how actions are combined and structured. It is crucial for a plot to have a unifying principle, he claims, but this should not consist of focusing the story on one person, since a number of things could befall that person that are irrelevant to the overall action of the story.[158] Rather, the unity of the plot consists of every incident being a necessary part of the whole: "For that which makes no perceptible difference by its presence or absence is no real part of the whole."[159]

Based on Aristotle's notion of plot, I will suggest that the plot of the liturgy is the combination of acts that tells the story of creation and redemption.[160] However, as already stated, the liturgical acts of worship are not attempts at imitation, but enactments that make present the promises of the biblical narrative (e.g., the enactment of the Eucharist makes present

---

153. Aristotle, *Aristotle*, 35.

154. Ibid., 36.

155. McCall, *Do This*, 87.

156. Ibid., 86. As these marks vary between church confessions, I do not go into which marks are essential for it to be called liturgical worship. Obviously, this is not because it is an unimportant question, but rather the opposite: the question is of such an importance that I cannot do justice to it here. Rather, I refer to the example of the Eucharist as a common Christian liturgical practice that also symbolizes the ecclesial differences when it comes to the question of marks or sacraments.

157. Aristotle, *Aristotle*, 37.

158. Ibid., 39.

159. Ibid.

160. McCall, *Do This*, 97.

the redemptive promise of the cross and the resurrection of Christ).[161] In simultaneously pointing backward to Christ's resurrection and forward to the eschatological resurrection, the Spirit holds together the *tempora* of past and future with the present by being present and active in the Eucharistic enactment of the church. Recalling the pneumatological categories of rationality, relationality, and *dunamis*, I would argue that these properties are relevant to the Spirit's agency in the worship of the church.[162] Regarding the holding together of the *tempora* in the enactment of the Eucharist, it is the Spirit of *dunamis* at work.

The Spirit also ensures the *telos* of liturgy. While Aristotle suggests the *telos* of tragedy is the catharsis of emotions, such as pity and fear, in the beholder, the *telos* of the church's liturgical worship is the transformation of worshippers, by the Spirit of relationality. Such a transformation does not consist primarily of emotional catharsis but of discovering how to live according to the plot enacted in the liturgy and in the less-obvious plot structure of everyday liturgical living.[163] As such, the liturgical worship of the church is the precondition for both the practices of RD and meeting the marginalized. In the liturgical performance of worship, the church is transformed by the Spirit of relationality to live liturgically in relation to humans and creation as a whole when sent out from the Eucharistic table. Following Hauerwas, it is only by being liturgically shaped that the church is able to see the world rightly, which I would add is a relational capacity that entails seeing both the continuity and discontinuity between the church and the world.[164]

From this brief analysis of Aristotle's considerations of the literary form of tragedy, I have gathered that liturgical worship can be understood

---

161. Without going into the confessional divergences regarding the Eucharist, I will continue to address its role in the liturgy, together with the pneumatological agency, as issues relating to the many Christian denominations in their liturgical practices. However, I do not intend for the reflections to attempt liturgical or theological uniformity but rather to be a starting point for customized conversations in congregations of various confessions.

162. See Hütter, *Suffering Divine Things*, for a substantive treatise on the Spirit's agency in the church's liturgy and sacramental enactment.

163. McCall, *Do This*, 97.

164. Similar to the previous argument about the Spirit of relationality bridging the discontinuity between the church and the world, my assumption is that the Spirit of relationality also bridges the discontinuity between liturgical worship and everyday liturgical living. Another way of looking at it would be to consider the Spirit of relationality as enabling us to see the complexities of Christian existence both *as* the church and the world, as well as *in* the church and the world, and how they are interrelated. However, I choose to maintain the terminology of continuity and discontinuity, while acknowledging the complexities that might not be fully covered by it.

as the enactment of the redemption story, having as its *telos* the transformation of worshippers so that they might live liturgically when sent out from the Eucharistic table. Liturgical worship is thus understood primarily as action rather than recital, and liturgical living as everyday practices that are empowered by eschatological promises made present by the Spirit of *dunamis*.[165] Consequently, practices such as RD and meeting the marginalized are motored by the liturgical worship of the church, and their particularity consists of a Christian's intentions, seeing the worship of God as her *telos* for living liturgically. Liturgical worship also has a crucial formative role, as emphasized by Hauerwas. However, following Yong, it is the Spirit who ensures that the worshippers are transformed and empowered to live liturgically and therefore, the enactment of liturgical worship in and of itself is no guarantee of the Christians living liturgically.

12.3.3 Preliminary Summary

In this chapter, I have explored what it means to claim that the church's liturgical worship is the heart of its performance. First, I turned to Hauerwas and Yong, who both emphasize the importance of the liturgy, although with a different focus. Hauerwas argues that it is only by being liturgically shaped that the church can rightly see the world and act accordingly. His emphasis on the importance of the church to *see* Christian existence rightly is in accordance with Taylor's intuition about the importance of how we *experience* life in a secular age. If Taylor's claim about religious belief being disembodied is recognized by the church, Hauerwas's call for liturgy to shape how the Christian sees her existence is a way to counter this disembodiment.

Following Yong's pneumatological insight, I suggested that it is the Spirit of *dunamis* who ensures that the liturgical worship becomes a formative practice for the character and faith of Christians. The Spirit works both in the liturgical worship and in the everyday liturgical performance of Christians by holding together the *tempora* and the events of creation, salvation, and eschatological redemption. Turning to Aristotle's literary critique of the tragedy, I queried the embodied and performative character of liturgical worship. Thus, I will argue that the church's practice of living liturgically counters the disembodiment of belief in understanding the liturgy as embodied and performative *action*.

---

165. It seems to me that it is possible to also understand the liturgical practices as anticipations of the practices of liturgical living in the following manner: confession anticipates forgiveness, communion anticipates hospitality, hymns anticipate exhortations, prayers/intercessions anticipate diaconal ministry, and preaching anticipates truthful speech.

While RD addressed the secular challenge of deconstructed truth, and meeting the marginalized was related to the challenge of the detached self, liturgical living firmly denies the possibility of belief being disembodied. In the attempt to further the understanding of the church's liturgical worship as embodied, Aristotle provides an action-oriented terminology from literary critique that underwrites the performative aspects of liturgy. His attention to the experience of the audience, which he describes as "catharsis of such emotions [as pity and fear]",[166] and considers the intended accomplishment of the tragedy, concurs with Taylor's concern about the excarnation of religion.

As previously noted, Taylor argues that such excarnation results in a religious life residing in the head; that is primarily concerned with proper beliefs.[167] Opposing this reductionist disembodiment of religious belief, he emphasizes that religion is embedded in bodily forms of ritual, worship, and practice, and thus he avers that religious beliefs also consist of altered life experiences.[168] The liturgical worship of the church both embodies belief and defines how the worshippers experience life. Also, Taylor's claim about the secular human stance as being independent of any transcendent powers is relevant to Yong's assertion that the church's liturgy nurtures in the worshipper a proper stance before God and creation. I would add that it is the liturgical experience of acknowledging and worshipping God, by the Spirit of relationality and *dunamis*, which empowers the worshipper to live liturgically.

12.4 A Final Outlook: Doing Theology and Being Church in Norway

The objective of this chapter has been to employ the findings from the pneumatological reconstruction of Hauerwas's ecclesiology in relation to concrete church practices, which is particularly relevant in a secular age. All three practices—RD, meeting the marginalized, and liturgical living—are public, and as such, examples of my conviction that theology and the church are public endeavors. Notwithstanding the critical charges of sectarianism against Hauerwas, I will argue that his work, and the traction it continues to garner, demonstrates his commitment to the public nature and relevance of both theology and the church.[169]

---

166. Aristotle, *Aristotle*, 35.

167. See chapter 3.3.

168. Taylor, *ASA*, 613.

169. In the field of public theology, there has been an ongoing argument about the proper public relevance of theology as a subject. Not surprisingly, Hauerwas has

Before moving on to the conclusion of this book, I would like to make a few comments about the context in which I am doing theology and the potentially immediate relevance to what is currently going on in the church(es) in Norway.[170] Since the amendment of our Constitution in 2012 that divorced the Church of Norway from the State of Norway, there has been an ongoing debate concerning the democratization of the Church of Norway (Den norske kirke), and the folk-church's (*folkekirken*) role and intention in contemporary Norwegian society.[171] This present book is relevant to that conversation, as it offers an ecclesiology that seeks to engage the secular challenges, and attend to the particular community of the church as being storied, defining, and performative.

Furthermore, I think it is important that the ongoing conversation about the role of the church and Christianity in Norway also involves Norwegian Free Churches[172] of various denominations, as this secures mutual learning and engagement, and possibly contributes to the ecumenical endeavor, perhaps even serving as a learning experience for further inter-religious dialogue. History shows that it can be equally challenging, if not more so, to conduct imaginative and hospitable dialogue among Christians from various denominations than among believers from different religious traditions. However, with regard to such efforts, this book may provide valuable input both methodologically and ecclesiologically. The Free Churches are also challenged by a secular society and a shifting ecclesial landscape, and

---

not been a big proponent of public theology, as he is rather critical of the underlying premises that he suspects have been shaped by a modern liberal order of religion and politics. However, John Berkman claims that Hauerwas in fact has contributed to a redefining of what constitutes "public theology" (Hauerwas, *The Hauerwas Reader*, 3, 90). For a further introduction into the conversation of public theology, see Forrester, Storrar, and Morton, *Public Theology for the 21st Century*.

170. Again, as mentioned in the introductory chapter, "the church" does not refer to a particular denomination. In this discussion, I differentiate between "the church in Norway," which refers to all Christian communities in Norway, and "the Church *of* Norway," which is the noun referring to the Evangelical-Lutheran Church, previously the state church, and currently with the constitutional designation "Norway's folk church."

171. Harald Hegstad has argued that the Church of Norway, or the folk church, is in need of rethinking its self-understanding in light of the ongoing political and societal changes in Norway (Hegstad, "Kirken som fellesskap"). I have also reflected on the church's role in the Scandinavian context, in the article "Folkekirken som mer enn en velferdsprodusent" (title translation: "The Church as More than a Welfare-Agency").

172. I use "Norwegian Free Churches" as an inclusive term for the Protestant congregations and denominations outside the Church of Norway. The capitalization follows Miroslav Volf's work on developing a Free Church ecclesiology (Volf, *After Our Likeness*).

thus they might find it fruitful to engage in processes of (re)defining self-understandings in negotiation with these developments.

Finally, the (many and varied) church statements on various public matters, be it environmental issues, political questions, or ethical arguments, need to be founded on a dynamic self-understanding, related to both theological (and other relevant) research and the actual practice of the church community. This is why I, in this final part, have attempted to engage in and further interdisciplinary conversations about the church's identity and practice in a secular society. This explorative effort, however, is in need of further critical engagement, not least with ethnographic studies and research.

13

In the End

THERE EXISTS NO BLUEPRINT or neat answers to what it means to be and to practice church in a secular age. Rather, this is an ongoing quest that engages Christians and theologians from a broad spectrum of church confessions. I am therefore not the first to ask how the church should navigate the challenges that this secular age presents, nor am I the first to think that Hauerwas's ecclesiology might offer resources on this matter. However, the main research contribution of this book is a result of the way I have pneumatologically reconstructed Hauerwas's central ecclesiological features while relating this ecclesiology to Taylor's framework of secularity.

Starting out with the question of how a particularistic ecclesiology might help the church in navigating the challenges of a secular age, it was pertinent to obtain a framework for secularity in order to articulate the challenges. Thus, I outlined what Taylor calls the immanent frame in the first part of the book, including the closed world structures (CWS) that Taylor claims prevent secular people from holding transcendent beliefs within the immanent frame. Part II of the book introduced Hauerwas's project, and in analyzing his ecclesiological arguments, I found them relevant to the challenges of the secular age in the following ways:

1. Church as a storied community navigates the secular deconstruction of truth by understanding truth as storied, and premised on communal practices and tradition. Hauerwas, subscribing to Taylor's type of opposition against modern epistemological priority relations, argues that truth can only be intelligible and verifiable in the context of story and community.

2. Church as a defining community navigates the secular detachment of the self. Hauerwas argues that the church is defining for both the world and the character of Christians by virtue of its particular language and tradition. The Christian self is defined by its relations to God and to others, and thus it critically corrects the secular notion of the detached self.

3. Church as a performative community navigates the secular disembodiment of belief by presupposing that Christian belief must be embodied in liturgical worship and peaceable practices. In his emphasis on the performative character of the church, Hauerwas acknowledges the necessity for reversing what Taylor calls the "excarnation" of religion.

In this systematic analysis of Hauerwas, some inconsistencies and weaknesses were noted, and in part III these were further deliberated by bringing prominent critics of Hauerwas into the discussion. I structured the critical discussion topically under the three most common charges: fideism, sectarianism, and pragmatism. Obviously, I could not extend into the larger debates on these issues in various fields, so I focused on the particular arguments against Hauerwas that relate to fideism, sectarianism, and pragmatism. The results of the critical discussion prompted my suggestion that Hauerwas's ecclesiology would benefit from a shift of agential emphasis.

I then argued that Hauerwas's lopsidedly communitarian way of constructing Christian agency is one of the foundational shortcomings of his work, and a focal shift of agency might prove fruitful. In order to explore this option, I turned to the foundational pneumatology of Amos Yong, and his pneumatological categories of rationality, relationality, and *dunamis*. Reconstructing Hauerwas's ecclesiology by reading him through Yong's pneumatological categories, I attempted to address both the challenges of a secular age and the critical questions outlined in the preceding chapter. My intuition was that by developing the agency of the Spirit in relation to Hauerwas's ecclesiology, it would allow me to retain his emphasis on Christian particularity while critically developing the pneumatological continuity between the church community, the world as creation, and the promised kingdom. I think this intuition was verified in the reconstruction of 1) church as a storied community by the Spirit of rationality; 2) church as a defining community by the Spirit of relationality; and 3) church as a performative community by the Spirit of *dunamis*.

This pneumatological reconstruction allowed a crucial shift of agency from the church, and its story and tradition, to the Spirit as being the one who acts in and through the church. Although Hauerwas allows the Spirit's agency, it has not been sufficiently developed in his work to counter the charges of fideism, sectarianism, and pragmatism. Considering my primary aim for this book, it was important to argue that the pneumatological reconstruction offers better ecclesiological resources for the church in navigating the challenges of a secular age. Also, the pneumatological reconstruction is an attempt to develop the pneumatological intuitions in Hauerwas's work, which has been a recurring proposal among his critics and readers in general. When the Spirit as rationality, relationality, and *dunamis* is acknowledged as the agent who makes God's truth intelligible through the church's story, who defines the self through human relations with both God and neighbour, and who makes God's promise present through the church's performance, then my concluding claim was that the tension between the particularity of the church and the whole of creation is appended by the continuity that the Spirit represents and enforces.

Finally, in part IV I turned to practice and took a more explorative approach in order to apply the pneumatologically reconstructed ecclesiology. Querying what might be the crucial practices for a storied, defining, and performative church that is attempting to navigate the challenges of a deconstructed truth, the detached self, and disembodied belief, I ventured an interdisciplinary deliberation on the practices of RD, meeting the marginalized, and liturgical living. While I did not present these as exclusive practices, I argued that they must be considered crucial for the church in a secular age. Starting with RD, I claimed it to be a required practice for any church challenged by the deconstruction of truth as propositional and homogeneous. If the church is storied by the Spirit of rationality it is also endowed with the potential to recognize God's truthful presence (or, alternatively, absence) in other stories, and therefore I argued that new approaches to the practice of RD should be further developed. As a tentative contribution, I suggested how Ricoeur's metaphorization process could offer useful perspectives on the method of RD.

Second, the practice of meeting the marginalized was explored through the case of mental disability. Utilizing Hauerwas's and Yong's work on disability theology, I suggested that a robust theological anthropology drawing on Smith's work on the self and human dignity, could offer valuable insight into the importance of the church meeting and including the marginalized. Finally, I argued that the practice of liturgical living, through both the liturgy of worship and everyday liturgical practices, embodies the church's faith in the eschatological promise. It is the Spirit, however, who holds together the *tempora* and the promises of the past, present and future, and who reminds the church of this through liturgical living. By so emphasizing the role of the Spirit, and by employing and expanding on the work of the Pentecostal scholar Amos Yong, I have also attempted to demonstrate the relevance and creative potential of the pneumatological efforts of Pentecostal theology.

How then can a particularistic ecclesiology contribute to the church in navigating the challenges of a secular age? This can be done by offering a way for the church to understand its distinctiveness as a Christian community, both in tension and continuity with the secular age as part of the created world. While the secular age certainly presents the church with challenges, these challenges may also contribute to expand the church's imagination of how to live truthfully in our time, by the Spirit.

Bibliography

Abbey, Ruth. *Charles Taylor*. Philosophy Now. Princeton, NJ: Princeton University Press, 2000.
Adams, Richard. *Watership Down*. New York: Macmillan, 1972.
Albrecht, Daniel E. *Rites in the Spirit: A Ritual Approach to Pentecostal/Charismatic Spirituality*. Journal of Pentecostal Theology Supplement Series. Sheffield: Sheffield Academic, 1999.
Albrecht, Gloria. "Article Review: In Good Company: The Church as Polis." *Scottish Journal of Theology* 50/2 (1997) 219–27.
———. "Myself and Other Characters: A Feminist Liberationist Critique of Hauerwas's Ethics of Christian Character." *Annual of the Society of Christian Ethics* (1992) 97–114.
———. *The Character of Our Communities: Toward an Ethic of Liberation for the Church*. Nashville: Abingdon, 1995.
Aristotle. *Aristotle on the Art of Poetry*. Translated by Ingram Bywater. Oxford: Clarendon, 1920.
Asad, Talal. *Formations of the Secular: Christianity, Islam, Modernity*. Cultural Memory in the Present. Stanford: Stanford University Press, 2003.
———. *Genealogies of Religion: Discipline and Reasons of Power in Christianity and Islam*. Baltimore: Johns Hopkins University Press, 1993.
Baumann, Gerlinde. *Love and Violence: Marriage as Metaphor for the Relationship between Yhwh and Israel in the Prophetic Books*. Collegeville, MN: Liturgical, 2003.
Bennett, Jana Marguerite. "Being 'Stuck' between Stanley and the Feminists (the Proverbial Rock and a Hard Place)." In *Unsettling Arguments: A Festschrift on the Occasion of Stanley Hauerwas's 70th Birthday*, edited by Charles R. Johnson, Kelly S. Pinches, and Charles M. Collier, 229–45. Eugene, OR: Cascade, 2010.
Bhargava, Rajeev. *Secularism and Its Critics*. Themes in Politics. New York: Oxford University Press, 1998.
Bjørndal, Silje Kvamme. "Folkekirken som mer enn en velferdsprodusent." *Ung teologi* 1 (2012) 42–52.
———. "Kirken som et sannferdig fellesskap." *Dansk Tidsskrift for Teologi og Kirke* 38/3 (2011) 45–51.
Browning, Don S. *A Fundamental Practical Theology: Descriptive and Strategic Proposals*. Minneapolis: Fortress, 1991.
Bunkholt, Marit. "'Den virkelige kirke' og embetet." *Nytt Norsk Kirkeblad* 38/6 (2010) 11–20.
Cavanaugh, William T. "A Politics of Vulnerability: Hauerwas and Democracy." In *Unsettling Arguments: A Festschrift on the Occasion of Stanley Hauerwas's 70th Birthday*, edited by Charles R. Johnson, Kelly S. Pinches, and Charles M. Collier, 89–111. Eugene, OR: Cascade, 2010.
———. *Theopolitical Imagination*. Edinburgh: T. & T. Clark, 2003.
Congar, Yves. *I Believe in the Holy Spirit*. 3 vols. New York: Seabury, 1983.

Eikelboom, Lexi. "Why Stanley Hauerwas Needs Blaise Pascal: Sin, Anthropology, and Christian Witness." *Studies in Christian Ethics* 27/4 (2014) 404–16.

Engelhardt, H. Tristram, and Daniel Callahan. *Morals, Science, and Sociality. The Foundations of Ethics and Its Relationship to Science.* Hastings-on-Hudson, NY: Hastings Center, Institute of Society, Ethics, and the Life Sciences, 1978.

Fagermoen, Tron. "Etter folkekirken?" *Tidsskrift for Praktisk Teologi* 31/2 (2014) 24–35.

Fenwick, John R. K., and Bryan D. Spinks. *Worship in Transition: The Liturgical Movement in the Twentieth Century.* New York: Continuum, 1995.

Forrester, Duncan B., William Storrar, and Andrew Morton. *Public Theology for the 21st Century: Essays in Honour of Duncan B. Forrester.* London: T. & T. Clark, 2004.

Frei, Hans W. *The Identity of Jesus Christ: The Hermeneutical Bases of Dogmatic Theology.* Eugene, OR: Wipf & Stock, 1997.

Frei, Hans W., George Hunsinger, and William C. Placher. *Types of Christian Theology.* New Haven, CT: Yale University Press, 1992.

Green, Garrett, and Hans W. Frei. *Scriptural Authority and Narrative Interpretation.* Philadelphia: Fortress, 1987.

Gregersen, Niels Henrik. "Dogmatik som samtidsteologi." *Dansk Teologisk Tidsskrift* 71 (2008) 290–310.

———. "The Fluid Mission of the Church: A Response to Stanley Hauerwas." In *Walk Humbly with the Lord: Church and Mission Engaging Plurality*, edited by Viggo Mortensen and Andreas Østerlund Nilsen, 74–84. Grand Rapids: Eerdmans, 2010.

Gustafson, James. "The Sectarian Temptation: Reflections on Theology, the Church and the University." *Annual of the Catholic Theological Society* 40 (1985) 83–94.

Haga, Joar. "Hegstad og den lutherske embetsteologien." *Nytt Norsk Kirkeblad* 38/6 (2010) 21–26.

Hagman, Patrik. *Efter folkkyrkan: En teologi om kyrkan i det efterkristne samhället.* Skellefteå: Artos og Norma, 2013.

Harder, Lydia. "Dialogue with Hauerwas." *Conrad Grebel Review* 13/2 (1995) 152–56.

Hauerwas, Stanley. *After Christendom? How the Church Is to Behave If Freedom, Justice, and a Christian Nation Are Bad Ideas.* Nashville: Abingdon, 1991.

———. *Against the Nations: War and Survival in a Liberal Society.* Minneapolis: Winston, 1985.

———. *A Better Hope: Resources for a Church Confronting Capitalism, Democracy, and Postmodernity.* Grand Rapids: Brazos, 2000.

———. *Character and the Christian Life: A Study in Theological Ethics.* Trinity University Monograph Series in Religion. San Antonio: Trinity University Press, 1975.

———. *Christian Existence Today: Essays on Church, World, and Living in Between.* Grand Rapids: Brazos, 2001.

———. *A Community of Character: Toward a Constructive Christian Social Ethic.* Notre Dame: University of Notre Dame Press, 1981.

———. *Dispatches from the Front: Theological Engagements with the Secular.* Durham, NC: Duke University Press, 1994.

———. *Disrupting Time: Sermons, Prayers, and Sundries.* Eugene, OR: Cascade, 2004.

———. "Failure of Communication or a Case of Uncomprehending Feminism." *Scottish Journal of Theology* 50/2 (1997) 228–39.

———. *Hannah's Child: A Theologian's Memoir.* Grand Rapids: Eerdmans, 2010.

———. *The Hauerwas Reader*. Edited by John Berkman and Michael G. Cartwright. Durham, NC: Duke University Press, 2001.
———. *In Good Company: The Church as Polis*. Notre Dame: University of Notre Dame Press, 1995.
———. *The Peaceable Kingdom: A Primer in Christian Ethics*. Notre Dame: University of Notre Dame Press, 1983.
———. *Performing the Faith: Bonhoeffer and the Practice of Nonviolence*. Grand Rapids: Brazos, 2004.
———. *Prayers Plainly Spoken*. 1st ed. Downers Grove, IL: InterVarsity, 1999.
———. *Sanctify Them in the Truth: Holiness Exemplified*. Nashville: Abingdon, 1998.
———. *The State of the University: Academic Knowledges and the Knowledge of God*. Illuminations—Theory and Religion. Malden, MA; Oxford: Blackwell, 2007.
———. *Suffering Presence: Theological Reflections on Medicine, the Mentally Handicapped, and the Church*. Notre Dame: University of Notre Dame Press, 1986.
———. *Vision and Virtue: Essays in Christian Ethical Reflection*. Notre Dame: University of Notre Dame Press, 1981.
———. *With the Grain of the Universe: The Church's Witness and Natural Theology*. Grand Rapids: Brazos, 2001.
———. *Without Apology: Sermons for Christ's Church*. New York: Seabury, 2013.
Hauerwas, Stanley, Richard Bondi, and David B. Burrell. *Truthfulness and Tragedy: Further Investigations in Christian Ethics*. Notre Dame: University of Notre Dame Press, 1977.
Hauerwas, Stanley, and Romand Coles. ""Long Live the Weeds and the Wilderness Yet": Reflections on *A Secular Age*." *Modern Theology* 26/3 (2010) 349–62.
Hauerwas, Stanley, and L. Gregory Jones. *Why Narrative? Readings in Narrative Theology*. Eugene, OR: Wipf & Stock, 1997.
Hauerwas, Stanley, and John Swinton. *Critical Reflections on Stanley Hauerwas' Theology of Disability: Disabling Society, Enabling Theology*. Binghamton, NY: Haworth Pastoral, 2004.
Hauerwas, Stanley, and Jean Vanier. *Living Gently in a Violent World: The Prophetic Witness of Weakness*. Resources for Reconciliation. Downers Grove, IL: InterVarsity, 2008.
Hauerwas, Stanley, and Samuel Wells, eds. *The Blackwell Companion to Christian Ethics*. Blackwell Companions to Religion. 2nd ed. Malden, MA: Wiley-Blackwell, 2011.
Healy, Nicholas M. *Church, World and the Christian Life: Practical-Prophetic Ecclesiology*. Cambridge Studies in Christian Doctrine. Cambridge: Cambridge University Press, 2000.
———. *Hauerwas: A (Very) Critical Introduction*. Interventions. Grand Rapids: Eerdmans, 2014.
Hegertun, Terje. "Menigheten i lys av den tredje trosartikkel: Elementer i en pentekostal ekklesiologi." In *Pentekostale Perspektiver*, edited by Knut-Willy Sæther and Karl-Inge Tangen, 165–86. Bergen: Fagbokforlaget, 2015.
Hegstad, Harald. "Den virkelige kirke og den virkelige lutherdom." *Nytt Norsk Kirkeblad* 40/2 (2011) 59–61.
———. "Kirken som fellesskap: Lutherske folkekirker i forandring." In *National kristendom til debat*, edited by Jeppe Bach Nikolajsen, 253–66. Fredericia: Kolon, 2015.

———. *The Real Church: An Ecclesiology of the Visible*. Church of Sweden Research Series 7. Eugene, OR: Pickwick, 2013.

Heide, Gale. *Timeless Truth in the Hands of History: A Short History of System in Theology*. Princeton Theological Monograph Series. Eugene, OR: Pickwick, 2012.

Heiene, Gunnar, and Svein Olaf Torbjørnsen. *Kristen Etikk*. Oslo: Universitetsforlaget, 2011.

Henriksen, Jan-Olav. "Mission: Invitation to Community." In *Walk Humbly with the Lord: Church and Mission Engaging Plurality*, edited by Viggo Mortensen and Andreas Østerlund Nilsen, 70–73. Grand Rapids: Eerdmans, 2010.

Herdt, Jennifer. "The Virtue of the Liturgy." In *The Blackwell Companion to Christian Ethics*, edited by Stanley Hauerwas and Samuel Wells, 535–46. 2nd ed. Malden, MA: Wiley-Blackwell, 2011.

Hill Fletcher, Jeannine. *Motherhood as Metaphor: Engendering Interreligious Dialogue*. Bordering Religions: Concepts, Conflicts, and Conversations. New York: Fordham University Press, 2013.

Hütter, Reinhard. "Ecclesial Ethics, the Church's Vocation, and Paraclesis." *Pro Ecclesia* 2/4 (1993) 433–50.

Jeanrond, Werner G. *Theological Hermeneutics: Development and Significance*. New York: Crossroad, 1991.

Jenkins, Philip. *The New Faces of Christianity: Believing the Bible in the Global South*. New York: Oxford University Press, 2006.

Johannesen, Halvard. "Menighetsutvikling for folkekirken." *Nytt Norsk Kirkeblad* 38/6 (2010) 5–10.

Johson, Kelly S. "Worshiping in Spirit and Truth." In *Unsettling Arguments: A Festschrift on the Occasion of Stanley Hauerwas's 70th Birthday*, edited by Charles Robert Pinches, Kelly S. Johnson, and Charles M. Collier, 300–314. Eugene, OR: Cascade, 2010.

Kallenberg, Brad J. *Ethics as Grammar: Changing the Postmodern Subject*. Notre Dame: University of Notre Dame Press, 2001.

Katongole, Emmanuel. *Beyond Universal Reason: The Relation between Religion and Ethics in the Work of Stanley Hauerwas*. Notre Dame: University of Notre Dame Press, 2000.

Kavka, Martin. "What Is Immanent in Judaism? Transcending *a Secular Age*." *Journal of Religious Ethics* 40/1 (2012) 123–37.

Kärkkäinen, Veli-Matti. *An Introduction to Ecclesiology: Ecumenical, Historical and Global Perspectives*. Downers Grove, IL: InterVarsity, 2002.

———. *An Introduction to the Theology of Religions: Biblical, Historical, and Contemporary Perspectives*. Downers Grove, IL: InterVarsity, 2003.

———. *Pneumatology: The Holy Spirit in Ecumenical, International, and Contextual Perspective*. Grand Rapids: Baker Academic, 2002.

Lindbeck, George A. *The Nature of Doctrine: Religion and Theology in a Postliberal Age*. 25th anniversary ed. Louisville: Westminster John Knox, 2009.

Lindbeck, George A., David B. Burrell, Stanley Hauerwas, and John W. Wright. *Postliberal Theology and the Church Catholic: Conversations with George Lindbeck, David Burrell, and Stanley Hauerwas*. Grand Rapids: Baker Academic, 2012.

Lord, Andrew. *Network Church: A Pentecostal Ecclesiology Shaped by Mission*. Global Pentecostal and Charismatic Studies. Leiden: Brill, 2012.

Lovibond, Sabina. *Realism and Imagination in Ethics.* Library of Philosophy and Logic. Oxford: Blackwell, 1983.

MacIntyre, Alasdair C. *After Virtue: A Study in Moral Theory.* Notre Dame: University of Notre Dame Press, 1981.

Marks, Darren C. *Shaping a Global Theological Mind.* Burlingtron, VT: Ashgate, 2008.

Mathewes, Charles T. *A Theology of Public Life.* Cambridge Studies in Christian Doctrine. Cambridge: Cambridge University Press, 2007.

McCall, Richard D. *Do This: Liturgy as Performance.* Notre Dame: University of Notre Dame Press, 2007.

Miles, Todd L. *A God of Many Understandings? The Gospel and a Theology of Religions.* Nashville: B & H Academic, 2010.

Mortensen, Viggo, and Andreas Østerlund Nilsen, eds. *Walk Humbly with the Lord Church and Mission Engaging Plurality.* Grand Rapids: Eerdmans, 2010.

Moyaert, Marianne. *In Response to the Religious Other: Ricoeur and the Fragility of Interreligious Encounters.* Studies in the Thought of Paul Ricoeur. Lanham, MD: Lexington, 2014.

Niebuhr, H. Richard. *The Meaning of Revelation.* New York: Macmillan, 1941.

Nikolajsen, Jeppe Bach. *The Distinctive Identity of the Church: A Constructive Study of the Post-Christendom Theologies of Lesslie Newbigin and John Howard Yoder.* Eugene, OR: Pickwick, 2015.

Njå, Ådne. "Den virkelige kirke og kirkens virkelighet." *Nytt Norsk Kirkeblad* 39/1 (2011) 46–52.

Østerlund Nielsen, Andreas. *Missional Transformation a Constructive Discussion Applying the Theologies of the Mission as Transformation Movement and Stanley Hauerwas.* Faculty of Arts. Aarhus: Aarhus University Press, 2012.

Oliverio, L. William. "An Interpretive Review Essay on Amos Yong's *Spirit-Word-Community: Theological Hermeneutics in Trinitarian Perspective.*" *Journal of Pentecostal Theology* 18 (2009) 301–11.

Pannenberg, Wolfhart. *Systematic Theology.* 3 vols. Grand Rapids: Eerdmans, 1991.

———. *Theology and the Philosophy of Science.* Philadelphia: Westminster, 1976.

Parsons, Susan Frank. *The Cambridge Companion to Feminist Theology.* Cambridge Companions to Religion. Cambridge: Cambridge University Press, 2002.

Rasmusson, Arne. *The Church as Polis: From Political Theology to Theological Politics as Exemplified by Jürgen Moltmann and Stanley Hauerwas.* Rev. ed. Notre Dame: University of Notre Dame Press, 1995.

Ricoeur, Paul. *Figuring the Sacred: Religion, Narrative, and Imagination.* Edited by Mark I. Wallace. Minneapolis: Fortress, 1995.

———. "The Metaphorical Process as Cognition, Imagination, and Feeling." *Critical Inquiry* 5/1 (1978) 143–59.

———. *The Rule of Metaphor: Multi-Disciplinary Studies of the Creation of Meaning in Language.* London: Routledge & Kegan Paul, 1978.

Sæther, Knut-Willy, and Karl-Inge Tangen, eds. *Pentekostale Perspektiver.* Kyrkjefag Profil 23. Bergen: Fagbokforlaget, 2015.

Scharen, Christian, and Aana Marie Vigen. *Ethnography as Christian Theology and Ethics.* London: Continuum, 2011.

Schmemann, Alexander, and Asheleigh E. Moorhouse. *Introduction to Liturgical Theology.* 3rd ed. Crestwood, NY: St. Vladimir's Seminary, 1986.

Sigurdson, Ola. "Beyond Secularism? Towards a Post-Secular Political Theology." *Modern Theology* 26/2 (2010) 177–96.
Singer, Peter. *Practical Ethics*. 3rd ed. New York: Cambridge University Press, 2011.
Smith, Christian. *What Is a Person? Rethinking Humanity, Social Life, and the Moral Good from the Person Up*. Chicago: University of Chicago Press, 2010.
Smith, Graham R. "The Church Militant: A Study of 'Spiritual Warfare' in the Anglican Charismatic Renewal." PhD diss., University of Birmingham, 2011.
Smith, James K. A. *Desiring the Kingdom: Worship, Worldview, and Cultural Formation*. Cultural Liturgies 1. Grand Rapids: Baker Academic, 2009.
———. *Introducing Radical Orthodoxy: Mapping a Post-Secular Theology*. Grand Rapids: Baker Academic, 2004.
Stassen, Glen Harold. *A Thicker Jesus: Incarnational Discipleship in a Secular Age*. 1st ed. Louisville: Westminster John Knox, 2012.
Stephenson, Christopher A. *Types of Pentecostal Theology Method, System, Spirit*. New York: Oxford University Press, 2013.
Stout, Jeffrey. *Democracy and Tradition*. Princeton: Princeton University Press, 2004.
Svenungsson, Jayne. "Transcending Tradition: Towards a Critical Theology of the Spirit." *Studia Theological* 62/1 (2008) 63–79.
Taylor, Charles. *The Ethics of Authenticity*. Cambridge, MA: Harvard University Press, 1992.
———. *Hegel*. Cambridge: Cambridge University Press, 1975.
———. *Modern Social Imaginaries*. Durham, NC: Duke University Press, 2004.
———. *Philosophical Arguments*. Cambridge, MA: Harvard University Press, 1995.
———. *Philosophy and the Human Sciences*. Philosophical Papers. Cambridge: Cambridge University Press, 1985.
———. *A Secular Age*. Cambridge, MA: Belknap, 2007.
———. *Sources of the Self: The Making of the Modern Identity*. Cambridge, MA: Harvard University Press, 1989.
Tolonen, Miika. *Witness Is Presence: Reading Stanley Hauerwas in a Nordic Setting*. Turku: Åbo Akademi University Press, 2012.
Volf, Miroslav. *After Our Likeness: The Church as the Image of the Trinity*. Sacra Doctrina. Grand Rapids: Eerdmans, 1998.
Vondey, Wolfgang, and Martin William Mittelstadt. *The Theology of Amos Yong and the New Face of Pentecostal Scholarship Passion for the Spirit*. Global Pentecostal and Charismatic Studies. Leiden: Brill, 2013.
Warner, Michael, Jonathan VanAntwerpen, and Craig J. Calhoun. *Varieties of Secularism in a Secular Age*. Cambridge, MA: Harvard University Press, 2010.
Welch, Sharon. "Communitarian Ethics after Hauerwas." *Studies in Christian Ethics* 10 (1997) 82–95.
Wells, Samuel. *Transforming Fate into Destiny: The Theological Ethics of Stanley Hauerwas*. Eugene, OR: Cascade, 2004.
Willimon, William H., Stanley Hauerwas, and Scott C. Saye. *Lord, Teach Us: The Lord's Prayer and the Christian Life*. Nashville: Abingdon, 1996.
Wilson, Edward O. *The Social Conquest of Earth*. 1st ed. New York: Liveright, 2012.
Wittgenstein, Ludwig. *Philosophische Untersuchungen [Philosophical Investigations]*. In German and English. Translated by G. E. M. Anscombe, P. M. S. Hacker, and Joachim Schulte. Rev. 4th ed. Malden, MA: Wiley-Blackwell, 2009.

Woodhead, Linda. "Can Women Love Stanley Hauerwas?" In *Faithfulness and Fortitude: In Conversation with the Theological Ethics of Stanley Hauerwas*, edited by Mark Nation and Samuel Wells, 161–88. Edinburgh: T. & T. Clark, 2000.
Yong, Amos. *Beyond the Impasse: Toward a Pneumatological Theology of Religions*. Grand Rapids: Baker Academic, 2003.
———. *The Bible, Disability, and the Church: A New Vision of the People of God*. Grand Rapids: Eerdmans, 2011.
———. "The Demise of Foundationalism and the Retention of Truth: What Evangelicals Can Learn from C. S. Peirce." *Christian Scholar's Review* 29/3 (2000) 563–88.
———. *Dialogical Spirit: Christian Reason and Theological Method in the Third Millennium*. Cambridge: James Clarke, 2014.
———. *Discerning the Spirit(s): A Pentecostal-Charismatic Contribution to Christian Theology of Religions*. Journal of Pentecostal Theology Supplement Series. Sheffield: Sheffield Academic, 2000.
———. *Hospitality and the Other: Pentecost, Christian Practices, and the Neighbor*. Faith Meets Faith. Maryknoll, NY: Orbis, 2008.
———. *In the Days of Caesar: Pentecostalism and Political Theology*. The Cadbury Lectures. Grand Rapids: Eerdmans, 2010.
———. "On Divine Presence and Divine Agency: Toward a Foundational Pneumatology." *Asian Journal of Pentecostal Studies* 3/2 (2000) 167–88.
———. "Performing Global Pentecostal Theology: A Response to Wolfgang Vondey." *Pneuma* 28/2 (2006) 313–21.
———. *The Spirit Poured out on All Flesh: Pentecostalism and the Possibility of Global Theology*. Grand Rapids: Baker Academic, 2005.
———. *Spirit-Word-Community: Theological Hermeneutics in Trinitarian Perspective*. Ashgate New Critical Thinking in Religion, Theology, and Biblical Studies. Aldershot: Ashgate, 2002.
———. *Theology and Down Syndrome: Reimagining Disability in Late Modernity*. Waco, TX: Baylor University Press, 2007.
———. *Who Is the Holy Spirit? A Walk with the Apostles*. A Paraclete Guide. Brewster, MA: Paraclete, 2011.
Zizioulas, John D. *Being as Communion: Studies in Personhood and the Church*. Contemporary Greek Theologians. Crestwood, NY: St. Vladimir's Seminary Press, 1985.

Index of Authors

Abbey, Ruth, 19n1
Adams, Richard, 76, 76n51, 153
Albrecht, Daniel E., 48n51
Albrecht, Gloria, 100–106, 100n4, 101n6, 101n8, 102n12, 102n14, 105n32, 105n34, 105n37, 106n38, 106n39, 107, 110, 111, 115, 139, 145, 146
Aquinas, Thomas, 54, 54n14, 61n57, 66, 77
Aristotle, 54, 54n14, 61n57, 77, 91, 116, 194, 198–201, 198n150, 199n153, 199n157, 202, 202n166
Asad, Talal, 23n19, 24n24, 195n130
Augustine, 27–28

Barth, Karl, 5, 5n15, 21n14
Baumann, Gerlinde, 177n47
Bennett, Jana Marguerite, 100n2
Berkman, John, 203n169
Bhargava, Rajeev, 22n17
Bondi, Richard, 144n28
Browning, Don S., 14n42
Bukholt, Marit, 12n35
Burrell, David B., 144n28, 171

Calhoun, Craig J., 7n23, 22n18
Camus, Albert, 32–33
Cavanaugh, William, 42n26, 116n97, 196n140
Coles, Romand, 7n23
Congar, Yves, 131, 131n8

Dawkins, Richard, 41
During, Simon, 22n18

Eikelboom, Lexi, 184n77

Fagermoen, Tron, 7n20
Fletcher, Jeannine H., 175n36
Forrester, Duncan B., 203n169
Foucault, Michel, 101, 105
Frei, Hans W., 52, 58, 58n36, 68n3, 145, 194n128

Green, Garrett, 68n3
Gregersen, Niels Henrik, 60n50, 107n47, 194n128
Gustafson, James, 64, 100, 107–11, 107n43, 107n48, 110n60, 128, 139, 145, 147

Haga, Joar, 12n35
Hagman, Patrik, 7n20
Harder, Lydia, 101n7, 107n46, 118n109, 121n128
Healy, Nicholas M., 11n30, 11n31, 12n33, 14n41, 119–25, 119n111, 122n129, 122n132, 122n136, 122n137–123n137, 129, 129n1, 158, 161, 162n26
Hegel, Georg W. F., 21, 21n14, 114n79, 137n41, 138n41, 142
Hegstad, Harald, 11n30, 12n35, 12n36, 203n171
Heide, Gale, 21n14
Heidegger, Martin, 29, 36, 37, 46
Helene, Gunnar, 181n63
Henriksen, Jan-Olav, 107n47
Herdt, Jennifer, 195n130
Hunsinger, George, 194n128
Hütter, Reinhard, 124n147, 125, 125n149, 125n150, 200n162

James, William, 64, 64n78
Jeanrond, Werner G., 13n39
Jenkins, Philip, 132n12
Jesus, 52, 58, 59, 64, 67, 75, 77, 80, 82, 85, 86, 87–90, 88n21, 93, 94–95, 127, 140, 146, 149, 150, 159, 160, 161–62, 170, 186
Johannesen, Halvard, 12n35
Johnson, Kelly S., 121n125
Jones, L. Gregory, 52n5, 64n75

Kallenberg, Brad J., 106n39
Kant, Immanuel, 21, 21n12, 21n14, 53
Kärkkäinen, Veli-Matti, 131n5, 132n9, 132n13, 171n14, 172n16
Katongole, Emmanuel, 108n53
Kavka, Martin, 7n23
Kierkegaard, Søren, 21n14

Lindbeck, George, 13n38, 13n40, 67, 67n2, 69–72, 69n15, 70n17, 70n18, 70n19, 71n26, 71n27, 81
Locke, John, 32
Lord, Andrew, 133n19
Lovibond, Sabina, 61–63, 61n59, 62n63, 70n18, 108, 108n53

MacIntyre, Alasdair, 61, 61n60, 75–77, 75n46, 81, 112–14, 113n75, 115, 116, 117, 118
Marks, Darren C., 133n15
Mary (mother of Jesus), 149
Mathewes, Charles T., 195n131
McCall, Richard D., 198n152, 199n155, 199n160, 200n163
McGrath, Alister, 30n52
Milbank, John, 112
Miles, Todd L., 179n55
Mittelstadt, Martin William, 133n20, 133n23, 136n31, 179n55, 180n62
Moorhouse, Asheleigh E., 194n126, 194n127, 194n129
Mortensen, Viggo, 2n5
Morton, Andrew, 203n169
Moyaert, Marianne, 175n35

Newbigin, Leslie, 93n47

Niebuhr, H. Richard, 5, 5n14, 179, 179n57
Niebuhr, Reinhold, 5, 5n14
Nietzsche, Friedrich, 30, 33
Nikolajsen, Jeppe Bach, 93n47
Njå, Ådne, 12n35

Oliverio, L. William, 132n14, 137n41
Østerlund Nielsen, Andreas, 2n5, 7n20

Pannenberg, Wolfhart, 131, 131n6, 142n16
Parsons, Susan Frank, 138n44
Pascal, Blaise, 184n77
Peirce, Charles Sanders, 151n10, 171
Placher, William C., 194n128
Plato, 27, 174

Rasmusson, Arne, 3n7, 5n11, 7n20, 129n2
Rawls, John, 22, 112
Ricoeur, Paul, 173, 174, 175–79, 175n37, 175n38, 175n39, 176n41, 177n47, 177n48, 177n52, 178n53, 207
Rorty, Richard, 112

Sæther, Knut-Willy, 132n12
Sartre, Jean-Paul, 174
Saye, Scott C., 196n133
Scharen, Christian, 122n131
Schleiermacher, Friedrich, 119–20, 119n111, 129
Schmemann, Alexander, 194, 194n126, 194n127, 194n129, 197n147
Sigurdson, Ola, 2n3, 48n49
Singer, Peter, 188–89, 188n108–189n108
Smith, Christian, 44n34, 181, 184n80, 187–91, 187n95, 187n97, 189n108, 189n109, 190n113, 192, 192n123, 197n146, 207
Smith, Graham R., 133n19
Smith, James K. A., 112n68, 195n130
Stassen, Glen Harold, 7n22

Stephenson, Christopher A., 133n23, 136
Storrar, William, 203n169
Stout, Jeffrey, 23n19, 81, 111–18, 111n63, 112n68, 112n69, 113n75, 113n76, 114n79, 115n87, 115n90, 116n95, 116n97, 116n99, 128, 149, 155
Svenungsson, Jayne, 155n32
Swinton, John, 80n85, 181n64

Tangen, Karl-Inge, 132n12
Taylor, Charles, 2, 2n3, 2n4, 3, 4, 6, 7, 7n22, 7n23, 8, 8n24, 8n25, 8n26, 10, 12, 19–33, 19n2, 19n3, 19n6–20n6, 20n7, 21n11, 21n13, 22n16, 23n19, 23n20, 24n25, 28n41, 29n48, 30n52, 34–48, 35n3, 35n4, 36n7, 41n23, 41n24, 42n27, 44n35, 44n37, 48n50, 65n82, 82n87, 83n88, 95, 96, 119, 126–27, 147, 156, 163, 164, 169n1, 173, 180, 193, 201, 202, 202n168, 205, 206
Tolonen, Miika, 7n20, 59n44
Torbjørnsen, Svein Olaf, 181n63

VanAntwerpen, Jonathan, 7n23, 22n18
Vanier, Jean, 181n64, 192n124
Vigen, Aana Marie, 122n131
Volf, Miroslav, 1n1, 203n172
Vondey, Wolfgang, 133n20, 133n23, 136n31, 179n55, 180n62

Warner, Michael, 7n23, 22n18
Welch, Sharon, 101n5
Wells, Samuel, 5n12, 78n62, 104n31, 122n136, 196, 196n134

Williams, Rowan, 90
Willimon, William H., 196n133
Wilson, Edward O., 44n36
Wittgenstein, Ludwig, 29, 29n47, 35, 36n5, 61, 62–63, 64n76, 71n26
Woodhead, Linda, 102n13, 106n42

Yoder, John H., 4–5, 4n10–5n10, 73, 89, 93, 93n47, 114, 115, 116, 117, 131n4, 155, 172
Yong, Amos, 9–10, 9n29, 126, 129–38, 132n14, 133n19, 133n21, 135n25, 135n26, 135n27, 136n28, 136n32, 136n33, 137n37, 137n38, 137n39, 137n40, 137n41–138n41, 138n44, 139–43, 139n1, 139n2, 139n3, 140n5, 141n13, 141n14, 142n17, 142n21, 145–47, 146n39, 149–52, 149n1, 150n4, 156, 156n34, 158–60, 158n2, 162–63, 162n27, 164, 169, 169n1, 170–74, 170n4, 170n5, 170n6, 171n12, 172n15, 172n17, 172n18, 173n22, 173n24, 173n27, 174n31, 174n34, 178, 179, 179n55, 179n56, 179n57, 179n58, 179n59, 180, 180n60, 180n61, 180n62, 181, 181n64, 182, 182n66, 184–86, 184n78, 184n81, 185n86, 190, 191–92, 191n122, 193n125, 194, 195–98, 196n141, 197n143, 197n145, 197n146, 197n147, 197n148, 201, 206, 207

Zizoulas, John, 131, 131n7, 132, 132n10, 151

www.ingramcontent.com/pod-product-compliance
Lightning Source LLC
Chambersburg PA
CBHW062023220426
43662CB00010B/1455